SOUTH AND MESO-AMERICAN MYTHOLOGY
A TO Z

Ann Bingham

Facts On File, Inc.

Library of Congress Cataloging-in-Publication Data is available on request from Facts On File, Inc.
ISBN 0-8160-4889-4

Facts On File books are available at special discounts when purchased in bulk quantities for businesses, associations, institutions, or sales promotions. Please call our Special Sales Department in New York at (212) 967-8800 or (800) 322-8755.

You can find Facts On File on the World Wide Web at http://www.factsonfile.com

Text design by Joan M. Toro
Cover design by Cathy Rincon

Printed in the United States of America

VB PKG 10 9 8 7 6 5 4 3 2 1

This book is printed on acid-free paper.

CONTENTS

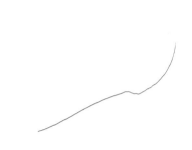

ACKNOWLEDGMENTS

With many thanks and grateful appreciation . . .

to Juan Carlos Flores and Maria Colorado for their critical reading of the content and for helping me find the right balance in dealing with sensitive and controversial topics . . .

to Dorothy Cummings at Facts On File for countless thoughtful suggestions and helpful questions . . .

to Kelley Beaurline and Amy Helfer for their thorough review and editing expertise, no easy task . . .

to Johanna Ehrmann for her copyediting magic . . .

to Audra Winston Bailey and the entire team in Wellesley, who make all these things possible . . .

and finally to all the people whose stories these are.

INTRODUCTION

The world from which the mythology of South and Meso-America emerged is a land of extremes. It is a land of high, snow-covered mountain peaks and low river basins; of barren, rocky, cold, and windy ocean coasts and hot tropical rain forests; of land that is fertile and lush, and land that is subject to drought or created with steep terraces so that crops could be grown. Volcanoes erupt. Earthquakes shake the ground—sometimes so violently that entire towns are flattened. Hail, wind, and driving rains destroy crops. The area covered by South and Meso-America gave rise to several major civilizations; today the land encompasses 21 countries. The mythology of this land is rich with stories of floods and fires, horrific monsters, and a host of gods and goddesses who are jealous, and kind, and evil, and arrogant. Some may be alternately kind and evil; some are so vast they have several names.

The realm of these gods and goddesses, and in fact of the people who revere them, is not linear. Time does not flow on a single path that goes from then to now. Space does not necessarily go from here to there. In this world, time and space merge so at any moment one can tap into the future or access the past. In South America, the INCA saw the cosmos as three concentric spheres—the past, the present, and the future. Humans, often with the help of a SHAMAN who could mediate with the inhabiting spirits, could learn from the past and future because they were always accessible. In Meso-America, too, the past and future merged with the present; it was possible to change the future by returning to the past. The Meso-American use of two or three CALENDARS, each operating on a different cycle—it might take as long as 52 years for a "date" to repeat—illustrate this perception of time and space as more fluid and multidimensional.

In the myths, time means little: Heroes help create a world before their fathers are born; people age or grow younger by ascending or descending a mountain. And because of this timelessness, the myths do make sense. They do explain why a CONDOR's feathers are black, what causes an earthquake, and how a much-played BALL GAME replays a cosmic fight. They also provide role models so strong that people both fear and live to serve them—even today. These gods and goddesses were real and infused every part of everyday life.

The myths of South and Meso-America reflect the themes found in the mythology of other places. Here you will find heroes who face ordeals or tests. You will read about paradise, the UNDERWORLD, SERPENTS, evil demons, the CREATION, and stories of how the EARTH became populated and how people got FIRE. Some believe that ancient people created myths to help them explain their world or construct their history—a world that we, in the age of information, try to explain through scientific and historical facts and theories. But there is little difference. Facts can be deceiving: As history teachers are quick to point out, history is more than a list of facts. It is the telling of a people's story.

SOUTH AND MESO-AMERICA: A BRIEF HISTORY

Historians believe that humans began to migrate from Asia across the Bering land bridge as long as 50,000 years ago. These humans brought with them a belief system that included shamans and the conviction that ANIMALS held spiritual power. People from several different groups made this trip, either gradually or in waves. Eventually, some groups arrived in South and Meso-America. We don't know much about these early people, but this we do know: Some had reached what is now Tierra del Fuego at the southern tip of South America by 9000 B.C.; by 8000 B.C people in the ANDES grew plants, probably to use to weave cloth; and by 7000 B.C. people in Meso-America farmed. The growing of crops for food in the Americas began in Meso-America and, from there, spread north and south.

Meso-America

The first communities in South and Meso-America were those of the Chincoro in northern Chile by 5000 B.C. However, scholars consider the first significant civilization in the Americas that of the OLMEC, who dominated the Gulf coast of Mexico by 1200 B.C. This society was an organized one; it had a class structure, highly developed arts, an extensive trade network, a calendar, writing in the form of pictographs, and deities and spirits who regulated rain and the fertility of humans and crops. The Olmec civilization continued until about 900 B.C. and its influence was widespread.

Other groups also settled in Meso-America. They lived in small villages and interacted with each other through trade and war. Gradually these settlements grew and became ceremonial centers or cities that boasted huge stone temples, monuments, palaces, and gardens; some of them had populations of thousands of people. These population centers were the heart of a chiefdom. Some were cosmopolitan cities—home of people from all classes of society. Others were places where only rulers, PRIESTS, the nobility, and the people and slaves that served them lived. In these settlements, most people lived in outlying villages where they hunted, farmed, or created goods to support themselves and the city center. The city reflected the Meso-American concept of the universe. Just as gods were at the center of the universe, the temples to the major gods stood in the center of the city. Villages and homes also had ceremonial centers—each village had one or more temples and each home had an altar. Ultimately, the people lived to serve the gods who had created humans to serve them. As a cultural area grew, or as a chiefdom expanded either by war or through trade, its group of deities became more complex. Gods were timeless. They did not die, and because the people both revered and feared them, they respected and often adopted the gods of the people they conquered. This was true in South American cultures as well.

In Oaxaca, the ZAPOTEC built the great ceremonial center Monte Albán that was later used by the MIXTEC. The Mayan civilization emerged around 2000 B.C. and peaked around A.D. 900. By around 300 B.C., the MAYA began to build hundreds of cultural centers out of stone in what is now central Mexico, the Yucatán, Guatemala, Honduras, and Belize. In the Valley of Mexico, the dominant center was TEOTI-HUACÁN, a city of more than 150,000 people. It was believed to have been one of the largest cities in the world at that time. As these three (Zapotec, Teotihuacán, and Maya) began to decline, the TOLTEC empire was flourishing at TOLLAN. As the Toltec empire declined, the GUACHICHIL, who had migrated into central Mexico from the north, were settling, establishing communities, and creating the ceremonial centers that would form the structure of the AZTEC (Mexica) empire. All of these civilizations followed the Olmec tradition of building huge, stepped PYRAMIDS that were topped with temples to honor their gods.

The gods of these cultures continued to be those of fertility, agriculture, the SUN, and rain and WATER; there were also gods of war, FIRE, the seasons, the planet VENUS, and others. The Maya alone may have had as many as 166 gods. Beginning perhaps with the Olmec, Meso-American cultures worshiped a serpent god best known today as QUET-ZALCOATL. This deity was known as Nine Wind to the Mixtec, KUKULCAN to some Mayan groups, and GUCUMATZ to the Quiché Maya. The serpent was not the earliest or most powerful god but was a highly influential day-to-day presence; he was the patron of priests and artisans and was associated with war and death, weather, and WRITING and learning.

Life in South and Meso-America changed in the 1500s with the arrival of the Spanish. The Spanish set out to destroy the native cultures: conquering the cities, tearing down the temples and monuments, burning books and records, and killing the people through disease, overwork, and outright violence. The nature of the gods changed at this time as well. In an effort to "cleanse" the native souls, the Spanish and other colonizers were determined to convert them to Catholicism, often holding mass baptisms to achieve this goal. In part, it worked. However, it is not clear whether or not the natives converted. They may have really adapted the Catholic concepts of Jesus, the Virgin Mary, and the saints to fit their needs or they may have simply maintained their own beliefs under different names.

Through the rebellions that both preceded and followed independence from European domination, a blend of native and Christian practice has developed in many places in Meso-America since the 1500s. For example, Easter celebrations may include dancers wearing DEER masks to celebrate spring, and the week-long DAY OF THE DEAD celebration in late October and early November combines ancient ancestor worship rituals with Catholic practice. For many, the significant aspects of the gods and goddesses and the power of the stories surrounding them have not significantly changed. An omnipotent god rules, regular ceremonies and rituals keep the presence of a belief system intact, and the telling of stories helps link the people to their heritage.

South America

Throughout South America, groups of people began settling, scholars believe, at least 13,000 years ago. They formed settlements along the Atlantic coast and in the AMAZON basin, along the Pacific coast and eastern side of the Andes south into the Patagonian pampas, and into the highlands of the Andes (except at the highest elevations). They farmed and, where necessary, built water management systems, either to control flood waters or to provide water for crops. These people believed that creator gods were responsible for their living where they were; that animals and often natural features had powerful spirits; and that shamans or priests mediated between humans and the deities. Sun and rain gods often were supreme, especially along the slopes of the mountains. As in Meso-America, the gods and beliefs of a conquered group were tolerated and sometimes adopted.

About 800 B.C., while the Olmec culture flowered in Meso-America, another great civilization began to emerge along the Pacific coast in the Andes around a ceremonial center at CHAVÍN DE HUÁNTAR. The CHAVÍN dominated the region. Like the Olmec, their influence was wide because of extensive trade networks up and down the Pacific coast and throughout the mountains. Some 600 years later, the Chavín civilization collapsed as the MOCHICA and NAZCA societies were growing. The Mochica and Nazca were separate warring tribes who joined together around A.D. 1 and became a strong unit along the north coast of Peru. The Mochica were farmers who were also dependent on the sea. The Nazca, also farmers, occupied the southern coast of Peru. They had a ceremonial center at Cahuachi but lived in individual villages with no central government or ruler. These civilizations were followed by TIAHUANACO on LAKE TITICACA, Huari in southern Peru, and CHAN CHAN, the Chimú center along the coast in northern Peru.

In the 1100s, the Incan empire began to grow at Cuzco. The Inca would become the largest of the pre-Colombian civilizations in the

Americas. Ruled by a succession of leaders believed to have descended from the Sun, the Inca eventually controlled a stretch of land that included cities and settlements and was some 2,500 miles long and more than 200 miles wide. Once the Spanish arrived, it took very little time for this empire to collapse. As in Meso-America, the people became impoverished and experienced a rapid population decline from disease, inhumane treatment, and overwork.

SOURCES OF SOUTH AND MESO-AMERICAN MYTHOLOGY

For hundreds of years, most of what we have known about the people in South and Meso-America has been colored by the interpretation and perspective of the Spanish and other early European settlers. In Meso-America, most of the existing native CODICES (books) were destroyed. Also destroyed were thousands of STELAE (monuments) covered with carved symbols and pictures known as pictoglyphs that told the histories and stories of the gods. Although the major civilizations in South America, including the Inca, had no system of writing, there are a series of painted murals in the Incan capital of Cuzco that may have served as the Incan recorded history. The Inca and other Andes highland people also literally wove their stories into intricate textiles and passed them along in a rich oral tradition of poetry and song.

In any case, much of what serves as ancient history in both South and Meso-America comes from the letters, diaries, and other writings of, first, the conquerors, and then, the clerics of the church and those sent from Europe to colonize. Inscriptions on monuments that did survive also add to these records. In Meso-America, native people did continue recording their history, which includes their myths, after the conquest. Many of these books have survived or were translated before the originals were lost.

Significant writings for the Maya include four surviving codices, the POPUL VUH, and the writings of Diego de LANDA (ca. 1524–1579), a Spanish priest. There are several codices written in pictoglyphs by the Aztec after the Conquest; also significant are the writings of Bernardino de Sahagún (1499?–1590), a Catholic priest whose writings in Nahuatl, the language of the NAHUA people, were later translated and are known as the Florentine Codex. Writings about the Inca include those written in Spanish by Sarmiento de Gamboa (1532–1592) and in QUECHUA, the language of the Inca, by Francisco de Ávila (1573?–1647?); both are transcriptions of orally told myths and legends. But again one must wonder, how well do these tell the ancient stories? The Indian perspectives on the universe and time so differed from those of the Europeans that a reliable interpretation might not be possible. Another question is, how readily would the native priests—who knew the stories best and were the scholars of a culture, responsible for preserving and protecting it—share their secrets with those bent on destroying it?

PRONUNCIATION GUIDE

The usual pronunciation of the vowels in Maya, Nahuatl (Aztec), and Quechua (Inca) is as follows:

- *a* sounds like *ah*
- *e* sounds like *eh*
- *i* sounds like *ee*
- *o* sounds like *oh*
- *u* sounds like *oo*.

The consonants and accented syllables vary slightly. In Mayan words, the accent is usually on the last syllable, and the following pronunciation rules apply:

- *c* sounds like *k*
- *ch* is pronounced like the *ch* in *chair*
- *u* before a vowel sounds like *w*
- *x* sounds like *sh*.

In Aztec/Nahuatl words, the accent is usually on the next to last syllable. Consonants are pronounced as follows, with double consonants pronounced separately:

- *c* before *e* or *i* sounds like *s*; other times *c* sounds like *k*
- *ch* is pronounced like the *ch* in *chair*
- *hu* before a vowel sounds like *w*
- *j* is pronounced like the *h* in *hat*
- *qu* before *e* or *i* sounds like *k*
- *x* sounds like *sh*
- *z* sounds like *s*.

In words from Inca/Quechua, the accent is usually on the next to last syllable and exceptional consonants are pronounced as follows:

- *hu* sounds like *w*
- *qu* sounds like *k*.

HOW TO USE THIS BOOK

The entries in this book are in alphabetical order and you may look them up as you would look up words in a dictionary. Entries include names of deities (gods, goddesses, and other beings, such as the mythological horse of the ARAUCANIAN people, CABALLO MARINO), cultural groups (such as the Aztec, Maya, Inca, Araucanian, and KOGI), primary geographic features (such as Andes and Amazon), and important objects, symbols, and ideas (such as ASTRONOMY, BAT, and RESURRECTION). Go directly to the alphabetical listings or use the Index at the back of the book, which will direct you to the pages with information about the topic you want.

Cross-references to other entries are written in SMALL CAPITAL LETTERS. Some topics with entries in this book are known by more than one name. Alternate names are given in parentheses after the entry headword. Those given in full capital letters are variations of the names from the original language; those appearing in upper and lower case letters are English translations.

Time Line for South and Meso-America

50,000 B.C.	Humans begin to migrate over the Bering land bridge.
2250–300 B.C.	Olmec settle and dominate the Gulf coast in Mexico.
1500 B.C.–A.D. 750	Zapotec civilization develops and grows in the Oaxaca region of Mexico.
850–200 B.C.	Chavín culture flourishes in the Andes highlands.
400 B.C.–A.D. 1100	Mayan civilization grows and spreads throughout the Yucatán peninsula (Mexico, Guatemala, and Belize).
200 B.C.–A.D. 600	Nazca culture flourishes along the southern coast of Peru.
100 B.C.–A.D. 650	Teotihuacán grows and becomes the cultural and religious center of the Teotihuacán culture in central Mexico.
100 B.C.–A.D. 750	Mochica civilization in the Andes highlands grows and reaches its height.
100 B.C.–A.D. 1200	Tiahuanaco civilization on Lake Titicaca, in Bolivia, thrives and influences the region.
A.D. 900–1200	Toltec dominate central Mexico, first at Tollan, then at Chichén Itzá.
A.D. 900–1600	Mixtec thrive in southern Mexico.
A.D. 1300–1470	Chimú culture flourishes in the Andes highlands.
A.D. 1300–1521	Aztec (Mexica) dominate central Mexico.
A.D. 1400–1532	Incan empire grows and dominates the Andes.

MAP OF SOUTH AND MESO-AMERICA

TEOTIHUACÁN

Yucatán
peninsula

NORTH
ATLANTIC
OCEAN

CHICHÉN
ITZÁ

Antilles

TENOCHTITLÁN

AZTEC

Caribbean
Sea

MAYA

Andes

Amazon
basin

TRUJILLO

CHAN CHAN

MACHU PICCHU

CUZCO

TIAHUANACO

Mato
Grosso
Plateau

PACIFIC
OCEAN

INCA

Pampas

SOUTH
ATLANTIC
OCEAN

Patagonia

Tierra
del
Fuego

A-to-Z Entries

A

AB KIN XOC The Mayan god of poetry. Ab Kin Xoc was also known as Ppiz Hiu Tec.

ABORE A hero to the Warau Indians of Guyana in South America for teaching humans how to live in a civilized society. Once the slave of the frog woman Wowta, Abore planned his escape when she announced plans to marry him. Knowing how she loved honey, he filled a hollowed-out tree with honey to attract her. Greedy for the honey, Wowta got stuck in the hole, enabling Abore to jump in a canoe and paddle away to live with humans.

ACLLAS (Chosen Women, Virgins of the Sun) Young maidens chosen for their beauty and purity to marry nobles, become priestesses, serve the Inca royal family, or be sacrificed. Four thousand *acllas* lived in the Acllahuasi, the Convent of the Sun Virgins, a school and living quarters built by the great INCA ruler Pachacuti (emperor 1438–71). The *acllas* were under close watch all the time and were never able to leave the Acllahuasi alone.

The *acllas* were actually a part of Incan society. The following story, however, is a legend: One day an exceptionally beautiful *aclla*, Chuguillanto, met a young shepherd while taking an evening walk with another *aclla*. Chuguillanto and the shepherd fell in love but knew they could not be together. Not only was Chuguillanto one of the Chosen Women, but with her beauty and golden hair she was so highly regarded that she was destined to be sacrificed to INTI, the sun god. Alone and apart, Chuguillanto and the young man pined for each other. He became so ill that his mother, who knew a bit of magic, turned him into a walking stick. When Chuguillanto and her friend came again to look for him, the shepherd's mother gave Chuguillanto the stick and told her the

young man had died. Grief stricken, she returned to the Acllahuasi. The guards, who were ever on the lookout for trinkets the *acllas* might have been given by men, overlooked the stick. That night, the stick changed into the shepherd, who declared his love for Chuguillanto. From then on, each night the shepherd assumed his real form so the two could be together; he changed back to a stick at daybreak. When the day came for Chuguillanto to be sacrificed, the two decided to escape and join a neighboring people high in the mountains. This, of course, did not please the gods, who changed the lovers into stone pillars at the top of a mountain pass where they remain: piles of rocks on opposite sides of the road, facing each other but forever apart.

AFTERLIFE The human life experience after DEATH. For most groups in South America, the gods influenced human life on Earth but had little influence after death. The INCA, for example, believed that some kind of life existed after death. They buried their dead sitting up with the pots, food, and tools needed to continue working in case the afterlife was similar to life on Earth. The good, which was most people, went to an afterworld called Hanac-paca. Those that had lived less than good lives on Earth went to a cold, dark UNDERWORLD. The CHIBCHA also believed that after death the soul went to live in an underworld in the center of the Earth, traveling there in boats made of spider webs.

In Meso-America, what happened after one died depended less on one's life on Earth than on the manner in which one died and/or on tests put to the dead person in the underworld. According to the MAYA, the dead descended into the underworld and went through a series of tests. This is similar to the experience of the HERO TWINS as described in the Mayan sacred book the *POPUL VUH* when they battled the underworld gods to free their father and uncle. The AZTEC, too, believed that for most people, death involved performing tests in the underworld. But some—women dying in childbirth, warriors, suicides, sacrificial victims, or others dying a violent death—went directly to a layer in the above world. Not all groups believe the afterlife happens in an underworld: The Miskito, of the Caribbean coast of Honduras and Nicaragua, believe souls follow the MILKY WAY to a land at its end; the SERI, of Mexico's Sonoran Desert, believe the afterlife lies north of the point of sunset in the west.

AHARAIGICHI The highest god of the Abipone people of South America. The Abipone believed Aharaigichi appeared in the heavens as the constellation PLEIADES. Out of respect, they referred to him as Grandfather. According to Abipone belief, when the Pleiades disappeared below the horizon in the fall, Grandfather was ill. The people celebrated when he reappeared in the sky in the spring, fully recovered.

AH KIN (AH KINCHIL, He of the Sun) Another name for KINICH AHAU, the Mayan SUN god and JAGUAR god; also the name for a Mayan high priest.

AH MUN A Mayan CORN god, usually shown with an ear of corn in his headdress. Ah Mun is also known as YUM KAAX and is identified as the LETTER GOD E.

AH PUCH (AHPUCH, AHAL PUH, AH-PUCHAH, To Melt, To Dissolve, To Spoil) A Mayan god of DEATH and the patron of the number 10, Ah Puch ruled Hunhau, the lowest underworld layer. As a LETTER GOD, he is known as God A. He was also associated with war. When Ah Puch is pictured, the flesh on his large body is shown decaying; his head might look like a skull, or he might be holding a skull and wearing a necklace of eyeballs around his neck or twisted in his hair. He is shown with bells and various symbols of death—a Moan bird (VULTURE), a screech OWL, or a DOG. Mayans today know him as the lord of death, YUM CIM or Yum Cimil, who moves about to bring illness and death. In one myth

he sets the soul on fire after a person dies, then throws cold water on the FIRE when the soul cries out in pain. Because the soul cries again from the cold water, Ah Puch sets it to burn again. Again and again he sets the soul afire and abruptly extinguishes it until the soul dissolves. Ah Puch is also known as Cizin to the Yucatán Maya and appeared as the twins Hun Came and Vucub Came (One Death and Seven Death; named after days of the sacred CALENDAR) to the Quiché Maya.

AH RAXA LAC (The Lord of the Green Plate) A Mayan earth god. The MAYA saw the Earth as a great green plate, the sky as an inverted bowl.

AH RAXA TZEL (The Lord of the Green Gourd or Blue Bowl) The MAYA believed the sky was an upside-down bowl. Ah Raxa Tzel was the sky god.

AHTOLTECAT A Mayan silversmith god. Ahtoltecat was also the patron of the TOLTEC, who produced elaborate silverwork.

AHULANE A Mayan god worshiped by warrior followers; he governed the course of arrows in battle.

AIOMUN KONDI (AIMUN KONDI, God of the Heights) The supreme and creator god of the ARAWAK of Guyana. According to their myth, long ago, Aiomun Kondi made the Earth, the sea, the heavens, and the wind. Then he made the great silk-cotton tree that spread wide and tall so its branches reached the sky. When twigs and bark fell from it, fish and birds and all kinds of animals, including humans, grew. They all lived in harmony. Because the people ate wild fruit and plants, there was no need to hunt the animals—which played with the children. The fathers and mothers taught the children how to hunt and fish and farm, even though there was no need for these skills.

The Arawak population grew. After a time, jealousies formed. Envy and all kinds of wickedness took hold. Aiomun Kondi was very unhappy. He warned the people that he would send a great fire. The few who listened saved themselves by digging caverns in the ground. The survivors were kind and true, but as the population grew again, wickedness again slipped in. And again Aiomun Kondi warned the people, saying that this time he would send a flood. But the only person who listened was Marerewana. He built a great boat, which Aiomun Kondi told him to tie to the silk-cotton, or CEIBA tree. The flood came, and all were washed away except for Marerewana and his family, who were safe in the boat tied to the silk-cotton tree. When the flood waters subsided, they were near the place they had lived. There they returned to live and began to repopulate the land.

AMAZON   A 4,000-mile-long river that empties into the Atlantic Ocean. Its source is in the Peruvian ANDES. An early Spanish explorer, Francisco de Orellana (ca. 1490–ca. 1546), named the river after the women warriors of Greek mythology. According to legend, Orellana and those traveling with him along the river were attacked several times by fierce women warriors. At the time the Spanish and Portuguese first made contact in the Amazon basin, a large population of native people lived along the river and its lowlands. But as Europeans took land, spread disease, and captured Indians for slaves, many tribes moved deeper into the forest to escape. Some still live there but with increasingly less isolation.

The mythologies of the Amazon tribes differ, although they center on the Earth and the water—either rivers or sea—on which the people depend. Although Amazon peoples have rain and thunder gods, given the abundance of rain there is little need to routinely appease them. The rivers and sea are familiar, and the Earth is supreme; therefore, the people pay the most attention to the spirits who guard their well-being. Primary among them is KORUPIRA, the protector of game animals, and the legendary *cobra grande*, the protector of fish (see SERPENT).

An exact code of ethics reflects their relationship with the natural world: The laws and rules for living must be followed carefully or disaster will befall all the people. This is illustrated through myths that tell how an earlier world was populated with jaguars who ruled supreme, while humans had little knowledge and no power. Through careful change—transformations of humans and animals—the current world was created. The lives of many people of these tribes are governed by powerful spirits and a reliance on SHAMANS to heal as well as to interpret the spirit world.

In some cases, traditional beliefs are challenged by influences from non-Indians. Some groups have little to do with non-Indians while others work closely with them. The cultures and ways of life of many people of the Amazon basin reflect traditions inherited from their ancestors as well as activities and objects from the "outside" world. Someone may, for example, consult with shamans and attend a Catholic mass in the same way a person might farm or fish traditionally yet use a motor boat to travel the rivers.

ANCHANCHO   Spirits considered by the Colla of the Andean highlands to be wicked. These wailing, moaning spirits were thought to inhabit lonely places in the mountains, especially at dusk and during storms. This is where they might cast an evil eye on solitary travelers, charm them, and then enter their bodies and suck out their blood. The Anchancho were considered responsible for all illness, capable of possessing a body and soul, leaving the person spent and dying. The Anchancho were the opposite of EKKEKKO, a spirit which brought good fortune. Both types of spirits were believed to be children of a powerful prince: Ekkekko was the son of the prince's wife and Anchancho the sons of a woman the prince was not married to. The Colla had other evil spirits called Machulas. Sometimes the Anchancho and Machulas were referred together as the SUPAY.

ANDES   The longest mountain range in the world, running some 4,500 miles down the length of South America, with peaks that are exceeded in height only by the highest peaks of the Himalayas. At their widest, the Andes are 400 miles wide. This mountain range is home to numerous indigenous people, many living in almost the same way their ancestors did hundreds of years ago. The name *Andes* comes from *anti*, the Quechua word for "copper." The Andes has one of the largest deposits of copper in the world.

ANHANGA   The devil to Amazonian Indians of Brazil. Anhanga is a shape-shifter, taking forms that include an evil-looking man and a white deer with fiery eyes. Its appearance—in dreams, by sound, or as a presence—foretells death. When seen in dreams, it presents the dreamer with a horrid picture of the

The bat was often linked with death. This urn with bat is from the Toltec. *(The Art Archive/National Anthropological Museum Mexico/Dagli Orti)*

form of a monkey when the gods decided it was too silly.

Some animal sounds were considered ominous. A dog's howl or an owl's hoot both indicated that someone would die. Seeing an animal that a SHAMAN or sorcerer used—a lizard, snake, toad, spider, or moth—was also thought to bring bad luck. The INCA particularly watched the activities of spiders.

The belief that animals possessed spirits did not keep them from being eaten. The AZTEC hunted lizards, coyote, deer, rabbits, hares, fish, and ducks for food. They raised ducks, turkeys, and dogs to eat and kept bees, both for the honey and for wax. Native groups in the rain forests of South America danced or performed other rituals before fishing or going out on a hunt to ensure success. Although the Incan diet included some meat, it was based on corn and potatoes. They ate LLAMA (which was jerked, or dried), deer, guinea pig (which they raised), rabbit, partridge,

afterlife. Anhanga also plays tricks on humans and is said to steal children.

ANIMALS Most tribes and civilizations believed animals had powers that could both help and hinder them. Humans could tap into this power by owning a part of the animal—either literally or by wearing a symbol or likeness of it. After death, common people were thought to become insects, while the nobility were thought to become birds and animals. Animals were often NAHUALS, or personal spirits, and animal symbols appeared in carvings and were painted on objects. The MAYA, for example, showed a fish held in the mouth of a heron or CAIMAN. They also often depicted a turtle and a frog.

Certain animals, such as the QUETZAL, a brightly colored bird of the Meso-American rain forests, had special significance. The Maya believed that the JAGUAR was the form the Sun took when it dipped below the horizon at night. The OWL was a symbol of death; the BAT was a symbol of the UNDERWORLD; ants (or a DOG, a coyote, or an OPOSSUM, depending on the myth) first led humans to CORN, the foundation of many diets. The black howler MONKEY was once the sacred animal of the Maya and, according to myth, had once been human; it was changed to the

The condor, a vulture native to the Andes, is considered intelligent and strong. This bottle is from the Nazca. *(Birmingham Museums and Art Gallery/Bridgeman Art Library)*

and some ducks and geese. With respect to hunting deer or killing llama, which were domesticated animals, Incan law was very specific: Females were not to be killed.

ANIMISM The belief that objects such as rocks, rivers, plants, and natural phenomena such as thunder and earthquakes have spirits or souls. These objects and phenomena were revered not because of what they were but because of the spirit of the gods within them. In many cases, the object personified the god.

Many scholars believe that animism is the starting point of religious thought for all human groups. The concept that there is an ultimate spirit (or spirits) is thought to spring from the belief that all things seen have a spirit or soul.

APIZTETL (Hungry God) The AZTEC god of famine. It was the Aztec custom to wash in a spring or running stream after eating flesh in sacrificial rituals. Those that did not were said to be too close to Apiztetl.

APOCATEQUIL (Chief of the Followers of the Moon) To the Huamachuco Indians in Peru, the god of night, also referred to as the Prince of Evil. (This name may be more from the connection to night than from being bad.) Apocatequil's twin is the god of day, Piguerao (White Bird). According to Huamachuco myth, Apocatequil and Piguerao were born among the underground people, the Guachimines. Their mother was a Guachimine and their father was Guamansuri, the first man sent to Earth by the creator god Atagudu. The Guachimines killed both parents before the twins were born, but when Apocatequil touched his mother's dead body she came back to life. Then Atagudu helped Apocatequil kill the Guachimines and told him to use a golden spade to dig a hole to the above ground. This hole enabled the Huamachuco to escape and populate the land.

Apocatequil was also considered the god of lightning and thunder, which he made by throwing stones with his sling. The small round stones became thunderbolts, and were thought to be Apocatequil's children. Villagers collected them to ensure fertile soil for growing crops. The stones were also considered charms for success in love.

APOIAUEUE Rain spirits of the Tupí Indians in Brazil. The Apoiaueue bring rain to end a drought.

ARAUCANIAN People of the southern ANDES, from the Pacific Ocean to the pampas (grassy plains) of Patagonia. There were four main groups: Pichunche, Huilliche, Mapuche (known as the people of the land because they farmed), and Pehuenche (people of the pines). The Araucanian put up the most resistance of any group against both the INCA, who never conquered them, and the Spanish. They had a supreme deity, GUINECHE (Master of the Land), a mostly kind creator of all forms of life who also controlled the forces of nature. Evil came through Guecuf from whom the Araucanian protected themselves with magic. The Araucanian believe they are the sole survivors of a battle Guineche waged with Guecuf long ago, when both took the form of serpents (see TEN-TEN AND CAI-CAI).

The Mapuche believe the gods recreate the Earth every 70,000 years after it collides with another world. They believe that they, as a people, were created when a man and a woman emerged from a hole in a volcano to worship a stone figure that had been shaped by rays from the Sun and the Moon.

ARAWAK A peaceful people with a defined class structure who migrated from the upper AMAZON to the Greater Antilles in the Caribbean about 3,500 years ago. The Arawak farmed in raised beds, growing MANIOC, sweet potato, peanuts, cotton, and tobacco. Through interactions with people in Meso-America, they later grew CORN, squash, and beans. In the Caribbean, three groups dominated: Taino Arawak (Cuba, Jamaica, Hispaniola), Borequio or Borinquen (Puerto Rico), and Lucayan (Bahamas). Throughout all Arawak groups, the chieftains were responsible for the daily and religious life of the people. The Arawak believed that all plants and animals had good spirits. In addition, each person had one or more guardian spirits from whom he or she sought advice. The chief's guardian spirits were thought to be particularly powerful and were worshiped as the tribe's gods. Guardian spirits were usually animals and had supernatural or humanlike qualities. In the following story, the spirit-helper is a tree frog.

Once when the hunting was thin around their village, three brothers and their sister went deep into the forest. They set up a camp near a river. The sister stayed at the camp to tend the fire while the brothers went off looking for game. Near the camp lived a tree frog, who splashed in a small puddle of water in a hollowed-out old tree and sang with joy. The young woman was annoyed at the sound and unkindly told him to be silent. The tree frog knew her annoyance came from her hunger, so he changed himself into a man and went hunting. He knew her brothers wouldn't have much luck, so he brought plenty of meat, and they all feasted well. Though the tree frog had assumed the form of a man, he was strange looking—he had bulging eyes and striped skin. The brothers were suspicious of him, but they were hungry and he had provided well. The next day, he taught them how to know when animals were nearby, how to quietly stalk them, and how to shoot their arrows with more accuracy. When the family returned to their village, the tree frog–man went along as the young woman's husband.

All was well for a long time, but one day the woman asked her husband to take a bath with her in the river. He refused, saying he only bathed in rainwater caught in tree hollows. She teased and teased and finally threw handfuls of water over him. This, of course, turned him back into a tree frog. Ashamed at what she had done, she told her brothers only that her husband had gone away. Thereafter, she spent many evenings sitting beneath a hollow tree hoping the tree frog would sing.

See AIOMUN KONDI for an Arawak CREATION MYTH.

ARICONTE AND TAMONDONAR (ARICOUTE AND TIMONDONAR, AROTEH AND TOVAPOD) Twin brothers who the Tupí-Guaraní of Brazil believe brought men and women above ground to live. They were sons of the creator MONAN. Ariconte was the god of night; Tamondonar was the god of day. The brothers argued repeatedly. One dispute was so heated that their village was sent to the heavens. When Tamondonar stamped his foot hard as he made a point, a great spring welled up and

flooded the land. The brothers managed to climb a tree and were saved. In other myths, the creator's anger at how humans lived—their wastefulness, their jealousies—brought on a great fire, which the magician Irin Mage put out with the flood.

ASPECT A side, appearance, or form of a god; a manifestation. Many gods had more than one aspect. For example, the AZTEC wind god EHECATL was an aspect of the FEATHERED SERPENT god QUETZALCOATL. Although they were the same god, they took on different forms depending on the situation.

ASTRONOMY The studied observation of the Sun, Moon, planets, and stars. The movement of heavenly bodies was central to the lives of the pre-Conquest people in South and Meso-America. Without the "dimming" effect of artificial light, the nighttime sky was huge and alive. It moved with an even flow that was powerful and awe-inspiring—literally the work and movement of the gods. People watched the sky to better understand the gods and what they did. Sky watching was also a defense of sorts, for by understanding the heavens and making predictions based on the cycles of heavenly movement, the people could not only prepare themselves for what was to come but find comfort from it. What happened in the heavens, they believed, would be played out on Earth. If the cycles repeated themselves—if the right signs appeared that showed that the movements of the heavens continued—then chaos would be averted on Earth.

Considering that astronomical observations were made without telescopes, they were very exact. The MAYA, for example, accurately predicted when eclipses would occur and determined that the solar year was 365.2420 days long. Twentieth-century astronomers have measured it at 365.2422 days. Because the PLEIADES passed directly overhead, the AZTEC used it to "reset" their solar calendar to account for the extra quarter day at the end of each year. How did they make such accurate observations? They did it by noting the movement of a heavenly body at the horizon, such as its rising and setting. They also used movements measured against other fixed objects, such as a mountaintop or a building. The temples to the Aztec rain god TLALOC and the supreme god HUITZILOPOCHTLI on top of the TEMPLO MAYOR exactly framed the rising Sun on the equinoxes. Markers on the mountains that surrounded the capital of the INCA, Cuzco, measured the movement of the Pleiades and other heavenly bodies that the Inca used to determine seasonal changes that regulated their planting schedules.

The Sky and Mythology   At the Mayan capital, CHICHÉN ITZÁ, during the spring and fall equinoxes, a snakelike shadow appears along one side of the Mayan temple to KUKULCAN, the FEATHERED SERPENT god. This happens only during the equinoxes, and the shadow's snakelike movement along the temple stairway is regarded as an earthly appearance of this god. Usually, however, proof of the gods' existence and their activities remained in the sky. The activities of the Aztec rain god, Tlaloc, are one example. Tlaloc's moods in the heavens determined the life of those on Earth, for Tlaloc had the power to provide good rain as well as drought or deluge. And the sun god was thought to have a difficult journey across the heavens during the day and a perilous one through the UNDERWORLD at night—so perilous, in fact, that Meso-Americans believed it entirely possible that some day he would not have the strength to be reborn. The old Meso-American cultures built temples to their gods on top of pyramids, symbolic mountains, in an effort to get them closer to the sky and therefore closer to their gods.

Some groups in the Amazon basin of South America believe the stars are their ancestors, and their priest-chiefs climb on poles to consult with them. The Inca believed that their rulers were direct descendants of the Sun, that the stars were the children of the Sun and Moon, and that the animal constellations seen in the Milky Way were the protectors of those animals on Earth. To people in the highlands of the ANDES, the stars in Orion's belt are three old women who escaped when fire destroyed the Earth. The four-star constellation the Southern Cross, which is only seen in the Southern Hemisphere and contains three of the 25 brightest stars, is believed to be two heavenly hunters and their dog chasing their prey. And the Bororo people of Brazil believe the stars are tears from their lost children. According to Bororo legend, long ago a young boy was so proud of

the help he gave his mother and other women in the garden that he decided he deserved a reward. So, he stole a little flour as his grandmother ground it. He hid the flour, and stole more and more, until he had quite a lot. Then he took the flour to his grandmother and asked that she make cakes for him and his friends. He lied about where he had gotten the flour, saying that the women had given it to him. But once the boy and his friends had eaten the cakes, he did not feel very well. He had eaten too much, of course, and he was beginning to feel guilty about his stealing and lying. The boy's friends were feeling guilty too, because they knew the truth. The boys thought that they should hide somewhere, so they all climbed a vine that grew into the sky. When the parents climbed to get them, the vine broke. The children were left in the sky, crying at night for their parents and for what they had done.

For other stories about heavenly bodies, see CON, COYOLXAUHQUI, EHECATL, FIRE, HUICHOL, IAE, MILKY WAY, SERI, SIBU, SUN, TECCIZTECATL, YAMANA, ZAPOTEC.

ATLACAMANC   An AZTEC storm god, the male complement of CHALCHIHUITLICUE, the storm goddess.

ATLAUA (Water, Arrow)   An AZTEC water god. Atlaua was also identified with arrows.

AUNYAIN-A   An evil magician of whom the Tupí were wary. Lizards, CAIMANS, and iguanas grew out of his body after the people on Earth tricked him into climbing a vine and he fell to Earth. Vultures ate the rest of his body. He had tusks and was believed to eat children.

AZTEC   A people whose civilization dominated what is now central and southern Mexico from about 1300 until the empire collapsed to the Spanish in 1521. The Aztec are believed to have come from northwestern Mexico. From there, they migrated slowly into the central valley and stayed for a while at TOLLAN, the TOLTEC capital. Then some of them moved on to settle on islands in LAKE TEXCOCO. There, they founded their capital city TENOCHTITLÁN, which grew to be a city with a population of as many

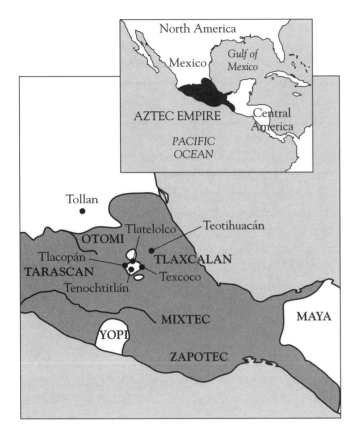

At its peak, the Aztec empire controlled most of what is now central Mexico. *(James Jarvis)*

as 225,000 people. Tenochtitlán was a city of stone buildings and pyramids surrounded by floating gardens.

When the Spanish arrived, the Aztec empire was still growing. A hundred years before, under the ruler Itzcoatl (ruled 1428–40), Tenochtitlán and the city states of Texcoco and Tlateloco had formed the Triple Alliance for mutual defense. This gave the Alliance control over central Mexico. Eventually, Tenochtitlán dominated. By 1519, the empire covered 80,000 square miles and included nearly 40 provinces, making it a vast area to govern effectively. The Aztec openly welcomed the Spanish explorer Hernando Cortés (1485–1547) and his soldiers because they believed they were the returning god QUETZALCOATL and his attendants. Seizing the opportunity, the Spanish captured the Aztec ruler MOCTEZUMA II and set out to take over the city. Within three years, aided in part by native tribes who were not happy with Aztec domination, the Spanish had captured Tenochtitlán and effectively seized an empire.

The Aztec society had a strict CLASS STRUCTURE. At the top were the rulers, priests, and warriors; slaves were at the bottom. It was an organized, prosperous society that believed in the myth-legend that foretold its greatness (see AZTLAN). Religion was at the center of daily life. The Aztec may have worshiped as many as 1,000 gods and goddesses, all of whom had a hand in controlling one's destiny. Deities were not worshiped as role models or in hopes of becoming a "better" person. They were placated in hopes they would influence fate: bring rain for crops, ensure healthy children, provide a favorable outcome to a BALL GAME or battle, and so on. All aspects of daily life were in the hands of the gods. The two-cycle CALENDAR used by many Meso-American cultures, including the Maya, set the structure of ceremonies that the priests organized to make sure the gods stayed happy. Some of these ceremonies may have involved bloodletting or SACRIFICES of humans or animals, although scholars are unsure to what extent this happened.

The Aztec adopted most of their gods and beliefs about them from other cultures—those that preceded them, those that they conquered, and those that they came into contact with through trade. The chief Aztec deities included HUITZILOPOCHTLI, the god of war and the only deity that was purely Aztec; TLALOC, the god of rain; COATLICUE, the goddess of the Earth; Quetzalcoatl, the multifaceted creator god; and TEZCATLIPOCA, the smoking mirror god, patron of warriors, and the god of darkness.

The Aztec Creation Account The Aztec believed that the universe and everything in it, including the people and the gods, was created by the four sons of the primordial god and goddess OMETE-CUHTLI AND OMECIHUATL. Tezcatlipoca, in the form of the Sun, ruled the first world, or Sun, as the Aztec called it. Giants lived in this world; they were drab, coarse beings that ate twigs and berries.

Unhappy with his "dark" brother's sunny form and control of the world, Quetzalcoatl batted Tezcatlipoca out of the sky. Ever unpredictable, Tezcatlipoca changed into a jaguar and ate the Earth.

Now it was Quetzalcoatl's turn: He recreated the Earth and repopulated it. But Tezcatlipoca was still angry. He defeated Quetzalcoatl and caused a great wind to surround the Earth. The wind destroyed everything but a few people, whom Tezcatlipoca changed into howler MONKEYS.

The rain god Tlaloc changed himself into the Sun and created the world of the Third Sun. Quetzalcoatl destroyed that world with a fire that burned everything but a few people who escaped by becoming birds and flying off.

The Fourth Sun began with the water goddess CHALCHIHUITLICUE becoming the Sun. This world was also unsuccessful; floods overcame it and left the few survivors as fish.

We are now in the Fifth Sun—the age of the Sun. This world was formed because of the sacrifice that all the gods made to put the Sun in the sky and have it make its daily east-to-west journey. The Aztec strived daily to achieve the balance that would keep the world going, although they knew that it would end by earthquake. At that time, a Sixth Sun would begin. See also AZTEC SUNS; EHECATL; NANAUTZIN.

AZTEC SUNS   The AZTEC told their history and recounted their mythology in eras, or ages, called SUNS. These have also been referred to as worlds. The present era is called the Fifth Sun. Each of the previous Suns ended with a massive catastrophe that destroyed all humans and most forms of life. The world of the First Sun, "Four Jaguar," was consumed by a jaguar; the Second Sun, "Four Wind," was destroyed by a hurricane; the Third Sun, "Four Rain," by a rain of fire; and the Fourth Sun, "Four Water," by a flood. The world of the Fifth Sun, "Four Earthquake," will be destroyed by an earthquake.

AZTLAN   (White Land)   The legendary place of the seven tribes who developed the cultures of the Valley of Mexico, including the AZTEC. Aztlan originated at the beginning of the Fifth Sun. Also known as the Place of the Seven Caves, Aztlan was a land of plenty where no one suffered, no one went hungry, and no one ever got old. Many myths with varying details tell how the Aztec came to leave Aztlan. In one version a bird tells the people to leave; in another, it is HUITZILOPOCHTLI, the Aztec supreme god, who speaks directly to the priests. Depending on the story, the seven tribes leave one at a time, with the Aztec leaving last, or all leave together.

In the following myth, it is a bird that cues the people to leave. (This bird may actually be Huitzilopochtli since the god's name means "hummingbird of the south.") One day a man heard a bird calling to him, saying, "Go now, go now." When the man told the chief about the bird the chief was relieved. He had known his people must find a new land, their own land, but had waited for a sign. So the people gathered and began a long march. They followed an idol of Huitzilopochtli that the priests carried. As they went, Huitzilopochtli spoke through the priests and prepared the people for the greatness of their empire to come. He explained that they should travel until they came to a large lake; there, they should look for another sign—an EAGLE in a cactus. The journey took 200 years, and the people settled for a while in the TOLTEC capital of TOLLAN. Some people stayed in Tollan and some moved on. From time to time, Huitzilopochtli changed himself into a white eagle to inspire the people, and they traveled until they came to LAKE TEXCOCO and saw a great eagle sitting on a cactus, holding a SERPENT. There they built TENOCHTITLÁN, the city that became the capital and center of the Aztec empire.

The image of the eagle, serpent, and cactus continues as an important symbol to the Mexicans. It is shown in the center of the Mexican flag and on all paper money.

B

BACABS (Erected, Set Up) Mayan gods that stand at the four corners of the world and hold up the heavens. In spirit, the Bacabs were one god, the son of ITZAMNA and IX CHEL, who appeared as four parts and who survived the destructive flood that CHALCHIHUITLICUE sent that ended the Fourth Sun (see AZTEC SUNS). The Bacabs protected the heavens by holding them above the swirling floodwaters. They were sometimes pictured as JAGUAR gods, with their hands over their heads. Each Bacab stands at a cardinal direction, is identified with a color, and influences a specific period in the Mayan CALENDAR. Each Bacab dies at the end of his period and the next one is reborn.

Direction	Color	Name
East	red, the rising Sun	HOBNIL
North	white, the cold	Can Tzicnal
West	black, the darkness after sunset	Zac Cimi
South	yellow, the Sun shining on cornfields	Hozanek

The MAYA of some Yucatán cities also looked to the Bacabs as the patrons of beekeeping and believed they regulated how much rain fell. Others, however, believed the four-part god CHAC. regulated the rain and held up the sky while the BALAMS were in charge of bees. Most agree, however, that the Bacabs were able to see into the future, and even today a Mayan might consult the Bacabs about weather concerns.

See also CEIBA TREE.

BACHUE (She of the Large Breasts) The mother goddess of the CHIBCHA Indians of Colombia. A creation goddess and protector of crops, Bachue came from a lake at creation and, with her husband, populated the land. Then they returned to the lake where they lived as snakes.

BALAM (Jaguar) The everyday gods that protected the MAYA, including protecting a village from disease or outsiders.

BALAM-QUITZE (Smiling Jaguar) To the Quiché MAYA, the first of four men whom the gods created from CORN after GUCUMATZ (some say HURAKAN) created the universe. The others were Balam-Agag (Nighttime Jaguar), Mahucutan (Famous Name), and Iqui-Balam (Moon Jaguar). These four men are considered the ancestors of all Quiché; they taught the people what they needed to know to survive.

BALL GAME Called *pok-a-tok* by the MAYA and *tlachtli* by the AZTEC, ball games were a major pastime of precontact Central and South Americans and are still played in some form throughout Meso-America. The rules may have varied slightly from place to place and through time but everywhere the game was played on an I-shaped court. The court had rings set 20 to 30 feet off the ground in the center of the two long sides and a line drawn across the floor from ring to ring. The court size varied; some accommodated one player per side and some as many as seven. The object of the game was to score points by driving the six-inch hard rubber ball across the line and into the end zone of the opposing team. Players were allowed use only their wrists, elbows, or hips to move the ball. They wore padding to protect themselves not only when hitting the ball, but also while scrambling across the hard floor after it. The ultimate object of the game was to send the ball through one of the rings. When a player did this, his team automatically won, regardless of the end-zone scores. The player who made the ring shot could take any possessions, including clothing, of any spectator he caught, which made for hasty exits from the audience as soon as a ring shot was made.

Ball games drew large crowds of spectators, who often bet on the outcome. The games were serious business and they connected the people and players to the mythic world. Symbolically, for the Maya, the ball represented the Sun, Moon, or planets, and the court represented the cosmos. The ball game represented the sacred game of the gods played out on Earth. It was a reenactment of the too-noisy game played by the HERO TWINS (and their twin father and uncle) that got them called to the UNDERWORLD. In

This ball goal is from the remains of a Mayan court in the Yucatán. *(Erich Lessing/Art Resource, NY)*

fact, the ball court was considered an entrance into the underworld. For the Aztec, the game was the reenactment of the daily trial of the Sun: rising in the morning after being born again from a nighttime of battling the underworld.

BAT Symbol of the UNDERWORLD, DEATH, destruction, and often associated with sacrifices. Bats appear in many stories with morbid themes, including blood-sucking, a behavior that in reality is characteristic of only two vampire bats that live in the tropics. (There are more than 100 species of bat in Meso-America.) Because bats are active at night it is natural that the bat is associated with death and the underworld.

A modern-day myth from the southern Mexico state of Oaxaca explains the nocturnal habit of bats: Once long ago, Bat, who was jealous of the brightly colored feathers of the birds, grumbled to God about always being cold. God took pity on Bat and dressed him in feathers he gathered from the birds. With his new feathers, Bat was quite lovely. He flew around night and day, bragging how *he* was the most beautiful now. Disgusted by—and tired of—Bat's bragging, the birds complained to God, who summoned Bat. Happy to have a new audience, Bat bragged to God—a big mistake, for as he boasted his feathers fell out. Humiliated, Bat now comes out only at night searching for his feathers.

BEE Both the Maya and Aztec kept a stingless variety of bee in their houses for the honey and for wax. The Aztec offered the following prayer when gathering honey:

> I, who come to do this unfriendly act, come compelled by necessity, since I am poor and miserable; thus I come only to seek my maintenance, and so let none of you be afraid nor be frightened of me. I am only going to take you so that you can see my sister the goddess Xochiquetzal—she who is called Precious Branch!

Like other people the world over, ancient Meso-Americans respected the "busy bee." The Maya considered the bee to be a symbol for those who were particularly hardworking. The Mayan god of bees was HOBNIL, the chief BACAB.

BINDING OF THE YEARS See NEW FIRE CEREMONY.

BOCHICA Sun god and founder god of the CHIBCHA Indians in Colombia; husband of CUCHAVIVA, the rainbow goddess. In the guise of a bearded old man with piercing blue eyes and wrapped in a blanket, Bochica traveled the Earth to teach the people how to live. He taught a strong moral code—do not lie, do not steal, and, above all, be kind to others. He also taught the skills necessary for living—such as how to build a house, make pots, and weave. His work done, Bochica disappeared into the west, leaving Earth to return to the realm of the gods; his footprints left great caves in the mountains. When HUITACA, the goddess of excess, teased humans to live more casually, to be merry and carefree, Bochica changed her into an owl. Apparently it was not enough of a lesson, however, for she then enlisted the help of CHIBCHACUM, the god of work, who flooded the land. The people asked Bochica for help, and he returned in a rainbow and brought the Sun to stop the rain and dry up the land. Then he cut a passage through the mountains to drain the water from the land.

BUNDLE A pack of objects, carried by priests, that was sacred to the followers of a god, particularly in nomadic tribes. A sacred bundle might contain fabric thought to be from clothing worn by a god. The fabric was thought to help the priest interpret the word of the gods and to access their power. Followers added other sacred objects thought to be powerful, such as JAGUAR teeth or JADE objects. Bundles are also shown in stone carvings on STELAE, or monuments, near the image of a god to indicate his or her responsibility—or, as one scholar phrased it—"the burden of office."

Family members prepared bundles to accompany the dead on their journey through the other world. These might contain food and jewelry or tools the person needed to continue working.

BUTTERFLY A symbol of joy and rebirth to the Maya.

C

CABALLO MARINO   The wondrous sea horse the witches in Araucanian myths ride to get to the phantom ship *EL CALEUCHE*. Caballo Marino is huge—about 13 feet high. It has a long, golden mane and a back that is long enough to seat 13 witches comfortably. It gallops through and over the waves and goes to the beach or the ship when the witches whistle for it.

CABAUIL   The word *God* in the language of the Quiché Maya of Guatemala.

CACAO   A tropical American tree, *Theobroma cacao* (food of the gods), native to southern Mexico and Central America. Its seeds are processed to make cocoa, chocolate, and cocoa butter. While the OLMEC and MAYA traded and raised cacao, the TOLTEC and AZTEC got cacao in trade because the Valley of Mexico was too dry and cold to grow cacao trees. As they expanded their empire toward the Gulf coast, the Aztec gained control of lands where cacao was native. By using a system of irrigation, a team of gardeners was able to keep cacao trees and other tropical plants in the courtyard of MOCTEZUMA II's palace.

The early Maya worshiped cacao as an idol. Later, their god Ykchaua (Ek Chuahin for the Yucatán Maya) was the patron of cacao producers. The Toltec and Aztec believed QUETZALCOATL brought cacao to the people to give them wisdom and power. Chocolate was believed to be so powerful that extreme care was taken in its preparation. (The process includes roasting, and chocolate does burn easily.)

The tree has long oval-shaped ribbed fruits that grow from its trunk and older branches. The beans contained in the fruits are high in food value and were used as medicine for fever and coughs and to help relieve pain during childbirth. They were also used to make cocoa butter and, of course, chocolate.

The word *cacao*, which the Anglicized word *cocoa* comes from, is Spanish. It comes from the NAHUATL word *cacahuatl*. We get the word *chocolate* from the Nahuatl word *xocolatl*, which is a compound word made up of *xococ*, meaning "bitter," and *atl*, meaning "water." The chocolate that was eaten was indeed bitter. It was often combined with hot pepper and other spices, including vanilla, to make a drink that packed an energy-giving punch. The Mayan chocolate beverage contained corn flour. Chocolate beverages were most often drunk by the upper classes. Farmers were more likely to grow it, literally, as a cash crop: Both the Maya and Aztec used cacao beans as money.

Today, chocolate is produced in huge quantities in manufacturing plants run by computers; in ancient times, chocolate was made by hand. However, the actual process for turning the cacao beans into chocolate has changed very little. The fruit, or pod, is opened and the beans taken out. After they have fermented, they are cleaned and dried. Then they are roasted, which cracks the outer shell. The "nib" inside is ground, which changes the cocoa butter in the nib into a thick paste. This paste is known as the "chocolate liquor" and it is the essence of the chocolate. As the chocolate liquor cools, it hardens. In that hardened state, it is the unsweetened chocolate that we use in baking. Ground to a powder, it becomes cocoa powder. When sugar and perhaps milk and flavorings are added, or when some of the cocoa butter is removed, it becomes sweetened chocolate or milk chocolate.

CACHIMANA The great spirit of the Orinoco of South America. Cachimana watched over the seasons and crop harvests. His evil opposite was Iolokiamo, who was more active but was thought to have less power (see DUALITY).

CAHA-PALUNA (Standing Water Falling from Above) The wife of BALAM-QUITZE, whom the Quiché Maya believed to be the first man.

CAIMAN A reptile of the tropics, smaller than but related to the alligator. Some Maya and Aztec believed that the world rested on the flat back of a caiman that floated in cosmic water. The four corners of the world were the four outstretched legs. Entrance to the underworld was through the mouth. The OLMEC believed the caiman or other alligator-type reptiles were responsible for providing good crops. The Aztec continued this belief and gave the reptile, which it named Cipactli, a day on the CALENDAR.

CALENDAR A system for determining the beginning and length of a year and how it is divided. Most groups in South and Meso-America kept some form of calendar to keep track of the passing of time and to schedule planting and harvesting times and ceremonial days.

Meso-America A two-cycle calendar was used in Meso-America. Although it was probably first developed by the ZAPOTEC it was refined by the MAYA. The calendar was important for many reasons. It kept track of the time and honored each god on a regular basis. It was also important for making predictions for the future and making decisions about scheduling events. The two cycles were the 260 named day cycle (20 weeks of 13 days) and the solar year of 365 days. (The solar year had 18 months of 20 days each; the extra five days were placed at the end and considered "bad omen days.") These two cycles are often pictured as interlocking, rotating gears that aligned to create a 52-year cycle before repeating. Each 13-day week *and* each of the numbered days of the week was watched over by a god or goddess—sometimes more than one. All time, therefore, was controlled by the gods, which meant that the priests were kept busy organizing the rituals and ceremonies

Day Signs of the Aztec 260-day Calendar

Name	God or Goddess
Alligator (cipactli)	TONACATECUTLI, highest god
Wind (ehcatl)	QUETZALCOATL as EHECATL, god of wind
House (calli)	TEZCATLIPOCA as Tepeyollotl, heart of mountain
Lizard (cuetzepalin)	Hueyhuecoyotl, old coyote
Serpent (coatl)	CHALCHIHUITLICUE, goddess of WATER
Death (miquiztli)	TECCIZTECATL, moon god/goddess
Deer (mazatl)	TLALOC, rain god
Rabbit (tochtli)	MAYAHUEL, goddess of PULQUE
Water (atl)	XIUHTECUHTLI, FIRE god
Dog (itzcunintli)	MICTLANTECUHTLI, god of the UNDERWORLD
Monkey (ozomatli)	XOCHIPILLI, prince of flowers
Grass (malinalli)	PATECATL, god of medicine
Reed (acatl)	TEZCATLIPOCA as Izquimilli (Lord of the Smoking Mirror)
Jaguar (ocelotl)	TLAZOLTEOTL, goddess of filth and love
Eagle (cuauhtli)	XIPE TOTEC (Flayed Lord)
Vulture (coz-caquauhtli)	ITZPAPALOTL (OBSIDIAN Butterfly)
Motion (ollin)	XOLOTL, god of twins
Flint (tecpatl)	TEZCATLIPOCA (Lord of the Smoking Mirror)
Rain (quiauitl)	TONATIUH, god of the Sun
Flower (xochitl)	XOCHIQUETZAL, goddess of flowers

that were necessary to honor them appropriately. The end of the 52-year-cycle was called "The Binding of the Years" and was particularly important to the AZTEC. They held their NEW FIRE CEREMONY at that time, in which they extinguished and then relit all fires. The Maya also had a LONG COUNT calendar that covered the years from the creation in 3114 B.C. to an end date in A.D. 2012. The long count calendar was used primarily by priests.

Incan Ceremonial Calendar

Festival	When Celebrated (equivalent months)	What Was Honored
Inti Raymi, Feast of the Sun	June, solstice	Inti, sun god
Chahua-huarquiz, the time for plowing and preparing fields	July	*Huaca* that contained the spirit to provide irrigation water for crops
Yapaquis, the time for sowing crops	August	All *huacas* received sacrifices to provide for good weather: Sun, rain, no frost or heavy winds
Coya Raymi, Feast of the Moon	September, equinox	Moon; purification rituals were performed
Uma Raymi	October	Most important *huacas* honored for the crops, especially for needed rain
Ayamarca, Festival of the Dead	November	Mummies or icons of the dead, particularly rulers and nobility
Capan Raymi, Glorious Festival	December, solstice	A formal religious festival symbolized by gold and silver
Camay quilla	January, new Moon to full Moon	Continuation of Capan Raymi festival but with fasting and personal sacrifices; then all sacrificed objects were discarded
Hatun-pucuy, Ripening	February	Sun and Moon; sacrifices made
Pacha-puchuy, Earth Ripening	March, equinox	Crops, ready for harvest
Ayrihua, Festival of the Inca	April	Royal family; the Sun
Aymoray, Cultivation	May	Corn harvest; major celebration

Meso-American priests used the 365-day solar calendar for festivals and agricultural purposes. The 260-day calendar was used for predictions—the days that would be best to hold a wedding or the official naming day for a newborn baby. The Aztecs called this the TONALMATL (The Book of Days). The numbers 1–13 "aligned" with a day sign, giving each day a calendar name: 1 Deer, 2 Rabbit, 3 Water, and so on. Named days and numbers were considered either neutral, lucky, or unlucky, which made planning ahead especially important—all part of pleasing the gods.

South America Not much is known about calendar systems for many groups including the Inca, although it is believed they primarily functioned to keep track of planting and harvesting of crops. The Incan calendar had 12 lunar months, each of which had three nine-day weeks. Every third year had 13 lunar months. Each day was honored at its HUACA, or sacred place. The Inca also had a ceremonial calendar, which honored specific deities at specific times.

CAMAHUETO A sea monster of the Araucanian in Chile that is responsible for destroying boats. The Araucanian believe that Camahueto is a young silver bull with a single gold horn that spends his childhood in marshes or shallow lakes. When fully grown Camahueto moves to the sea, destroying gardens as he goes. The people of the Chilean island of Chiloé believe Camahueto can only be controlled by a wizard who wraps sea kelp around his neck and leads him away.

CAMAXTLI The AZTEC god of fate, war, and the hunt and a tribal god of the GUACHICHIL. One of the four gods believed to have made the world. According to some accounts, Camaxtli was responsible for giving the world FIRE.

CAMAZOTZ (CAMALOTZ) A vampire BAT god of the Quiché MAYA in Guatemala. He was usually shown holding his victim and a knife. The Maya considered him a terrible god who served death and ruled twilight. He lived in bloody caverns and other dark places which people tried to avoid for fear of disturbing him. Enduring the house of Camazotz was one of the tests put to the HERO TWINS in their UNDERWORLD ordeals. They tricked him by first hiding in their blowguns to protect themselves.

CANNIBALISM The eating of human flesh for ritual or for food. As with human and animal SACRIFICE, cannibalism may have been practiced in South and Meso-America, but to what extent scholars are not sure. Most of what we know about the early civilizations has been influenced by the Spanish and early European colonists, many of whom viewed the people they conquered and their traditions as uncivilized. Consequently, the practices of the native people may have been exaggerated or distorted to justify the Europeans' insistence on converting them to CHRISTIANITY. Considering these qualifications, in Meso-America, cannibalism may have been a ritual, part of a human sacrifice and possibly practiced most by the Aztec. The late Mayan groups may have learned the custom from the Aztec. Some scholars believe that the practice of eating human flesh grew out of the Aztec belief that their gods demanded human sacrifice. The practice may also have grown because the scarcity of animals to hunt in the Valley of Mexico made finding another source of animal protein necessary. The pre-Conquest Aztec did not raise large domestic animals for food, although they did raise turkeys and small dogs.

The Aztec believed that everything on Earth, including the human body, stood for or reflected some aspect of the gods or the universe as a whole. The human head represented the highest layers of heaven; residing in the head was *tonalli*, the energy force necessary for growth. The heart represented the lower layers of heaven and contained *teyolia*, the soul, the energy that contains memory, knowledge, and emotion. The liver represented the UNDERWORLD and contained *ihiyotl*, the part of a human soul that gave humans the energy to love, to have courage, and find happiness. They may have believed that eating a portion of the liver of sacrificed victims, who often were well-regarded enemy warriors captured in battle, would provide some of that warrior's courage.

Cannibalism may also have been practiced in South America, but not by the Inca. In fact, the Inca tried to stop it as their empire widened. In South America, cannibalism appears to have been practiced not for food but for ritual, such as to show kinship and to transfer the power and spirit from one individual to another. Some evidence exists that human bones may have been ground and added to MANIOC beer. Those related to the dead person then drank the beer. This practice reflected the belief that the spirit and power of a person was contained in every part of the person. Therefore, eating the flesh or bones of an individual would give these qualities to the cannibal. The ritual eating of flesh may also have been done as an act of humiliation to those defeated in war. Warriors in tribes that did practice cannibalism believed they had the spirit of the JAGUAR, which made them hunt and eat prey.

CARIB Tribes migrating from Guyana and Venezuela to the Antilles around 1300. They were warlike and may have practiced CANNIBALISM. The Carib gradually migrated north and captured, slaughtered, and assimilated the ARAWAK and even Europeans. Their gods included Mama Nono, the Earth Mother, who created humans by planting stones in the fields, from which people grew; Auhinoin and Couroumon, the star gods; and Icheiri, a household goddess.

CAT Wild cats in South and Meso-America include the JAGUAR, ocelot, and puma. South and Meso-Americans regarded cats as powerful, fierce (particularly the jaguar), and mysterious because of their aloofness. They appear symbolically in carvings and decorations; the inner city of the Inca capital Cuzco was arranged in the shape of a puma. Much evidence supports the existence of jaguar cults, but scientists are not certain that they existed. However, the jaguar as an apparent religious figure is so common that some archaeologists believe it might have been a very powerful god. The devil, or a comparable evil figure, often appeared to shamans in the form of a cat. Today, some groups believe that killing a jaguar with only a wooden spear and no help from others is a sign of great strength and warriorship. The Chiriguani believe that the green tiger Yaguarogui causes solar and lunar eclipses by trying to eat the Sun and the Moon. See also CCOA.

CATEQUIL (CHOKE ILLA) Incan thunder and lightning god who served INTI and MAMA QUILLA. He was usually shown carrying a mace and a sling and was important enough that children may have been sacrificed to him.

CCOA According to the Quechua tribes of the highlands in Peru, a flying catlike spirit. The *ccoa* is said to be the most dangerous of the animal companions of the mountain god INKARRI. It is considered bigger than a domestic cat and thought to be gray with black stripes. When threatened, it hisses hail, urinates rain, and throws lightning from its shiny eyes. Though a malevolent spirit, the *ccoa* does not bite the hand that feeds it. Hence the *ccoa* is more likely to harm the crops of the poor: The noble and rich can feed it well and many farmers make daily offerings to propitiate it.

This stone carving reflects the Mayan belief in the power of the jaguar. *(Banco Mexicano de Imagenes/ Bridgeman Art Library)*

The Aymara in Bolivia believe a puma spirit has the same power as the *ccoa* and symbolizes both the destructive and creative powers of their creator god VIRACOCHA.

CE ACATL (One Reed) A warrior ASPECT of QUETZALCOATL. Ce Acatl was Quetzalcoatl's calendar name. The AZTEC believed that Quetzalcoatl would return by sea from the east in a year designated as One Reed, which was 1519. This strengthened the Aztec's belief that Hernando Cortés (1485–1547) was indeed their returning god.

CEIBA TREE The silk-cotton tree and to the MAYA a sacred symbol of rebirth. Some Mayan groups believed four BACABS stood at the corners of the world and held up the heavens on their up-stretched hands. In the center grew a huge ceiba tree, whose roots grew in the UNDERWORLD and whose branches grew into the heavens. The tree was a "road" used by the gods and the souls of those who had died to travel between the levels of the universe. This arrangement of objects in four corners and the center is called a QUINCUNX.

CEIUCI (Starving Old Woman) To the Tupí Indians along the Amazon River in Brazil, a witch who eats people. Ceiuci is believed to be one of the stars of the PLEIADES who came to Earth to fish because she was starving. When a young man appeared along the bank of the river, she ordered him in the water but he refused. He did dive into the water, however, after she sent a swarm of red ants to attack him. Ceiuci snared him, of course, and took him home to cook. But before she could cook him, her daughter set him free and they ran off together. Furious, Ceiuci chased them but they hid their tracks with branches they cut from trees; these changed into the first animals to inhabit the Earth. The daughter finally stopped running, but the young man ran on—still pursued by Ceiuci—through his entire life. Finally, as an old, old man, he arrived at his mother's house; she was able to protect him from Ceiuci.

CEQUES Straight lines that radiate from Coricancha, the Sun Temple in Cuzco, along which are HUACAS, sacred shrines. The Sun was the center of the Inca's universe and the father of their rulers. The Sun Temple was in the heart of their capital, Cuzco. The *ceques* radiated from the temple and spread the Sun's power throughout the four quarters of the Inca empire. For the most part, the *ceques* were not obvious. They were not paths that could be seen and used but were considered to be spiritual connections between the *huacas* and the Sun Temple. The *ceques* were assigned to social groups who maintained the *huacas* along them. These groups received the power from the sun god INTI via the *ceque*. The Inca had a shrine or idol for every day of the year. Those who cared for the *huacas* had to be very familiar with the calendar and the relationship of their *huacas* to it in order to prepare for the rituals associated with those days. Other Inca towns may also have had *ceques*.

CHAC Mayan god with four parts, each identified with a color and a cardinal point. Chac was the lord of rain, thunder, lightning, wind, and fertility. He was patron of the NUMBER 13, which was considered lucky. As a LETTER GOD, Chac is known as God B. He was the most frequently illustrated of the Mayan gods; he was usually shown with two long, curling fangs and with tears running down his face. The four parts of Chac and the names and colors associated with them are as follows:

North	Sac Xib Chac	White Man
South	Kan Xib Chac	Yellow Man
East	Chac Xib Chac	Red Man
West	Ek Xib Chac	Black Man

The colors are standard for the directions throughout Mayan mythology. Each of the four parts of Chac is responsible for providing rain from that direction. Chac's closest companions were frogs that croaked before rainstorms. During rainstorms, Chac threw stone axes to the ground to make thunder and lightning and emptied gourds of WATER to make rain. Today, in a Mayan Ch'a-Chak ceremony for rain, four men who represent Chac sit at the four corners of an altar. They clap sticks together, roar thunder, and sprinkle water on young boys who hop around as frogs do in a rainstorm. A shaman tends a smoky fire in the center of the altar and offers prayers as he moves around them all.

The Maya believe that it was Chac who broke open a rock and discovered CORN. They also believe that Chac continues to provide corn for the people by sending the rain that helps it grow.

CHACMOOL (CHAC MOOL) A large sculpture honoring the Mayan god CHAC made for receiving sacrificial offerings. A *chacmool* is a humanlike figure sitting with its knees up and leaning back on its elbows and arms. Its head is always turned to look sideways. Some *chacmools* have a flat abdomen on which an offering bowl was placed. In others, the abdomen is carved out slightly to form a built-in bowl. In the Yucatán Maya center at CHICHÉN ITZÁ, there are more than 12 *chacmools*.

CHACO The Argentine pampas, or plains. The two main groups of the Chaco were the Chamacoco and the Macobi. The Chamacoco had a supreme goddess, mother of all, who also controlled the Sun and provided for all living things. The Macobi's overall good spirit Cotaa created the Earth and kept the cosmos running. Once, the Macobi believed, a great tree connected the Earth to heaven and men regularly climbed the tree to hunt. When a spiteful woman burned the tree, those left in the sky became the stars.

Throughout the Chaco, sky objects were carefully considered. The Sun was female, the Moon male. The constellation PLEIADES was a kind figure referred to as Grandfather. Rainbows, however, were suspect because they killed people with their tongues and whisked children away.

CHACS Old men assistants to Mayan priests during ceremonies. Four *chacs* usually assisted a priest. Many *chacs* did live in the temples in the religious centers, of course, but some were skilled craftsmen who lived in villages and helped the priests in rituals and ceremonies there. *Chacs* were knowledgeable and highly regarded, and they may have been the most accessible religious figures in the MAYA's everyday world.

CHALCHIHUITLICUE (CHALCHIUHTLI-CUE, Jade Skirt, Lady Precious Green) AZTEC goddess of rivers, lakes, oceans, storms, and whirlpools. Chalchihuitlicue was the wife of TLALOC and both the creator and destroyer—by flood, of course—of the Sun of Water. The Sun of Water was the Fourth Sun, or fourth age, in Aztec mythological history. Chalchihuitlicue was considered to be the embodiment of youth and beauty and was thought to watch over the ill and newborn children. On an infant's naming day, attendants rinsed his or her mouth with water as a midwife assured the child that Chalchihuitlicue had washed away evil and misfortune. This practice was not unlike the Christian baptism ritual.

Chalchihuitlicue was sometimes depicted as a flowing river that had a prickly pear tree heavy with fruit growing out of it. She has also been identified as the female aspect of ATLACAMANC, the male storm god, and as Chimalma, who was the mother of QUETZALCOATL in his incarnation as CE ACATL, a god of war. Chalchihuitlicue was known as Matlalcueyeh in Tlaxcala, a small state that stayed independent of the Aztecs. See also TLALOC; TLALOCAN.

CHALCHIUHCIHUATL (Precious Woman) An AZTEC CORN goddess. She was the adult form of the young corn goddess XILONEN.

CHALMECACIUATL The AZTEC paradise for children who die young. The concept of such a paradise may be an adaptation of the Christian concept of Limbo, a place for innocent souls.

CHAMALCAN The BAT god of the Cakchiquel MAYA, who were neighbors and frequent enemies of the Quiché Maya.

CHAN CHAN The most populous city in South America before the Spanish CONQUEST, it was a great cultural center of the CHIMÚ. Chan Chan occupied a beautiful valley. It was a city of straight roads and a complex irrigation system for its lush gardens. It also seemed to be a city obsessed with theft. When Chimú rulers died, their property and possessions were closed off and so closely guarded that, in time, the city took the appearance of a city of huge cemetery vaults. The INCA took over Chan Chan between 1465 and 1470 and adopted much of the Chimú culture.

Chacmools were huge stone carvings on which the Maya placed offerings. This *chacmool* was excavated in Chichén Itzá. *(© Doug Bryant/DDB Stock)*

The ruins of Chavín de Huántar as they are today. Still considered a sacred site, Chavín de Huántar was the center of the Chavín culture in the Andes. *(© Charles & Josette Lenars/CORBIS)*

CHASCA A young person with long, curly hair who served the sun god INTI and symbolized the planet Venus in Incan myths. To the INCA, Chasca was Inti's attendant, serving him he rose and set. Some believe Chasca is a page, a young man; others believe it is a young woman who is also the goddess of dawn and twilight and watches over girls and virgins.

CHAVÍN The first great civilization in the ANDES, prominent from 800 to 200 B.C.; their influence throughout the Andes is similar to that of the OLMEC in Mexico. The Chavín were centered in the north central highlands of what is now Peru. Although they did not use the wheel and had no written language or armies, they were highly skilled builders and engineers. They greatly influenced what is now Peru. The Chavín lacked a highly unified system of government. Unlike the INCA, who were not allowed to look directly at their rulers, the Chavín did not fear their rulers. The Chavín did not worship

their ancestors or plan for an afterlife, but their ceremonies and rituals did connect the mostly agricultural people, who were dependent on the weather and climate. As their influence spread, they met little resistance because they coexisted with any local belief and practice. The gods of the Chavín were awe-inspiring. A small caste of priests dressed as animals—particularly JAGUARS, CAIMANS, EAGLES, and hawks—perhaps to attract the power of the gods whom the priests hoped would possess them. The Chavín may have been the earliest tribe in South America to have an organized priesthood and temples.

CHAVÍN DE HUÁNTAR The cultural and ceremonial center of the CHAVÍN in the coastal ANDES. Chavín de Huántar was well situated "vertically and horizontally," as one writer described it, among the coastal kingdoms. People came to this city of about 2,000 not only from the surrounding villages that supported it, but from farther away as well. This was partly because of the oracle thought to speak through the SMILING GOD, one of the three remaining statues of the Chavín. The STAFF GOD is also located there. Work in the city, particularly on the temples, is thought to have been required of members of the Chavín. Today, Chavín de Huántar is still a pilgrimage site for Andes cultures and draws people from Meso-America as well.

CHAY OBSIDIAN stone in the stories of the Cakchiquel MAYA. *Chay* was revered by the Maya and used to make tools. The Maya believed that *chay* could tell them about good places to settle.

CHENUKE An evil spirit of the ONA Indians of Tierro del Fuego that was killed by the hero Kwanyip.

CHERRUVE To the Mapuche ARAUCANIAN Indians in Chile, the spirits of shooting stars. The Mapuche believed that shooting stars were monsters, flying SERPENTS with human heads, or ghosts.

CHIA (CHIBCHO) The CHIBCHA Moon goddess and possibly a form of the evil goddess HUITACA.

CHIBCACHUM (CHICCHECHUM) To the Chibcha Indians of Colombia, the god of work and the patron of merchants and laborers.

CHIBCHA A pre-Conquest civilization in the lowlands of what is now Colombia, north of the Orinoco River. BACHUE was their mother goddess; BOCHICA, their sun god and chief deity; CHIA, the moon goddess; and CHIBCACHUM, the god of work. The Chibcha were conquered by the Spanish in the 1500s.

CHICCANS Giant snakes thought by the Chorti, the MAYA of eastern Guatemala, to hold up the world. *Chiccans* lived in lakes at the four corners of the world and, like the Mayan wind gods, the BACABS, were associated with a direction and color. An infinite number of smaller *chiccans* lived in lakes, running streams, and rivers but spent the dry seasons deep in the Earth in natural mountain springs. When the rains came, they returned to their lakes and rivers, causing them to flood if too many were in the water

at once. The Chorti also believed the *chiccans* caused earthquakes when they turned over as they slept in the mountains. The Yucatán Maya believed the earthquake god MAM caused earthquakes as it slept.

CHICHÉN ITZÁ (Mouth of the Wells of Itza) A great city in the Yucatán peninsula founded by the Itzá, an early Mayan people, in the early 500s. The Itzá migrated there from central Mexico. The city was abandoned around 670 and then rebuilt around 1000 when the Itzá returned. The TOLTEC took over the city and ruled from there until their civilization collapsed around 1200. The buildings in Chichén Itzá reflect both the Mayan and Toltec cultures. One building, the Caracol (Snail), is round and was likely built as an observatory specifically to view Venus, a planet of utmost importance to the Maya. When at war, the Maya apparently scheduled attacks to coincide with Venus as it rose. Today, Chichén Itzá is a great archeological site and draws tourists from all over the world.

CHICHIMEC See GUACHICHIL.

CHICOMECOATL (Seven Serpent) An adult form of the AZTEC goddess XILONEN, the young CORN goddess, and the female aspect of the Aztec corn god CINTEOTL. Chicomecoatl was the goddess of sustenance and fertility. Each fall, the Aztec sacrificed a young girl dressed as Chicomecoatl to ensure a good crop. In art, the goddess was often shown as a young girl surrounded by flowers, a woman who would kill you with a hug, or a motherly woman holding a sunlike shield. Chicomecoatl was not all good, as evidenced by her ability to kill with a hug. The Aztec believed that poor crops due to drought were the result of a collaboration of Chicomecoatl and CHALCHIHUITLICUE, the Aztec goddess of water.

CHICONQUIAHUITL (Seven Rain) An AZTEC slave in costume who played the role of a god during feasts for XOLOTL, lord of the evening star. Slaves taking the roles of gods on feast days were honored as if they were actually the gods. However, they may have been sacrificed at the end of the festivities.

CHILAM BALAMS (Books of Spirits, Book of the Tiger Priests) Books recording the histories of towns and the lineages of ruling families of the MAYA. The full name of a particular book, such as *The Chilam Balam of Chumayel*, refers to the town or region whose history it recorded. The original books no longer exist. Written in glyphs, they were translated after the Conquest.

CHILAN A priest who spoke for the gods of the MAYA, interpreting what they wanted as well as predicting what would happen. During religious ceremonies, the *chilan* went into a trance to receive the messages from the gods. He spent days preparing for this ritual, alone and without food, in order to purify his body. The ritual itself was held in a small building. The *chilan* lay stretched out on his stomach on the floor and heard from the gods, who hovered just below the roof above him.

CHIMALMA To the AZTEC, mother of the FEATHERED SERPENT god QUETZALCOATL in his CE ACATL form. She has also been identified with CHALCHIHUITLICUE, goddess of rivers, lakes, oceans, streams, and whirlpools.

CHIMINIGAGUA The creator god of the CHIBCHA Indians. It is said that Chiminigagua created the universe and then sent large, black birds to carry light over the mountains. These essentials completed, he gave the other deities, especially BACHUE, the task of creating the rest of the world.

CHIMÚ A South American civilization that flourished between 1300 and 1470, just before the rise of the INCA (1400–1532). The Chimú had a very structured society that included a ruling aristocracy that was believed to have descended from the stars. (Other people, they believed, descended from two planets.) The Chimú had no creator god but held that they were created by Taycanamo, a mysterious man who floated to land on a balsa log. He was likable, with a smooth tongue that convinced the people he had been sent to rule them. And, indeed, he did start a dynasty that lasted 500 years. It ended when it was overtaken by the Inca. The center of the Chimú civilization was at CHAN CHAN, which today is an

archaeological site in Peru that is considered endangered. The Chimú religion was practiced along with that of local cults and included celebrations with feasts and dances during which the gods appeared. It included magic and oracles. The people relied on SHAMANS to connect them to their individual guardian spirits.

The Chimú had no written language but were organized and highly skilled engineers who built cities of stucco buildings, canals, and mass-produced goods. They were particularly skilled metalworkers who employed techniques such as hammering, casting, soldering, gilding, and plating that are still used today. Their influence was widespread. When the Inca conquered the Chimú, they took many fine metalworkers back to their capital at Cuzco to teach Incan artisans their craft.

CHIN Moon goddess of the Muysca Indians in Colombia, believed to flood the Earth when unhappy. Chin symbolized the destructive power of women.

CHIPIRIPA Rain god of the Panamanian Indians.

CHONCHON A vampire with big ears and a human head that uses its ears as wings to fly and look for prey. Chonchon was feared by the ARAUCANIAN Indians in Chile.

CHRISTIANITY After the CONQUEST (1521 in Meso-America, 1532 in South America), the native people throughout South and Meso-America were forced by the Spanish and later colonists to convert to Christianity. The Europeans viewed the people they conquered and their traditions as uncivilized. Eager to impose their values on the conquered people, the Spanish destroyed most temples, writing, and monuments of existing religions; banned their traditional ceremonies; and conducted mass baptisms of native people. The AZTEC, MAYA, and INCA, as well as their predecessors, had generally absorbed the gods of the people they overtook. The belief was that gods are greater than anything else; they may take on another name but they cannot die. So, as Christianity was forced on them the indigenous people took on the principal figures: Jesus, Mary, and the saints. Parallels—a supreme god that cannot be seen, for more specific similarities, such as the Aztec ceremony of rinsing the mouth of an infant on its naming day and the Christian baptism (see CHALCHIHUITLICUE), and the fact that the Aztec, Inca, and Catholics confessed their sins.

What developed in many places to various degrees was a blend of ancient and traditional rituals with Christian practice. Those living in the Andes of Peru, for example, may worship in the Catholic Church on Sunday and still put out offerings to CCOA, the catlike spirit that sends hail and destroys crops. Thousands of people form a human snake that curls up the mountain Colquepunku in Peru every spring on the feast of Corpus Christi. They do this to both celebrate the Catholic feast day and to honor the constellation PLEIADES as it begins its three-month disappearance from the nighttime sky. In western Mexico, during a festival at Easter, church bells celebrate the Resurrection. As part of this celebration, a dancer in a traditional costume dances as Judas, the man who betrayed Jesus. At the same time, the dancer is also dancing to celebrate, or to give thanks for, a successful deer hunt.

In many places, the saints in the blended Church that evolved took on a slightly different form than in the Catholic Church. The traditional Catholic saints all actually lived and were canonized by the pope to act as intercessors—to pray to God on behalf of a person on Earth. In the "People's Church," as the blended Church is sometimes called, saints often are worshiped directly, not as middlemen. Some saints have churches of their own and are treated as the ancient people once treated the gods. Many are particular to a town or area and serve the same function as a patron deity did long ago.

That a blended Church evolved is no surprise. The South and Meso-American concept of the universe was different from that of the Spanish. Native peoples adapted Catholicism to suit their needs through their own view of the world. Also, priests were few and far between, perhaps visiting a village only a few times a year. This left the people to create what they needed to deal with the weather, crops, childbirth, and the rest of everyday life. In some areas, such as El Salvador, little remains of traditional practices, so the blend primarily reflects Christianity.

This gold ceremonial knife is of the Chimú god Naylamp. *(Museo del Oro, Lima, Peru/Bridgeman Art Library)*

example—eased the process. The traditional religions worshiped more accessible gods and goddesses as well, and had gods who were patrons of occupations and activities. Christians worshiped Jesus and Mary, and the Catholics have patron saints. There were even

Saints can appear to the people anywhere—in the woods or a cave—or in any form—as a beggar or a merchant, depending on the circumstances and the message. Two Virgins have appeared as well: the VIR-GIN OF GUADALUPE, who is considered the patron of Mexico and is much revered, and the Virgin of Ocotlan, who helps those in need, as well as curing illnesses with water from a spring that appeared at her feet. Throughout, there are both public and private shrines for the saints where they are worshiped, prayed to, and given offerings.

CIBONEY Nomadic hunter-gatherers of the Greater Antilles in the Caribbean and possibly the first inhabitants of the West Indies. The Ciboney may have migrated from Central America or Florida. As no evidence of the language remains, there is no way of tracing its roots or the roots of the people. It is also not possible to know the name that the people used to refer to themselves. The name *Ciboney* comes from the ARAWAK: *siba*, meaning "cave," and *eyeri*, meaning "man." Some sites in Cuba that have been identified with the Ciboney may be 6,000 years old; in Hispaniola, 4,000 years. Spanish records contain little mention of the Ciboney and, in fact, they disappeared soon after Europeans arrived. It is believed that they were sun worshipers, and some possible ceremonial stones have been identified.

CIHUACOATL (QUILAZTLI, Snake Woman) Earth mother to the TOLTEC and AZTEC. Cihuacoatl was a powerful goddess who was very active in the lives of humans. She presided over both births and battles, and her thunderous call was the signal for war and an omen of death. Women giving birth prayed to Cihuacoatl to help them through childbirth by sharing her strength and courage in the same way warriors prayed to her before going into battle. The perceived connection between childbirth and battle was such that tying the middle finger of a woman who had died in childbirth to a shield was thought to make a warrior more powerful.

Cihuacoatl was also considered the goddess of life's difficulties and was thought to wander over the land predicting disasters. She is often identified with the earth goddess COATLICUE, the mother goddess TONANTZIN, and the VIRGIN OF GUADALUPE, a Catholic patroness honored throughout Mexico. With the FEATHERED SERPENT god QUETZALCOATL, Cihuacoatl created new men and women at the beginning of the Fifth Sun. They were made from blood Quetzalcoatl had sacrificed and the meal she made from grinding the bones of those who had lived during the Fourth Sun. Quetzalcoatl had brought those people up from the UNDERWORLD.

CIHUATETEO (*CIUAPIPILTIN, CIUTEOTO*) The spirits of women who died while giving birth. The AZTEC considered such a death an honor. *Cihuateteo* were often shown with a skull for a head and claws for hands and feet. The Aztec believed that the *cihuateteo* lived in the western paradise where each day they carried the Sun from overhead on its afternoon descent to the UNDERWORLD. After spending four years in paradise, they could return to Earth; however, they could come out only at night, either as moths or as demons who brought catastrophe to those who saw them. The *cihuateteo* also brought illnesses to children. When the *cihuateteo* were thought to be about, people made offerings to them, often in the form of butterflies, and children were not allowed outside.

CINTEOTL (CENTEOTL) The AZTEC god of CORN. Cinteotl was the male aspect of the corn gods and was specific to corn. Because corn was primary in the lives of the Aztec, the spirit of Cinteotl was very much present, and the Aztec really wanted to keep him happy. For this reason he may also have been closely connected with other gods. There are various stories concerning Cinteotl: He was considered an aspect of the FEATHERED SERPENT god QUETZAL-COATL; has been said to be both a child of and sister to TLAZOLTEOTL, the goddess of sex and vice; and was thought to be the husband of XOCHIQUETZAL, the goddess of flowers. The powerful rain god TLALOC protected Cinteotl. In the spring, the Aztec collected bunches of reeds, sprinkled blood on them, and arranged them in their homes to ensure the fertility of the corn they planted.

CIPACTLI A sea monster so ancient that it existed before the beginning of time and was thought to have swum in an ocean of stars. From it, the AZTEC believed, the gods made the Earth. Cipactli was also known as TLALTECUHTLI.

CIZIN Another name for AH PUCH, the Mayan god of death.

CLASS STRUCTURE Throughout South and Meso-America, rulers had absolute power. In the larger civilizations, a middle class was generally made up of administrators, engineers, and supervisors. Peasants and slaves made up the lowest class. Artists of all kinds may have been a separate class altogether. Class structure continued after death—common people were thought to become insects, while the nobility became birds and animals.

Aztec The ruler, who held the title *tlatoani* (He Who Speaks Well), was at the top of the Aztec social order. This was an elected post but, except for the earliest periods in Aztec history, the ruler always came from the same family, although it was not necessarily a direct descent. The *tlatoani* was elected by about 100 electors—the nobles and the most important warriors, priests, and government officials. In earlier times, the electors were the heads of the family clans. The ruler had an assistant who was in charge of the everyday workings of the government. Below the assistant were the military commanders, and then the city councils.

An Aztec's status as a member of the nobility depended more on the job he held than on the status of his parents or family. Jobs were not a right of birth. Even those born to slaves could become members of the noble class. Most commoners were part of a hereditary clan, and it was the clans that held land. They also paid the taxes and were primarily responsible for keeping the roads and public buildings maintained. At the bottom of the social order were the *mayeqyes*—free people who were not part of a family clan and, therefore, had no land. Slaves, although not free, did have the benefit of a place to live, food, and regular work. These benefits made it possible for them to move up in the social order: Through work, whether as a weaver or a pottery maker, or as foreman or overseer of an estate, a slave could achieve recognition and, perhaps, freedom. Slaves could also achieve freedom by escaping and successfully reaching the palace of the ruler.

Maya Mayan villages were ruled by a chieftain or lord who inherited the post from a father or older brother. The ruler distributed the land, which was held by the village, and received local taxes, which were paid both in crops and in service to the village. Only the peasants paid taxes. Noble and wealthy Maya had slaves who did all the manual labor. Beyond the villages were the *batabs*, government officials with great power who collected taxes from the peasants; made judgments in times of civil disputes; led a levy of soldiers during war; and relayed messages from the gods from the high priests to the villages.

Inca The Incan social order was very structured, even harsh, but it made for a stable society. People knew what was expected. The ruler, thought to be a direct descendent of the sun god INTI, was at the top of the social order. This *Sapa Inca* (Unique Inca) had divine right over the people in all the villages in the empire. Below him were the four *Apu* or Prefects, each of whom administered a quarter of the empire. They made up the Sapa Inca's Supreme Council. Under them were the provincial governors, the *Tocricoc Apu*, who lived in the outlying capitals and acted both as government administrators and as judges. Then came the *curaca*, native rulers of tribes or villages, and the *camayoc*, leaders of a district or community within a village. The taxpayer households were at the bottom of the heap. In a class of their own were the ACLLAS (the Sun Virgins) and the Yani, a class of servants who served only the royal family. The Yani came to be highly regarded; some scholars believe they were developing into a separate class equal in the society to artisans and skilled craftsmen.

COATLICUE (Serpent Skirt) Earth goddess, ruler both of life and of death, and the mother of the sun god HUITZILOPOCHTLI. The AZTEC believed Coatlicue was discovered by magicians, wrapped in a cloud. Because of her, humans could live and inhabit the Earth, which was necessary if they were to attain spiritual release. Despite Coatlicue's importance, the Aztec did not portray her as a beauty. She was often shown with loose and sagging breasts and with claws for hands and feet. She wore a skirt made of snakes, and around her neck hung a skull strung on a necklace of human hearts. Coatlicue was a DUALITY— both life-giving and cruel. Mexicans still honor her as

Coatlicue's serpent skirt represented the Earth. *(The Art Archive/National Anthropological Museum Mexico/ Dagli Orti)*

a symbol of the strength women possess and of how humans are influenced by their unconscious minds.

In one myth, a large ball of feathers floated from the sky and landed at Coatlicue's feet as she swept out her home one day. She picked it up and tucked it in her pocket. Doing so made her pregnant. Ashamed and horrified that their mother had so mysteriously become pregnant, Coatlicue's 400 sons, led by their sister COYOLXAUHQUI, prepared to attack her. But before they could, Huitzilopochtli sprang from her womb, fully grown, and killed them all. (In another version of this story, Coyolxauhqui is loyal to her mother but Huitzilopochtli does not realize this and kills her along with her brothers.) Huitzilopochtli sent them all to the sky, Coyolxauhqui to be the Moon and his brothers to be the stars.

In another myth, the Aztec ruler MOCTEZUMA I sent a group of priests to visit their homeland AZTLAN and they met Coatlicue. She told them that because the people had become such gluttons and had become so awed by their own lavish culture, they would soon be conquered and their empire would disappear. She gave the priests simple sandals and capes to take back with them in hopes that they would remind the priests of the Aztec's simple beginnings and inspire her son, Huitzilopochtli, who had led the Aztec away from Aztlan, to return and bring the people back.

To the Aztec, Coatlicue and her family represented the universe: She was the Earth, Huitzilopochtli the Sun, Coyolxauhqui the Moon, and her 400 sons the stars. The Aztec celebrated this earth goddess twice a year, in the spring to cure illnesses and in the fall to ensure good hunting.

COCA   The *Erythroxylum coca* bush, native to the ANDES, from which the narcotic cocaine is made. Fresh or dried coca leaves were chewed to bring on a trancelike state that made talking to the gods easier. Dried leaves were also used in mummifying priests and nobles.

According to one story, the people found the coca bush when they left their high mountain home. Seeking a warmer place to live where life would be easier, they settled in a tropical paradise on the eastern side of the Andes. There they burned trees to clear a place in the forest and after much work planted some crops. But the gods became angry, both because smoke from the fires the people built had dirtied the snow on the mountaintops and because the people had abandoned their mountain home, a gift of the gods. The gods sent a heavy rain to wipe out everything the people had grown. Thus defeated, most of the people wanted to give up and die. One young man, as tired and hungry as the others, found a shrub and ate some of its leaves. After eating the leaves, he felt much better. The others followed his example and also became joyful and optimistic. Grateful for another chance, the people gathered seeds from the bush and returned to the mountains.

Coca is still an important part of the lives of people in the high Andes, as it continues to help them endure life in the harsh mountain highlands. In some areas of South America and in other parts of the world, including Africa and southeast Asia, coca is grown to be turned into forms—such as crack—of the illegal and highly addictive drug cocaine.

COCIJO A ZAPOTEC rain god, also the god of lightning. Cocijo was powerful. At the time of creation, he blew on formless matter to create the Sun and other heavenly bodies, the seasons, plants, animals, days, nights, mountains, and rivers.

COCOPA Native people of Northern Baja California and the Colorado River near the Gulf of California. The Cocopa had no written language but did have a strong oral tradition. For the most part their religious practices were individual, not organized. They worshiped twin gods who were both good. Their names were Sipa, who gave them tools but also caused disease, and Komat, whose common sense made the world right. Dreams and visions helped the Cocopa tap into the supernatural and interpret what they experienced for themselves. They believed the soul decided when the person died; after death an OWL took the soul to a southern land where it lived for a time before dying itself. Ghosts of the dead were thought to haunt relatives, so great care was taken to mourn the dead and burn their belongings. The Kerauk, a funeral ceremony done a year after the death, is still practiced by American Cocopa.

Like many peoples, the Cocopa believed that the Earth was once completely covered with water. The creator twins, Sipa and Komat, lived in the center of the Earth inside the womb of their mother. When they decided to come out, Sipa came first. By this time, the land had begun to dry out; it was inhabited only by ants. The twins began to create humans. They made all kinds and did not agree on what they should look like. For example, Sipa thought each toe should have an eye. Komat believed that would be

foolish since the eyes would be useless when the people walked through mud, which the world had a lot of! Sipa had other good ideas, such as inventing a bow and arrow. When he shot it in the air, the falling arrow hit Komat, so Komat decreed that bows and arrows should only be used for hunting. Sipa also made a Sun, but it was so small that it was useless. Komat again stepped in, made it larger, and then threw it into the eastern sky. Together they made a much larger new Sun. Sipa's Sun became the Moon. The Moon decided the seasons and told the people when to plant and when to harvest. The Sun told the people the time of day, when to get up, when to work, and when to sleep.

CODICES Books of the MAYA and NAHUA painted primarily with glyphs that included explanations of the CALENDAR, rituals, history, lineages of some families, and prophecies. Some codices were created before the Spanish CONQUEST, some after it. The pre-Conquest codices were made from paper, skin, or cloth and were about seven inches high and as many as 13 yards long. They were folded accordion fashion to create a book. Most pre-Conquest codices were destroyed by the Spanish. Those created after the Conquest were bound books made of paper from Europe. The codices were named for a location, an owner, the person who found them, or the place where they originated.

Four Mayan codices written before the Conquest have survived: the Dresden Codex, which was concerned with the movements of the planet Venus; the Paris Codex; the Grolier Codex, which was also filled with astronomical calculations; and the Madrid or Tro-Cortésianus Codex. Also surviving is the *POPUL VUH*, the sacred book of the Quiché Maya. Two other important books, *The Annals of the Cakchiquels* and the *Books of Chilam Balam*, were written later and include records of the Conquest.

The 12 NAHUA codices include Codex Borgia (MIXTEC), which describes the Aztec calendar; Codex Fejervary-Mayer, which relates the gods to the calendar; and Codex Borbonicus, which includes a description of the AZTEC 260-day calendar of festival days (the *tonalamatl*) and instructions for foretelling the future (the *trecena*). In addition to these is the 12-volume Florentine Codex written by a Spanish priest,

Bernardino Sahagún (1499?–1590), which was completed about 1577. The Florentine Codex includes descriptions of the gods, the calendar, the people, and the natural world, as well as information—including riddles— about the everyday life of the Aztec, such as the following:

What is it that is a small blue gourd bowl filled with popcorn? One can see from our little riddle that it is the heavens.

What is it that bends over us all over the world? The maize tassel.

What is it that which follows along the gorge, going clapping its hands? The butterfly.

For two additional excerpts from the Florentine Codex, see TLALOC for a description of the rain god Tlaloc, and WATER for an excerpt from a prayer to Tlaloc.

COLLA   A culture of the highland plateaus (llama country) of what is now Bolivia that flourished from 300 B.C. to A.D. 400. The Colla was a very advanced society that built huge round stone structures and made elaborate stone carvings. The people were fierce fighters, skilled in using the *ayllus* or bola. This is a weapon made of three joined cords, with each end tied to a stone. When thrown, the *ayllus* tangles and trips an animal or an enemy. The Colla states were conquered by the INCA and became part of their empire.

The Colla creator god, Tutujanawin (The Beginning and End of All Things), was considered the energy that fills all life to keep it going. Associated with him was INTI/Pachatata, who created human bodies, animals, and the stars. Inti/Pachatata was married to PACHAMAMA, goddess of fertility, who made humans alive. And there was THUNUPA, a culture hero who was good and wise and apparently somewhat accessible to the people. None of these deities was a supreme being.

According to the Colla creation account, in the beginning there was no Sun, the Earth was completely dark, and there were no people. The creator appeared in human form out of LAKE TITICACA and made the Sun, Moon, stars, and then humans. He made groups of humans different from one another in dress and hairstyle. (These differences are still maintained in some parts of the mountains; it is a serious matter not to dress according to the place of one's origin.) The people came out of the Earth at different

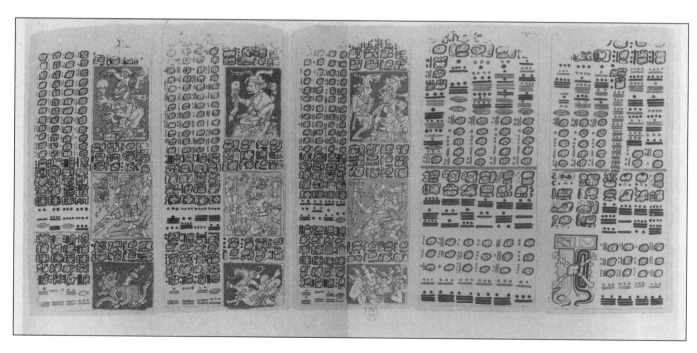

These pages from a 19th-century Mayan codex give information about eclipses. *(Bibliotheque Nationale, Paris, France/Bridgeman Art Library)*

places—from caves, streams, rocks, and trees—and the creator gave each group a language and taught the people how to live where he placed them. This is why groups of people or settlements have HUACAS, or sacred places: The *huacas* are where the people came out of the Earth at origin.

COLOR Most of the archaeological remains of ancient cultures are clay-colored, and little evidence shows the color originally used to paint temples, pots, and other objects. Color, however, was important and symbolic in ancient South and Meso-American cultures. Ancient people made paint from plants and applied it with pieces of pottery. The Maya, for example, had a wide use of symbolic colors that are still used in Guatemala in traditional weaving:

black	the color of obsidian; represents war
yellow	represents food, especially CORN
red	represents blood and life
blue	represents sacrifice
green	the color of quetzal feathers; represents royalty

The ancient Maya used these colors for a variety of purposes beyond purely decorative. Mayan males painted themselves black until they married; then they used red. Prisoners were painted with black and white stripes. Sacrificial victims were painted blue, as were instruments used in the sacrificial ceremony. Priests also painted themselves blue. Red, as a symbol of death and mourning, was used to stain tombs or burial markers and, sometimes, even bones.

Colors also represented the cardinal directions and the gods associated with them. When colors were adapted for Christianity, they took on slightly different meanings:

black	represents west and St. James
yellow	represents south, Mary Magdalene, and fertility
red	represents east, St. Dominic, and teachers
white	represents north, St. Gabriel, and judgment

CON (KON, CUN) To the Peruvian Indians of the ANDES, Con was the thunder god of the mountains, thought to be generally annoyed although he had little interest in humans. He moved fast but had no muscles, bones, or limbs. The people believe that drought comes because Con fought with his brother Pachacamac, who defeated him and sent him north, taking the rain with him.

CONDOR A large black vulture (*Vultur gryphus*) with a bare neck and a collar of white feathers that lives in the ANDES. An intelligent, strong bird that soars in the mountain air currents, the condor was very much respected by the INCA—and is still respected by South Americans living in the mountains. The name *condor* comes from the Quechua *kuntur*.

According to Incan myth, Condor was once entirely white, but grief changed his feathers to black. One day, Condor flew over a mountain pasture and saw a lovely young woman tending a flock; he fell in love with her immediately. When he swooped down to talk with her, she was afraid and ran off. Undeterred, he changed himself into a man and set off the next day to find her again. This time she returned his love. Condor complained to his love that his back itched, and she offered to scratch his back. When she did, he changed back to a condor and flew off with the young woman on his back. The view from the clouds overwhelmed the young woman and the idea of living at the top of the mountains appealed to her, so she agreed to marry him. But after a time of eating old and decaying meat and feeling always cold with nothing but a few feathers to keep her warm, Condor's wife grew very unhappy. One day, when her husband flew off, leaving the young woman to tend their eggs on the mountain ledge (condors do not build nests), a parrot flew up. The parrot brought news of the young woman's family and of how they missed her. The young woman climbed onto the parrot's back and went home. When her condor husband came and pleaded with her to come back, she threw a pot at him to chase him away. Condor became so sad that his feathers turned black and remained so, for he was always mourning his lost love.

CONIRAYA (CUNIRAYA) The all-wise and kind creator god of the Huarochiri (Warachiri)

Indians of coastal Peru. Coniraya was said to have taught the people how to build terraces and irrigate the land to farm; he also made the sea plentiful with fish. He knew the thoughts of humans and occasionally got involved if he thought a person was acting unwisely. As the influence of the INCA spread, the power of Coniraya merged into that of the Incan sun god INTI and Coniraya gradually disappeared.

CONQUEST The European invasion of South and Meso-America began in 1492 when Christopher Columbus (1451–1506) landed on the Caribbean island of Hispaniola. Two years later he returned and landed on Jamaica. The arrival was disastrous for the native people, the ARAWAK. A hundred years later, they were virtually extinct due to disease, overwork, and being killed by Europeans.

Similar scenes played out in mainland South and Meso-America. The Spanish, led by Hernando Cortés (1485–1547), landed in Veracruz, Mexico, in 1519. Within two years, they had arrested the AZTEC speaker, or chief, MOCTEZUMA II, and effectively dismantled the Aztec empire, claiming all its territories for Spain. A 16th-century Aztec song to the gods shows how they felt:

Flowers and Songs of Sorrow
Nothing but flowers and songs of sorrow
are left in Mexico and Tlatelolco,
where once we saw warriors and wise men.

We know it is true
that we must perish,
for we are mortal men.
You, the Giver of Life,
you have ordained it.

We wander here and there
in our desolate poverty.
We are mortal men.
We have seen bloodshed and pain
where once we saw beauty and valor.

We are crushed to the ground;
we lie in ruins.
There is nothing but grief and suffering
in Mexico and Tlatelolco,
where once we saw beauty and valor.

Have you grown weary of your servants?
Are you angry with your servants,
O Giver of Life?

It was a relatively easy victory for the Spanish. The Aztec had had prophecies that indicated their empire would collapse, and the arrival of Cortés reflected their belief that their feathered-serpent god QUETZALCOATL would return over the sea from the east. In addition, many groups that the Aztec had conquered were not happy under their rule and sided with the Spanish. The strong central rule of the Aztec meant that once the central government had been taken, the Spanish could assume control of all.

The Spanish had a more difficult time assuming control of the Yucatán territory. Acquiring the territory of the MAYA also proved to be difficult—there was no central rule, the people lived in smaller villages, and parts of the land were thickly forested. In much of South America, although there were about 30 million people, the population was more widely scattered, and the only major civilization was the INCA. Most of the groups that the Inca had conquered and made part of their empire were happy under Incan rule. Still, the taking of the king and the government proved to be easy for Francisco Pizarro (ca. 1475–1541) and his small army. Pizarro tricked the Incan ruler by asking him to meet with him, unarmed. Then, when the ruler showed up, Pizarro's men snatched him and blasted his attendants with cannons. The emperor agreed to use his gold as ransom for his life, but Pizarro still killed him as soon as the gold was in his possession.

Throughout South and Meso-America, the Spanish assumed the land and diligently destroyed the native cultures. The land, given to conquistadores and nobility as reward for service, was turned into large estates. The native people were treated as slaves and worked the plantations—primarily sugar and tobacco—and silver and gold mines. Many native people died of diseases brought by the Europeans and from overwork. Others undoubtedly died because of the immediate loss of their own culture and the total destruction of the life they had known. Central to this was the loss of the gods that had sustained them. The Spanish had systematically destroyed monuments, temples, and sacred books, and forced the natives to convert to CHRISTIANITY, specifically Catholicism.

COPÁN

One of the largest and oldest of the Mayan centers (see MAYA), possibly *the* center for studying the stars and heavens, making it a city closely associated with the gods. Copán was located in a valley along the Motagua River on the Guatemalan-Honduran border 2,000 feet above sea level. It was a city of elaborate temples, monuments, and plazas, many rich with glyphs. The 63-step Stairway of Hieroglyphics, for example, has more than 2,500 carvings. Copán has been widely restored and attracts visitors from all over the world.

COQUI-XEE

The creation god of the MIXTEC. According to some accounts, Coqui-Xee first made the Mixtec people. Then he created the deer god Cozaana and, finally, the deer goddess Huichaana. In other accounts, the deer gods were the first beings of the world that existed before the present world.

CORICANCHA (Enclosure of Gold)

The Sun Temple at Cuzco, the capital of the Incan empire. Indeed, this principal temple of the INCA was made of gold. It is said to have been 1,200 feet around, housing shrines not only to INTI, but to thunder and lightning gods, the Moon, and the planet Venus as well. The mummies of Incan rulers were kept there. The mummies had attendants, the *ACLLAS*, who kept them cleaned and fed and regularly made offerings to them. The image of the Sun was a gold sculpture four to five feet across with rays radiating out from its face. To its right was the golden image of VIRACOCHA, the creator. To the left was ILLAPA, the rain god. The walls of the temple were lined in gold. In addition, there were gold plates, each weighing four and a half pounds. The Spanish carried off all of these religious relics. By some accounts, the Spanish stole billions of dollars (in today's value) of gold from the Inca.

CORN (MAIZE)

A grain, botanical name *Zea mays*, that grows in fruits called ears along the main tall stalk of the plant. Corn was the main food of Meso-Americans. It was an important food to those living in the Caribbean and South America, who also relied on root crops, such as potatoes, squash, and MANIOC. It is believed to be the oldest, or one of the oldest, cultivated food plants; corn was farmed in Meso-America at least 7,000 years ago. Still a major food plant, corn is grown widely all over the world. The United States, China, Brazil, Mexico, and Argentina are the top five producers of corn.

Ancient Meso-Americans considered corn a gift from the gods, and corn itself was worshiped as a god. The people made sacrifices of ground corn at important occasions, such as coming of age ceremonies. At birth, males who were likely to grow corn as adults were given the dibbing stick used to plant it. Growing

Yum Kaax, the Mayan corn god, sustained life through the corn he provided. *(The Art Archive/British Museum/Eileen Tweedy)*

corn was a communal process; often as many as 20 men worked a cornfield. Farmers used a dibbing stick to make holes three or four inches deep, about 15 inches apart. Into each hole they planted four or five seeds, hoping that one would germinate into a plant. Once the corn germinated, the men tended the fields carefully, pulling competing weeds, which grew rampantly, making sure the corn had enough water, and protecting the plants from insects and animals. When the corn was mature, it was picked and prepared to be eaten—a time-consuming process. Corn needed to be husked, cooked for some time to soften it, and then ground into flour. The corn flour was used for making tortillas and dumplings or mixed with water and spices (sometimes CACAO) to make a beverage.

In corn, people saw the connection between the Sun and the life cycle. Planting corn represented birth; its growth, which was dependent on the Sun, represented life; harvesting and eating the corn represented death; and planting the seeds that had grown the season before represented rebirth. To grow and prepare corn correctly was to honor the gods and show gratitude. The Aztec corn deities included CINTEOTL, the male corn god; CHICOMECOATL, the female goddess; and XILONEN, the goddess of young corn. The Mayan corn gods included CHAC, who brought corn to humans; HOMSHUK, god of corn germination; and YUM KAAX, god of corn.

Contemporary Aztec believe their FEATHERED SERPENT god QUETZALCOATL brought corn to humans with the help of an ant and the rain gods. After creating humans at the beginning of the new age, Quetzalcoatl realized he needed to provide them with food. He watched an ant carrying a grain of corn across a field and into a large mountain. When Quetzalcoatl followed the ant into the mountain, he found it filled with corn. He called on the rain gods. They sent lightning bolts to split open the mountain and wind and rain to release the corn from inside. Corn became the people's first food and, because of their help, the rain gods gained control of the crops.

A HUICHOL myth shows how man came to appreciate corn. Long ago, the Corn Mother introduced a young man to her five daughters, each of whom was a color of corn: Yellow Daughter, Blue Daughter, White Daughter, Red Daughter, and Speckled Daughter. The young man ignored them until he was hungry.

Coyolxauhqui, the Aztec moon goddess, continues to be revered in Mexico. *(Banco Mexicano de Imagenes)*

Then, Corn Mother gave him a tortilla and some *atole*, a drink made from ground corn. He was so satisfied that he chose as his wife Blue Daughter, the most sacred and beautiful daughter of them all.

COXCOXTLI Husband of XOCHIQUETZAL and considered by the AZTEC to be the first man. Coxcoxtli and Xochiquetzal survived the flood that destroyed all life by going to the top of a mountain. (See TLALOC for another account.) Coxcoxtli is considered by some scholars to be an aspect of the supreme god TEZCATLIPOCA.

COYABA The ARAWAK land for the afterlife, where there was continuous feasting and dancing.

COYOLXAUHQUI (Golden Bells) The AZTEC moon goddess; daughter of COATLICUE and sister of HUITZILOPOCHTLI. Coyolxauhqui plays a strong role in many Aztec myths. Some of these myths imply that she is the goddess of the MILKY WAY. In one version of an important myth, Coyolxauhqui's 400 brothers wanted to kill their mother, Coatlicue, when she became pregnant by a ball of feathers. Coyolxauhqui opposed her brothers and went to Coatlicue to warn her of their plan. (In other versions of this myth, Coyolxauhqui led the attack on Coatlicue.) But the newborn Huitzilopochtli, thinking Coyolxauhqui was a threat, killed Coyolxauhqui before she could speak. Afterward, when Coatlicue told him that Coyolxauhqui was good, Huitzilopochtli chopped off his sister's head and threw it into the heavens to be the Moon. Thus Coatlicue could always look to the heavens to see her loyal daughter.

Another story tells about the Aztec's 200-year migration from their legendary homeland of AZTLAN to the Valley of Mexico: Coyolxauhqui (who, in this story, was still alive) wanted to remain in one of the places where the Aztec had temporarily settled. Huitzilopochtli, however, said it was time to move on. She was so insistent and he so adamant that he killed her. Then he broke down the irrigated gardens, which forced the people to leave because the land became too dry. Both stories show Coyolxauhqui as a woman who was strong and stood up for what she wanted. These were warrior qualities that the Aztec admired and which made Coyolxauhqui an EAGLE warrior woman. The NAHUA tradition of using the phrase "fallen warrior women" to describe a conquered city came from this story.

Coyolxauhqui is still respected. In 1978, when a large, carved stone honoring Coyolxauhqui was discovered at an archaeological site in Mexico City, the workers at the site stopped and sang a hymn to honor her.

CREATION MYTHS Stories that explain eternal questions, such as how a people came to live on Earth and in a particular place, how their world of plants and animals was made, and what the heavenly bodies are. Throughout history, humans have wondered about their creation and their world and how it came to be. The people of South and Meso-America were no exception. They believed without question that the gods were responsible, as their myths show, but their creation stories also reflect themes of cycles, life coming from death, and DUALITY.

The AZTEC had a PANTHEON, or network, of gods they believed were so powerful the gods could create and, therefore, destroy the world. They also believed that humans were created solely to support the gods—to worship them by making prayers and offerings and by making SACRIFICES. These gods were jealous and had huge egos. They not only became displeased with how humans treated them, they bick-

ered among themselves. This quarreling is at the heart of the creation and destruction of the AZTEC SUNS, or ages.

Self-importance drove the Quiché MAYA gods to create a world and humans to inhabit it. In fact, it took the gods several tries to make a human they thought was properly respectful of all they had done. (See GUCUMATZ.)

The INCA have several myths to account for their creation. This may reflect the fact that the Incan empire covered a large area and included many different tribes or groups of people. Some historians believe that Incan priests who were sent as teachers and leaders to a village after it had been conquered by the Inca adapted Incan myths to accommodate the beliefs of the people. Most myths reflect the belief that the world was created by the creator god VIRACOCHA.

See the following entries for creation stories of the groups listed.

Entry	Group
AIOMUN KONDI	Arawak
APOCATEQUIL	Huamachuco
ARAUCANIAN	Araucanian
AZTEC	Aztec
CIHUACOATL	Aztec
COCOPA	Cocopa
COLLA	Colla
EL-LAL	Tehuelche
GUCUMATZ	Maya
HUNAB-KU	Maya
INCA	Inca
KARUSAKAHIBY AND RAIRU	Mundurucu
KERI AND KAME	Bakairi
MAKONAIMA	Acawoios
MAMA OCCLO	Inca
MANCO CAPAC	Inca
MAYA	Maya
MILKY WAY	Maya
MIXTEC	Mixtec
MOON	Apinaye
OKONOROTE	Warau
SIBU	Bribri
TEN-TEN AND CAI-CAI	Araucanian
TLALTECUHTLI	Aztec
TUPARI	Tupari
VIRACOCHA	Peruvian Andes
XMUCANE AND XPIYACOC	Maya
YAMANA	Yamana
YANOMAMI	Yanomami

CUCHAVIVA The rainbow goddess of the CHIBCHA Indians in Colombia. Married to BOCHICA, she made fields fertile for planting and guarded women as they gave birth.

CUICHU (CUYCHA) The Incan rainbow god, who served the sun god INTI and moon goddess MAMA QUILLA. Cuichu was important to the Inca because of their dependence on rain for growing crops. He created a temple, complete with his seven colors painted across a golden arch, in the compound honoring Inti in Cuzco. The INCA considered rainbows to be two-headed SERPENTS that had their heads buried in springs deep in the Earth; they were capable of moving and causing trouble. Sometimes they entered humans—particularly women—and caused disease, which could be cured if the person unraveled a multicolored ball of yarn.

CULTURE HERO A figure in mythology, usually in human form, that helps people learn a culture. A culture hero, for example, might teach people how to make and use fire, cultivate and use important plants, or otherwise how to live on Earth. In some stories, the gods helped the culture hero, in others, the culture hero had to solve a problem presented by a deity or overcome obstacles deities threw in the way.

The culture heroes mentioned in this book include the following:

Culture Hero	Group
APOCATEQUIL	Humachuco
EL-LAL	Tehuelche
GAGAVITZ	Cakchiquel Maya
GUCUMATZ	Quiché Maya
HERO TWINS	Quiché Maya
Ixaitiung	TEPEHUAN
Kenos	ONA
KUKULCAN	Yucatán Maya
Maire-Monan (see MONAN)	Tupí-Guaraní
MANI	several groups in Brazil
OKONOROTE	Warau
QUETZALCOATL	Aztec
THUNUPA	several groups in the Andes, including the Collao and Inca
Yoaloh Brothers	YAMANA

D

DABAIBA Water goddess and Mother of Creation to early Panama people. She was also mother of the creator god and was so important that human sacrifices were made to her in hopes that she would always provide rain.

DAY OF THE DEAD An important modern-day festival, celebrated throughout Meso-America and South America, that combines traditional ritual with Christianity. Celebrated on November 2 (or November 3 if November 2 falls on a Sunday), the Day of the Dead coincides with the Catholic All Soul's Day. In many places Day of the Dead is celebrated as a three- or four-day festival that begins on October 30. The festival honors ancestors and welcomes—even encourages—their souls to return to Earth. The holiday reflects the time when dead relatives were thought to be messengers of the gods and had power over the living; this belief is still held by many. Traditionally, many NAHUA cultures had celebrations or performed rituals for the dead throughout the year. Since European colonization, however, it has come to be celebrated in the fall. This is largely because of the similarities between Day of the Dead and All Soul's Day. All Soul's Day is a day when prayers, offerings, and personal sacrifice in the form of observing the Catholic Mass are given to cleanse the souls of the dead and help them resolve any misdeeds so they can be released into heaven.

The Day of the Dead celebrations may include food, offerings, flowers, and new clothes. Central in many houses in Mexico is an *ofrenda*, an altar honoring the dead. The altar may include flowers; statues of the saints, the Virgin Mary, and Jesus; and pictures of the dead and skeleton statues engaged in activities dead relatives enjoyed. The flowers most associated with the day are marigolds, which have been used in rituals by Meso-Americans since ancient times; their round shape and bright orange or yellow color symbolize the Sun. Besides sharing food with family and neighbors, attending church, and making offerings, celebrants may hold all-night vigils in cemeteries or make a path of marigolds to help the souls find their way to the open doors of their houses.

Altars with offerings and skeletons are part of Day of the Dead celebrations. *(D. Donne/DDB Stock)*

DEATH What happens to people after death is a concern in virtually all human societies because it is unknown. Throughout Meso-America people believed that they had many souls or spirits that split up and separated after death. One stayed with the body, whether it was buried or cremated. Others went to the gods; became butterflies, birds, or clouds; fled and hid among the trees to terrify those still alive; and stayed with the person's name to be remembered by the descendents and passed along with the name to a new child. Honoring the dead was important, for their spirits had the power to cause harm or even death if they made themselves seen.

The Maya feared death. In fact, the root of the prayers and offerings to the gods that they made throughout their lives was the hope for a long and healthy life, which the Maya believed was entirely in the hands of the gods. When they died, objects such as tools or pots were often buried or burned with the body because they would be needed in the afterlife. Food and drink might be buried too to ensure some sustenance on the road to the next world.

The Inca believed that life did go on in some form after death (see AFTERLIFE). They did not believe in reincarnation—the moving along of a soul from one body to another after death. At death, a person's life was celebrated—a member of the nobility might be honored for as long as a year. During the Festival of the Dead in Ayamarca (approximately our November), the dead were specifically remembered and mummies were brought out on display.

DEER Some kind of deer is found throughout most of South and Meso-America, specifically mule deer, white-tailed deer, and brocket deer. In older times, these animals were important for both food and

This image of a deer being killed as a sacrificial offering is from the Aztec Codex Borgia. (*Biblioteca Apostolica Vaticana/Bridgeman Art Library*)

clothing, so important that the CALENDAR of some Meso-American cultures had a deer day.

In Meso-American myths, Deer can be highly symbolic or portrayed as a fool. One story in the Quiché Maya book the *POPUL VUH* tells of the HERO TWINS grabbing Deer by its tail when they found it nibbling corn in their garden. Ever swift, Deer bounded away, leaving its tail in the hands of the twins—which explains why deer have short tails. In South America, ANDES people also respect the deer's swiftness as well as its shy and somewhat aloof nature, and some associate the deer with HALLUCINOGENS, which can produce similar qualities. Being quick and somewhat apart are important when a person is trying to communicate with the gods through a trance.

DEFORMITIES Some scholars believe that the OLMEC may have revered deformities as if they were symbols of the will of the gods. Those with hunched backs or Down's syndrome and even those who were obese were thought to have magic powers. In their art, the Olmec showed great respect for humans with deformities. Some Olmec parents misshaped their babies' heads by strapping them between boards to create a deformity. The MAYA practiced this custom as well. Mayan parents also encouraged their children to develop crossed eyes or a squint by dangling a bead from the top of the child's forehead to between the eyes. Some Maya deliberately lengthened the ear-lobes, as did some groups in what is now coastal Peru. The INCA too were awed by—and even worshiped—oddities in nature such as a misshapen ear of corn, a physical deformity, and even the brightest of planets, Venus.

DOG To the people of Central and South America, the dog was associated with death. Some groups believed a dog was a companion for the trip into the unknown, often carrying the person over water to get to the UNDERWORLD. The Inca kept dogs as pets and believed that hearing a dog howl was a sign that someone close to you might die. Some Inca believed that dogs could also send messages to the gods; they tied their dogs and left them unfed in hopes that their howls would let the gods know that rain was needed.

In Meso-America, some myths say Dog discovered CORN; in others it was Ant, Coyote, Fox, or Opossum. Dogs were important in everyday life as working animals, not as pets, but their importance was unquestioned. They were sometimes buried with their owners to help the dead enter the underworld, and they were important sacrificial animals. The Maya raised small hairless dogs for food but used other breeds for hunting. As for the belief that dogs carried the soul over water after death, the later Nahua were very specific. They believed this could be done only by yellow dogs, thinking that black dogs carried only themselves across and that white dogs would refuse since they had just bathed.

DUALITY The concept present in many cultures that an essence has two sides; for example, death brings life. The concept of duality is shown in the gods throughout Meso-America: Many gods had both a male and female ASPECT and could be good and bad. One example is the Aztec earth goddess COATLICUE, who was both life giving and cruel. Similarly, rain gods could bring water for crops or bring the floods or waterborne diseases that would destroy them. Sun gods brought warmth and light as well as drought and thirst. Duality is also reflected in the theme that the material world complements the spiritual world.

EAGLE A symbol of day, the Sun, and a warrior. Eagle Knights were an order of AZTEC warriors. They were warriors of the Sun, which made them the highest order of warrior, higher even than the JAGUAR Knights. An Aztec woman who died while giving birth was also considered a warrior. She became an Eagle Woman, helping to carry the Sun down in the afternoon sky. An eagle holding a SERPENT was the sign for the Aztec to build their city on LAKE TEXCOCO. The eagle and serpent are still the national symbols of Mexico. See also FALLING EAGLE.

EARTH As shown by their myth traditions, the ancient people of South and Meso-America revered the Earth. The Earth was alive, the place that supported all life and therefore not to be taken for granted. Because the Earth gave life, it was regarded as female, and earth mother goddesses—such as the AZTEC CIHUACOATL, COATLICUE, and TETEO INNAN; the CARIB Mama Nono; and the Incan MAMA ALLPA and PACHAMAMA—were worshiped not only for their "earthly" properties but for personifying fertility of all living things. Besides earth mother goddesses, the PANTHEON of gods of early South and Meso-Americans included many earth-related deities to whom people gave offerings regularly, such as the following:

water and rain
CHAC and IX CHEL (MAYA)
TLALOC (Aztec and TOLTEC)
CHALCHIHUITLICUE (Aztec)
ILLAPA and MAMA COCHA (INCA)
CHIPIRIPA and DABAIBA (early tribes in what is now Panama)

hunting and animals
IZTACCIHUATL and OPOCHTLI (Aztec)
MIXCOATL (Aztec and Toltec)

corn and farming
CHALCHIUHCIHUATL, CHICOMECOATL, CINTEOTL, QUETZALCOATL, XILONEN, XIPE TOTEC, and XOCHIQUETZAL (Aztec)
YUM KAAX (Maya)
MAMA CORA (Inca)
ILAMATECUHTLI (Toltec)

In addition, there were earthquake gods—such as the Aztec HUEMAC and the Mayan CHICCANS and MAM—mountain gods, and gods of the UNDERWORLD, for the Meso-Americans particularly saw the Earth as part of the cycle of REBIRTH AND RENEWAL.

The people throughout South and Meso-America were dependent on the Earth, and as with cultures everywhere, their stories grew from it. To most of the people, albeit to varying degrees, all things on Earth had a spirit, and the Earth's spirit along with those of plants and animals and their own were intertwined, so great care and thought were taken to maintain the natural balance: Only what was needed was taken; crop land was carefully terraced on steep slopes to protect the soil, which was nourished with manures and waste materials (today's compost). This was in addition to the daily and seasonal prayers and offerings, for the people accepted their own responsibility in addition to asking for divine intervention.

As an example of how the Earth figures into both the mythology and daily life of a people, consider the Aztec, who believed that the gods Quetzalcoatl and TEZCATLIPOCA created the Earth from a many-mouthed female monster. (See TLALTECUHTLI for the story.) Whether as an Earth monster or not, the Aztec believed the Earth was alive. Earthquakes were not uncommon in Meso-America, and the Aztec kept records of when they occurred. They also made regular offerings to the Earth and took care to plow their fields gently and only in the spring, saying a prayer

This page from the Codex Mendoza shows the eagle on the cactus surrounded by images describing the beginning of the Aztec empire at Tenochtitlán. *(Library of Congress, Washington, D.C./Bridgeman Art Library)*

and kissing a handful of soil before beginning. Some NAHUA groups still believe that if people walk too hard or too much upon the Earth she gets tired, and one should not urinate on her or forget to make prayers of thanksgiving.

EHECATL The wind god and an ASPECT of the NAHUA and MIXTEC god QUETZALCOATL. Ehecatl has as his own aspects the four directions—the four sources of the wind. The AZTEC showed him as a black god wearing a beaked red mask. Around his neck he wore a necklace of a conch shell from which came the whistling of the wind. Ehecatl worked with the rain god TLALOC, clearing the air for the rain to follow.

At the beginning of the Fifth Sun (the current Sun or age according to Aztec belief), Ehecatl blew on NANAUTZIN, the god of light, and TECCIZTECATL, the moon god, after they sacrificed themselves in a FIRE to become the Sun and Moon. The wind from Ehecatl made the Sun and Moon move, as they still do; this is reflected in this age's calendar name, *Four Movement*. Because he was linked so closely with the rain gods—rain and wind often occur together—Ehecatl received sacrifices along with them. With his strong breath, Ehecatl also breathed life into newly created things. By falling in love with the beautiful MAYAHUEL, he gave humans the ability to love.

EK BALAM (EQUEBALAM, Black Jaguar) A god of the early MAYA in the Yucatán, possibly worshiped as a JAGUAR.

EK CHUAH (Black War Chief) In the belief of the MAYA, the god of war, particularly of those who die on the battlefield; of CACAO; and of traveling merchants. Ek Chuah is sometimes referred to as God M. (See LETTER GODS.) As a war god, he is shown carrying a lance or fighting another war god. As a merchant god, he is shown with a pack of items on his back to trade. He was always shown black with a black-rimmed eye and was often shown with a drooping lower lip and a scorpionlike tail.

EKKEKKO (EKEKO, EKAKO, EQ'EQ'O) An everyday, personal god of good luck, plenty, and wealth to the people in the highlands of what is now Peru. Miniature objects that represent things that people need or want are bought and placed on an Ekkekko doll in hopes of acquiring those objects within the next year. These desires might include a husband or wife, good crops, or a new home. Taking the miniatures off the doll is considered to be an invitation to bad fortune (see also ANCHANCHO).

EL CALEUCHE A phantom boat that the Araucanian in Chile believe carries sailors or fishermen to the bottom of the sea. It sails on top of or below the water's surface and is usually in the waters of the channel between Chiloé, an island in the Pacific off Chile, and the mainland. *El Caleuche* always sails at night and appears suddenly through the fog or mist, brightly lit. Under orders from EL MILLALOBO, master of the sea, *El Caleuche* guards the waters and punishes those who bring hardship to the sea or the creatures that live in it. The ship is crewed by witches who come and go from the ship on the back of the great sea horse CABALLO MARINO and by dead shipwrecked sailors, who are given an afterlife of happiness once they board the ship. On calm nights, it is said, music and laughter can often be heard coming from the ship.

EL DORADO (The Gilded One) A wondrous and perhaps legendary city of gold; also, a king. Legends abound about El Dorado: It is a city of gold that existed deep in the rain forests of the Amazon; or the place where Inca escaped with gold to save it from the Spaniards who demanded it all; or a king who covered his body with gold dust each year and then offered the gold to the gods by paddling to the center of a lake (possibly LAKE GUATAVITA) and diving into the lake to wash. Many believe the native people of South America told the Spanish about El Dorado in hopes they would look for the city and leave. Spanish, French, and Portuguese parties hunted deep in the Amazon and Orinoco rain forests but found no sign of a city of gold. Many of the expeditions ended in tragedy as local groups vigorously attacked the explorers.

EL EL The leader of the Quezuba, who were demons feared by the Puelcho of the pampas (plains) of Patagonia. Their purpose was to bring about the downfall of humankind.

In one legend of El Dorado, the legendary king rode a raft filled with gold across a sacred lake. This model made of gold is from the Chibcha culture. *(The Art Archive/Museo del Oro Bogota/Dagli Orti)*

EL-LAL A CULTURE HERO of the Tehuelche Indians of Patagonia. When his father, Nosjthej, threatened to eat him, the infant El-lal was carried to safety by a rat that raised him and taught him the ways of the natural world. (In some versions of the story, El-lal is saved by a worm when an evil god—variously named Keronkenken, Huendaunke, Maipe, or Azhjehen—kills his mother.) El-lal invented the bow and arrow and became a fearless hunter. He was generous to the core, sharing with humans all that he knew. He even shared his knowledge with his father, who still wanted to kill him. In a confrontation with a giant, El-lal changed himself into a dragonfly, flew into the giant's mouth, and killed the giant with a sting. When his love for the daughter of the Sun was spurned, El-lal left Earth on the wings of a swan to reside in an island paradise. Deciding he had done enough for humans, he declared that from then on, they would have to take care of themselves. In other stories, El-lal wins the heart of the Sun's daughter by winning a series of trials, which include slaying a monster and removing a ring from the inside of a dangerously poisonous egg.

EL MILLALOBO A golden seal that the people of Chiloé Island in Chile believe is the lord of the seas. El Millalobo is part man but with short golden fur, the lower body of a seal, and a shaggy wolflike head. It is said to live in the deepest waters, to control the tides and sea storms, and to make sure there are enough fish for those who fish to earn their living.

F

FALLING EAGLE To the Aztec, one of the pillars that supports heaven (see PILLARS OF HEAVEN). Falling eagle represents the power of the gods and heaven on Earth. The three other pillars are SERPENT OF OBSIDIAN KNIVES, RESURRECTION, and THORNY FLOWERS.

FEATHERED SERPENT A powerful mythic being that was a combination of the beautiful QUETZAL and a rattlesnake. In many Meso-American cultures, the serpent was part of the creation and was also involved in the people's everyday lives. See also GUCUMATZ; KUKULCAN; QUETZALCOATL.

FIRE Fire was immensely important to people in ancient South and Meso-America: it was used for cooking; for rituals, including cremating the dead; and, sometimes, for sacrifices. The INCA often threw extra food and drink into a fire as an offering to the Sun. Both AZTEC and Mayan priests tended the fires in temples. The MAYA believed the fire used in ceremonies must be pure, so priests began a new fire for each ceremony. A new fire represented the rebirth of time. This belief was particularly evident in the practice of the NAHUA, whose NEW FIRE CEREMONY (The Binding of the Years) every 52 years honored what they believed was the birth of a new Sun.

There are many myths throughout South and Meso-America about how the people got fire. One group from the Amazon believe that JAGUAR rescued a young man caught by the vines in a tree and carried him to its home. At the jaguar's home the young man learned about fire, stole a red-hot coal, and took it back to his people.

The Cora Indians in Mexico believed that long ago, Iguana took the fire from Earth when he quarreled with his mother-in-law. The people first sent Raven, then Hummingbird, then all the other birds to retrieve it, but they all failed to climb into the sky to reach Iguana. Then the people asked OPOSSUM to try. Opossum told them that he would throw the fire down and that they should catch it on their blankets so it would not burn the Earth. Opossum climbed a cliff, then a waterfall, and finally came to the sky where he found an old man sitting next to a fire. "Grandfather, please, I am cold," said Opossum, "may I warm myself by the fire?" The old man was hesitant but finally agreed. Opossum sat there for so long that the old man got tired. Before he drifted off to sleep, he asked Opossum to watch his fire. As the old man slept, Opossum quietly dragged off a burning stick. When he awoke, the old man saw that Opossum had stolen his fire and chased him. Opossum had already thrown the stick over the edge of the sky when the old man reached him. He beat Opossum soundly before throwing him over the edge as well. When the burning stick landed below, it started to burn the Earth because the people did not catch it in their blankets. When Opossum landed, the people thought he was dead and wrapped him in their blankets. When he came alive again, he saw that fire was everywhere. Opossum called on the Earth Mother to put it out, and she did—but she saved just a bit for the humans to use.

See GAGAVITZ for the story of how fire came to the Cakchiquel Maya; JAGUAR for another story about the great cat and fire; and TOHIL for a story of how this Aztec fire god provided humans with fire.

FLOWERS An AZTEC symbol of spiritual enlightenment, particularly the marigold, which is thought to have the warmth and power of the Sun.

FOX The fox frequently appears in South and Meso-American myths. Along the South American coasts, the fox is believed to have gotten the black tip on its tail by dragging it in water while escaping one of the floods that periodically wiped out all human life. It is one of the dark cloud animals the QUECHUA believe both give life to the MILKY WAY and affect their counterparts on Earth. The fox is one of the shapes that ancient people carved into the NAZCA plains.

In the Gran Chaco region of South America, Fox is often seen as a trickster, playing pranks and trying to trick every animal—VULTURE and Skunk included—usually unsuccessfully. When up against JAGUAR, however, Fox usually wins, for jaguars may be powerful and fierce, but they are not thought to be very bright.

Fox once watched Vulture sit in a tree for a long, long time without moving. Always exaggerating his abilities to himself, Fox bet Vulture that he could sit longer. So they sat and sat, and it got dark and cold. Fox shivered and just sat there but under the cover of darkness, Vulture hopped down so the rocks would protect him from the wind. In the morning when Vulture flew off to find some prey, Fox was still in the tree, frozen to death.

G

GAGAVITZ (Hill of Fire) The "first man," or father of all Cakchiquel MAYA, and a culture hero in part for bringing FIRE to the people. Gagavitz appears in the *Annals of the Cakchiquels*—written in the 1500s in Spanish from Mayan sources, it contains the legendary history of the Cakchiquel as well as an account of the Spanish CONQUEST. According to the *Annals*, Gagavitz was asked by the people to help them get fire from the great volcano Gagxanul. As one man threw pieces of the corn plant and water into the mouth of the volcano, Gagavitz climbed inside and, a long while later, emerged with fire.

GAME See BALL GAME.

GOLD The most malleable (easily worked) of the elemental metals, gold is easy to use and is not likely to rust or get worn with use. In other words, gold is stable. It is also naturally shiny and has a remarkable color. For all these reasons, gold has long been valued. Rich deposits of gold were found in what is now Mexico and South America, particularly Bolivia.

Of the MAYA, AZTEC, and INCA, the Maya had the least use for gold. They did value it but valued QUETZAL feathers and JADE more. The Maya were a Stone Age people; they did little metalwork. Had they worked more with metals, they might have had more regard for gold. They did use gold for fishhooks and some ornamental objects. Gold ornamental objects have been found, particularly at the bottom of *cenotes*, or natural wells. These were probably offerings to a rain god. Scholars believe that these objects came to the Maya through trade and that the later Maya had begun to recognize the value of gold as currency. They may have used it for betting at BALL GAMES. Most Mayan gold is believed to have come through trade from what is now Panama.

Aztec metalworkers, called *tolteca*, worked and cast gold into vessels and ornaments—including masks and jewelry—and created objects with moveable parts, such as tongues and tails. Shields carried by warriors were decorated with intricate gold and turquoise designs that were inlaid in the wood. XIPE TOTEC, the god of agriculture, rebirth, and the seasons, was the patron of goldsmiths. Aztec gold was mined in what is now Oaxaca and especially on the Pacific coast in Zacatula. The Aztec primarily panned gold from rivers, using gourds.

Of all the cultures, the Inca prized gold the most and considered it the "sweat of the Sun." Inca gold was both panned and mined, and the Inca developed their metalwork from the techniques of CHIMÚ. All gold was considered property of the government and taken to Cuzco. There it remained, except by permission of the Sapa Inca, the head of the empire. Only the nobility and priests used the gold. Peasants had no use for it or for any other form of money, since they were paid for their work with the food, clothing, and shelter they needed to live.

To the Inca, gold symbolized the radiance of the Sun, their supreme god. Gold was used inside and outside CORICANCHA, the main temple to the sun god INTI. It was used to line the walls of shrines and for ornamentation on the building. It was also used for statues, including a field of full-sized corn plants in the garden, which also contained statues of rabbits and snakes, butterflies and birds, foxes, and wild cats—all of gold and silver.

When the Spanish first arrived, an envoy from the Aztec leader MOCTEZUMA II presented gifts to them. The Aztec believed that the Spanish were their returning feathered-serpent god QUETZALCOATL and, therefore, believed they were making offerings to him and his attendants. The Spanish hunger for gold is reflected in the following eyewitness account of an Aztec.

> They gave the "gods" ensigns of gold, and ensigns of quetzal feathers, and golden necklaces. And when they were given these presents, the Spaniards burst into smiles; their eyes shone with pleasure; they were delighted by them. They picked up the gold and fingered it like monkeys; they seemed to be transported by joy, as if their hearts were illumined and made new.
>
> The truth is that they longed and lusted for gold. Their bodies swelled with greed, and their hunger was ravenous; they hungered like pigs for that gold.

The Spanish took so much gold from people throughout South and Meso-America that the economy of all of Europe was affected, causing rapid inflation.

GUACHICHIL   Nomadic hunter-gatherers who migrated into central Mexico from the north around 1200, as the TOLTEC civilization was collapsing. They dominated the area, settling there and blending with the Toltec, adopting their culture. The Guachichil, known as the Chichimeca by the Spanish, were fierce and often fought with neighboring tribes. The Sun was their supreme god, the Moon and stars lesser gods. They worshiped no idols and made no sacrifices or offerings except for those buried with the dead to help with the transition to the other world. There is some evidence that the Guachichil may have practiced CANNIBALISM, believing that one could take on qualities of people and animals by eating their flesh or by painting their likeness on one's own skin. They relied on SHAMANS as links to the supernatural world. As the Spanish moved in, Guachichil shamans burned the Spanish churches and attacked churchmen to fend off the onslaught of foreign culture.

GUAGUGIANA   (GUAGUYONA, VAGONIONA)   A trickster of the Taino Indians of Cuba.

GUALLIPEN   (HUALLEPEN)   A fantasy creature of the ARAUCANIAN of Chile that had the head of a calf on the body of a sheep. The Araucanian believed that a child would be born with deformities if the mother dreamed of *guallipens* three nights in a row while she was pregnant. The *guallipen* could also cause deformities in cows and sheep.

GUAYAVACUNI   (GUAYARAKONNY)   The creator and supreme deity of the Tehuelcho/Puelche of the Patagonian pampas (prairie). Although helpful and kind, Guayavacuni was considered remote and beyond comprehension, as most supreme gods are.

GUCUMATZ   (GUGUMATZ, Plumed Serpent)   A Quiché MAYA hero capable of changing himself into an EAGLE, SERPENT, or other animal. He is similar to QUETZALCOATL (TOLTEC and AZTEC) and KUKULCAN (Yucatán Maya), and the Quiché may have borrowed him from one of those cultures.

According to one interpretation of the POPUL VUH, the "council book" of the Quiché Maya, at the beginning of time there was just the sky and sea. Around and above it all were the creator gods Gucumatz and TEPEU. They talked about the world and realized they had the power to bring light and create land, which they did with the help of HURAKAN, the lightning and thunder god. They made animals, too, to roam the forests and mountains; birds to fly above the land; and fish and serpents to swim the waters. The world they created was so magnificent that the gods decided they wanted someone to worship them. Because the animals could not speak, they could not express their gratitude for the world the gods had created.

So the gods made humans. First the humans were created from mud, which did not hold its shape and dissolved when wet. Then, with the help of two older gods, they made humans out of wood. Although they held their shape, these humans had brains too stiff to be grateful for what the gods had done. In other words, they could not worship the gods in the way the gods wanted to be worshiped. The gods destroyed these wooden people by breaking them up, throwing them away, and burning them. Some escaped, however, and became monkeys.

Finally, Gucumatz, Tepeu, and Hurakan made humans from CORN. They made four wise and strong men—BALAM-QUITZE (Smiling Jaguar), Balam-Agag (Nighttime Jaguar), Mahucutan (Famous Name), and Iqui-Balam (Moon Jaguar)—who praised the gods for the world they had created. But these four were so wise that the gods thought they might not continue to be appreciative. Hurakan clouded the men's eyes so they could not clearly see into things and, thus, made them not quite as wise. Then the gods gave them sleep and women with whom they could create children and populate the Earth.

GUECUBU *(CUECUFU, HUECUVU)* Demons that can change form and become humans or animals. The ARAUCANIAN in Chile believe that the *guecubu* cause earthquakes, fill fields with crop-destroying caterpillars, bring disease to animals, and consume all the freshwater fish.

GUINECHE (GUINEMAPUN, Master of Men) The supreme god of the ARAUCANIAN. Guineche controlled the natural world, giving life to all. During a flood that threatened to drown all the people, Guineche made the mountains higher so they could climb above the waters.

GUIRIVILO *(NEGURUVILU)* A snake-fox monster of the ARAUCANIAN. The *guirivilo* lives in rivers. It snares humans with its long tail and drags them to the bottom of the river.

H

HACAVITZ A mountain god of the MAYA; also the name of the mountain where the Maya worshiped him.

HALLUCINOGEN A drug or other substance that brings on hallucinations when ingested. Hallucinogens were made from the leaves, flowers, or seeds of specific plants by priests, SHAMANS, and spiritual healers. These substances induced a trance or caused a vision that helped them communicate with the gods. Although hallucinogens were not used often, most cultures allowed their use only by those who had specific training. Many plants, such as COCA, were also used for medicinal purposes.

The Aztec made beverages from the buds of the maguey, a cactus, for medicinal purposes. The hallucinations brought on would explain the cause of the illness, which god or goddess was unhappy, and what the person or the people had done to make him or her so. The Aztec also dried and ate *teonanacatl,* a hallucinogenic black mushroom they considered sacred.

The Inca used the leaves from the coca bush, which they cultivated in plantations. The also used the leaves from the *wilka* plant and the seeds of the datura plant. The *wilka* brought on visions of the gods, while drinks made from the datura aided communication with dead ancestors.

HERO TWINS HUNAHPU and XBALANQUE, major figures in the stories of the *POPUL VUH,* the "council book" of the Quiché MAYA. The Hero Twins used tricks and magic to get the better of those intent on overthrowing HURAKAN, a creator god, and later to defeat the lords of the UNDERWORLD to get even with them for killing their father and uncle, One Hunahpu and Seven Hunahpu, who were also twins.

In the myths, One Hunahpu and Seven Hunahpu enjoyed playing the BALL GAME and played often, which disturbed the lords of the underworld, who thought that if the twins liked the game so much that they needed to make so much noise, they would be a good match for the underworld lords One Death and Seven Death. But in their travels through the underworld to the ball court, One Hunahpu and Seven Hunahpu failed a test the underworld lords put to them and were sacrificed.

As the Hero Twins, Hunahpu and Xbalanque, grew up, they too spent a lot of time playing ball—and they too made so much noise the lords of the underworld became angry and demanded they come below. After they arrived, the lords set the twins to six trials: in the Dark House, the Razor House, the Cold House, the Jaguar House, the Fire House, and the Bat House. With skill and cleverness, the twins passed the first five tests, but in the Bat House, Hunahpu literally lost his head: A bat cut it off and sent it flying onto the ball court. (This is the mythological world, remember, so losing one's head does not necessarily mean instant death.) The twins called for help from other animals, who brought a pumpkin, which OPOSSUM gave to Hunahpu to use for a head so the twins could play ball with the underworld lords. As the game progressed, Rabbit ran across the court, momentarily confusing the lords, and Hunahpu traded his pumpkin head for the real thing. When the game resumed, Xbalanque gave the pumpkin ball a hard kick, destroying it and winning the game for the twins.

The Hero Twins went on to have more adventures in the underworld, eventually defeating the underworld lords. Their extinction meant that the underworld no longer had great power over the lives of the people on Earth. Whereas once the underworld controlled everything and received magnificent gifts as offerings, now those in the underworld could focus their attention only on people who had behaved dishonorably and only insignificant gifts would be presented to the underworld as offerings. At the end of their adventures, the twins tried, unsuccessfully, to bring their father out of the underworld with them. Then they returned to the sky to become the Sun and the Moon.

The Hero Twins are tricksters, not gods, but that does not lessen their importance to the Quiché Maya. The Hero Twins and their actions are widely symbolic. Their actions on the ball court, for example, explain the movements of the Sun, Moon, and the planet Venus.

Twin Tales It is common for twin brothers to play a central role in myths. The role of the twins varies and includes twin gods, such as Sipa and Komat of the COCOPA; culture heroes, such as the Yoaloh Brothers (see YAMANA), who spread knowledge given by a supreme god; assistants to the creation itself, such as ARICONTE AND TAMONDONAR and KERI AND KAME; and magicians, such as the Hero Twins themselves, Hunahpu and Xbalanque.

HEX CHUN CHAN (The Dangerous One) A Mayan war god and demon spirit that still alarms the MAYA of the Yucatán.

HOBNIL The BACAB of the east and of the color red and thought to be the chief Bacab. Hobnil was also a Mayan BEE god and the patron god of beekeepers. He is usually shown with beelike features.

HOMSHUK The CORN spirit of the MAYA in Veracruz. At the beginning of time, the creator god HURAKAN did not accept Homshuk. When he saw how much life was dependent on corn, however, he changed his mind.

HUACA (GUACA, Holy Site) A sacred shrine of the INCA; a place in the landscape thought to have special mystery or sacredness. *Huacas* could be natural or human-built features. They included caves, mountains, tombs, springs, bridges, boulders, and crossroads. These were places that the Inca believed were given a special, even supernatural, spirit by their creator god VIRACOCHA, enabling them to help humans in times of dire need. After winning a battle against the neighboring people the Chanca, at the time considered more powerful than the Inca, the great Inca ruler Pachacuti (emperor 1438–71) said that he and his warriors had gotten help from the *huacas* who had changed themselves into soldiers.

Offerings made at a *huaca* occasionally included human sacrifice but were more likely other valuables: perhaps woven cloth, an object of carved stone or gold, or a llama or guinea pig, which was raised for food. Mountain *huacas* still receive simple offerings—usually flowers, a stone, yarn, or a cross.

In Cuzco, the center of the Incan empire, more than 360 *huacas* were arranged along imaginary lines called CEQUES that spread out from the Sun Temple. Each *huaca* corresponded to a calendar day and was the site for rituals or other ceremonies on that day. The most important of these was Huanacauri, a hill near Cuzco that was associated with the rainbow gods. Huanacauri was thought to be Ayar Uchu, a son of the god INTI and brother of MANCO CAPAC.

Many of the *huacas* were destroyed by the people after they converted to Christianity. Today the word *huaca* refers to jewelry or a small treasure.

HUATHIACURI The son of PARIACACA, the hero god of the Huarochiri (Warachiri) Indians of the Peruvian coast. According to myth, Huathiacuri was traveling through the land of a man who claimed to be the creator god. The man lived in splendor but was dying of a horrible illness. While walking along a road, Huathiacuri heard two foxes talking about the man's wife, who was keeping company with another man, and about a two-headed toad—a very bad omen—that was living under the stone the man's household used to grind corn. Huathiacuri realized that the actions of the man's wife had brought to the household the toad and the two great serpents that were eating the man's life. Huathiacuri confronted the wife and after she confessed, the serpents and toad disintegrated. The man recovered and allowed Huathiacuri to marry his daughter.

HUEHUETEOTL Oldest of the ancient Meso-American gods, the god of FIRE. The AZTEC saw him as an old man and held various celebrations to honor him. In one celebration, young boys offered lizards, toads, snakes, or frogs to the old men who served the fire god. Some festivals showed the aging of Huehueteotl. First he was shown as a young man; as the celebration progressed, he grew old and his costume changed from bright colors to red and black, to symbolize fire.

HUEMAC (HUEYMAC, Strong Hand) AZTEC god of earthquakes and a legendary ruler of the TOLTEC. Scholars are unsure whether Huemac was a separate god or an aspect of the FEATHERED SERPENT god QUETZALCOATL. According to some accounts, Huemac-Quetzalcoatl both founded the Toltec city of TOLLAN and later caused it to be destroyed to prevent it coming under the rule of the Chichimec.

HUEYTONANTZIN See TONANTZIN.

HUICHOL Indians of the Sierra Madre Occidental mountains in western Mexico. The Huichol still live and farm traditionally; they make 300-mile annual pilgrimages to their homeland, Wirikuta, in the desert of San Luis Potosi. There they gather peyote cactus and retrace and relive the migration of their ancestors. Until recently, they had little to do with the outside world. One source describes them as "self-sufficient and self-contained."

Spiritually, the Huichol still follow ancient traditions. They are the largest group in Mexico that has not been greatly affected by Catholicism. Where Catholicism is practiced among the Huichol, it is not to the exclusion of ancient ceremonies. Equal treatment is given to Catholic saints and traditional gods, which include deities of FIRE, SUN, DEER, EARTH, RAIN, and CORN. Other gods are Maxa Kwaxi (Deer Tail), considered the Great-grandfather; Tatewari, an old fire god, referred to as Grandfather; and Tayaupaq, a sun god, called Father.

Scholars have noticed that the myths of the Huichol reflect the effect of the seasons on their lives. The stories are divided between wet season stories (about growing corn and the flood, for example) and dry seasons stories (about fire and the Sun). One dry season story tells how the Sun came to be: Long ago only the Moon shone; it was very hard on the people, who had to live with much darkness. So, the people

convinced the Moon to give them her son. They dressed the boy in much finery and then threw him into a fire. The people thought he was gone, but he sneaked below the Earth. Several days later, he rose as the Sun in the east. He gave off constant great light and heat, which was hard on the animals that were accustomed to hunting at night. They stayed hidden in shadowy, cool places for a while but they became restless and hungry and angry. They shot arrows at the Sun to make him go away. The gray squirrel and woodpecker grew concerned that the Sun really would disappear and never come back. They put some corn beer at the horizon in the west as a gift for the Sun in hopes that it would encourage him to move from east to west across the sky. It did, of course, which is why the Sun disappears only for a night and always comes back.

HUITACA The goddess of excess and drunkenness and of joy in life to the CHIBCHA Indians of Colombia. Huitaca comes down to Earth to teach evil to humans, to destroy the good they have created, or to show them how to have a "wicked" good time. An appearance by Huitaca often followed a visit from the supreme god BOCHICA, who taught people how to live moral lives. Huitaca may also be the goddess of the Moon, Chia, who was married to Zuhe (possibly a form of Bochica, the Sun). In some stories, it is Chia who follows Bochica. She is so angry at him for not telling people how to bring joy into their lives that she brings on a great flood that drowns most of the people. Bochica throws her into the sky and she becomes the Moon.

HUITZILOPOCHTLI (Hummingbird of the South, Hummingbird of the Left) Warrior and sun god of the AZTEC; the most important god of the Aztec in TENOCHTITLÁN. Huitzilopochtli was a new god to the Aztec, not one evolving from earlier groups. The Aztec viewed the Sun's path across the sky as Huitzilopochtli's daily struggle with the UNDERWORLD—a victory in the morning as it rises, then defeat as it descends in the afternoon for its nightly journey through darkness. His name reflects the Aztec belief that when warriors die, their souls become hummingbirds that travel with the Sun. A myth about Huitzilopochtli's origin tells that he burst

This image of Huitzilopochtli, the Aztec sun god, is from the Florentine Codex. (*The Art Archive/Antochiw Collection Mexico/Mireille Vautier*)

out of his mother's womb as a full-grown warrior. (See COATLICUE.) In another myth, he is the hero-god who led the Aztec from their legendary home of AZTLAN in northwestern Mexico to the Valley of Mexico where they eventually built an empire. During the 200-year migration, priest rulers carried an idol of Huitzilopochtli, who prepared the people (through the priests) for the great civilization to come.

The temple to Huitzilopochtli in Tenochtitlán was on top of the main pyramid alongside that of TLALOC, the rain god. The juxtaposition symbolized both the people's need for the Sun and rain, without which they could not exist, and the yearly cycle of a war-filled dry season and a wet growing season. Stone skulls standing out against a red painted background decorated Huitzilopochtli's temple.

Huitzilopochtli was usually shown wearing a hummingbird helmet or with feathers on his head

and down his left leg. He held a snake, a mirror, or a warrior's shield. Because Huitzilopochtli was a new god, except for his temple, there were no monuments or stone sculptures of him. The helmet was his one distinguishing feature. This may have been one reason why the Aztec accepted the Spanish so readily at first: The helmets the Spanish conquistadores wore were remarkably like Huitzilopochtli's. In an ironic twist, the brutal massacre of the Aztec in Tenochtitlán by the Spanish occurred when the Aztec had gathered on Huitzilopochtli's festival day.

HUIXTOCIHUATL (UIXTOCIHUATL) A fertility goddess of pre-AZTEC Mexico. Huixtocihuatl was the older sister of the rain god TLALOC. After arguing with the rain gods, Huixtocihuatl went alone to live in the sea. She told people that they could get salt by filling pans with seawater and setting them out in sunlight.

HUNAB-KU (HUNAB KU) The Only God, the Unified God) Supreme god of the MAYA, equal to OMETEOTL, the earlier god of the NAHUA people, and either the father of or the same god as ITZAMNA. Hunab-ku does not appear until late in Mayan history—just before the Conquest and into the period of colonization. Itzamna makes an appearance at about the same time, but he is mentioned more often and later than Hunab-ku. It is not known whether these two, as creator and supreme deities, were actually Mayan or were Mayan names for the Spanish Christian god.

In any case, Hunab-ku was above all else. The other gods were aspects of him who looked after the everyday affairs of humans and their world. He brought back life to the world three times after it was covered with water that spurted from the mouth of the great sky SERPENT. Dwarfs lived in the first world, and it was the dwarfs who built the Mayan cities. The Dzolob, a little-known group of people, lived in the second world, and the Maya themselves lived in the third world. In the fourth world—the present world—all kinds of people live. As with the first three, this world will also end with a flood.

HUNAHAU To the MAYA, a lord of death and head of all demons. Some consider Hunahau to be an aspect of the death god AH PUCH.

HUNAHPU A CULTURE HERO of the Quiché MAYA who was one of the HERO TWINS. (His brother XBALANQUE was the other.) The Quiché Maya believed Hunahpu and Xbalanque were drawn into the underworld, as their father had been, but that the twins used tricks and magic to pass the six trials that the underworld lords set before them.

HURAKAN (HURACAN, JURAKAN, The One-Legged) A creator god of the Quiché MAYA who, according to some interpretations, created Earth from a watery mass, while other gods created animals and humans. Because the humans were thought to be too wooden, Hurakan sent a flood to destroy them, except for some that became the little forest monkeys. Then Hurakan created BALAM-QUITZE, Balam-Agag, Mahucotan, and Iqui-Balam who are the ancestors of all Quiché. (For another version of the creation story, see GUCUMATZ.)

Some sources say Hurakan is the god of fire, water, thunder, lightning, and heavy rain. This explains the association of his name with the word *hurricane*, which is derived from the Taino/Carib *hurakán*, meaning "god of the storm."

I

IAE The moon god of the Mamaiuran of the Brazilian Amazon who, along with his brother KUAT, brought daylight to humans. At one time, the world was dark because the wings of the birds completely shaded the Earth; the people had no way to see the wild animals that preyed upon them. Iae and Kuat were determined to change matters. They found a dead body to hide in and waited for Urubutsin, the king of the birds, to find it. When Urubutsin showed up to feast on the corpse, the brothers grabbed his legs and held on until he agreed to allow daylight through. Afterward, thanks to Kuat (the Sun) and Iae (the Moon), the Mamaiuran had both day and night.

IHUIMECATL To the NAHUA peoples, demons who helped TEZCATLIPOCA bring ruin to QUETZAL-COATL. Some sources give Ihuimecatl as another name for the warrior and sun god HUITZILOPOCHTLI.

ILAMATECUHTLI (Old Princess) To the TOLTEC and AZTEC, Ilamatecuhtli was the young CORN goddess XILONEN as a grown woman. She was often shown wearing a skirt covered with stars.

ILLAPA (ILYAP'A, Lightning) Incan god of rain, lightning, thunder, and storms. Illapa was one of the everyday gods of the INCA, closely held and much revered. According to myth, he filled a jug of water from the MILKY WAY and gave it to his sister to guard—in some accounts the Milky Way *is* Illapa's sister. It rained only when Illapa sent a lightning bolt to break the jug. Thunder was the sound of his sling sending the bolt. The movement of his clothes flashed and produced lightning. To inspire a storm, the Inca tied up and kept food from black dogs or llamas in hopes that their cries would make Illapa so sad that he would send rain.

Illapa was shown as a man wearing shiny clothes or as a man with a club and stones. The Quechua in the Peruvian Andes closely associated Illapa with Saint James, the patron saint of Spain. They celebrated both Illapa and Saint James on July 25. As the story goes, when the Spanish soldiers were about to charge, they would call out "Santiago!" Their flashing swords and the explosions from their muskets reminded the Inca of lightning and thunder.

INCA A people whose empire ruled the 2,000-mile Andes region in South America for 100 years prior to Spanish CONQUEST. The Inca were ruled by an emperor, Sapa Inca, who was thought to have descended from the Sun. The emperor looked out for the welfare of the people to the extent that the government owned everything and people had no need for money; the got what they needed as payment for work done. The Inca built terraces and used irrigation to successfully farm the steep mountain slopes. They grew corn, potatoes, squash, quinoa, and peppers, and raised llamas and guinea pigs for food. The Inca also used llamas as pack animals. They had no draft animals (animals that could pull loads), so they did not use the wheel. They were skilled metalworkers who worked especially with GOLD and silver. The Inca were also skilled engineers who built a network of roads that included tunnels, causeways, and bridges. The main routes ran for 3,450 miles along the ridge of the Andes and 2,500 miles along the coast. Secondary roads connected the main routes to each other.

The Inca may have made some human and animal SACRIFICES in gratitude to the gods. Worship of the Sun was the national religion. The principal gods included VIRACOCHA, all powerful and supreme but worshiped only by the nobility; INTI, the sun god;

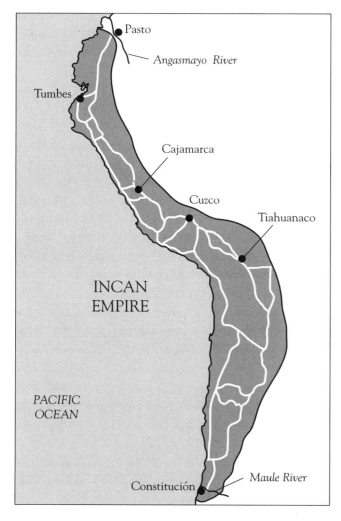

The empire of the Inca was connected by a vast network of roads. *(James Jarvis)*

MAMA QUILLA, the moon goddess; and ILLAPA, the god of rain, thunder, and lightning. The Inca looked for signs and omens to predict the future, especially before taking any important action. The conversion to Christianity is believed by some scholars to have been easy because the Inca had always been tolerant of, and had even assimilated, the religions of those they conquered.

The heavens—stars, weather, planets, Moon, and of course the Sun—all were spiritual beings. Many caves, mountains, springs, and boulders were also believed to be filled with the spirit of the creator god (see HUACA). The Inca made very accurate astronomical observations. They kept records of sunrises and sunsets and matched them to the movement and phases of the Moon. They believed that the movements of the heavenly bodies affected life on Earth. When the constellation Yacana (the LLAMA) fell below the horizon at midnight, for example, the Inca believed it was drinking water from the Earth. This helped prevent rivers and streams from flooding. The lives of the Inca descendants in the Andes today are still shaped by the heavens. Symbolic animals and birds in the sky (constellations) are held responsible for the well-being of those on Earth. Similarly, Andes dwellers believe that the Vilcanota River is the earthly form of the MILKY WAY. As such, it makes a continual flow of water between Earth and sky.

There are several stories that explain the origin of the Inca, but they all reflect the belief that their rulers are direct descendents of the Sun. In one story, four brothers and sisters emerged from the middle of three caves in a cliff and wandered the land looking for a place to live. They were unlike the other people in the land and were considered superior. One brother, Ayar Cachi, was particularly strong and clever, not to mention arrogant. He climbed the great mountain Huanacauri and hurled boulders at the surrounding mountains. This so angered the others that they tricked him into going back to the cave. Once he was inside they filled the entrance, trapping him there forever. The others settled at Tambu Quiru. Later, the spirit of Ayar Cachi appeared and told them to build Cuzco. The spirit again climbed Huanacauri and was turned to stone. The brothers, led by MANCO CAPAC, the son of the sun god Inti, then went to Cuzco, found the land perfect for a city, and settled there. Manco Capac and his sister/wife MAMA OCCLO ruled the city.

INKARRI The all-powerful but aloof creator god of the Quechua of the ANDES. In addition to creating the heavens and the Earth, including humans, Inkarri created the WAMANIS, the everyday spirit lords.

INTI The Sun, a godlike ancestor of the Incan royal family and, according to some myths, the ancestor of all Incan people. Worship of Inti, the Sun, was the state religion of the INCA. Inti, the son of the creator god VIRACOCHA and his wife MAMA QUILLA, was married to PACHAMAMA, the earth goddess. GOLD was the symbol for Inti; he was often portrayed as a golden disc surrounded by rays and with a human face. At the Sun Temple, CORICANCHA, in the Incan capital at Cuczo, fully dressed mummies of the dead emperors surrounded a golden image of Inti. Peruvians still celebrate the power and glory of Inti during the Festival of INTI RAYMI in Cuzco.

INTI RAYMI The Sun Festival, celebrated at Cuzco on June 24, the winter solstice. Inti Raymi celebrates the beginning of the new solar year—a time when the Sun returns to provide warmth for all life. Traditionally, the Incan kings sacrificed llamas as offerings to the Sun during the festival. Today, Inti Raymi draws tens of thousands from all over the world. Among South American celebrations, it is second only to *festival* in Rio de Janeiro. One of the highlights is the portrayal of Inca nobility by 500 actors who are adorned in gold and silver, as befits their rank. The actor portraying the Sapa Inca blesses the day and gives a speech in Quechua (the language of the Inca) that honors the Sun and all that it provides.

IOCAUNA The supreme deity of the Indians of the Antilles at the time of Columbus. Also known as Guamaonocon and Yochu Vagua Marorocoti, Iocauna was all-knowing, all-powerful, invisible, and everlasting.

ITOM AE (Our Mother) The great mother of all YAQUI and creator of the universe. Because Itom Ae is the world and everything in it, she has no originating story. The qualities of Itom Ae were transferred to the Virgin Mary as the Yaqui converted to Catholicism. Itom Ae is honored with bright ribbons—especially red ones—and dancers who hold feather wands and flowers. The Yaqui regard the land as sacred and an extension of Itom Ae. Therefore, when people are buried they are said to be "with our mother."

ITZÁ A powerful Mayan people who may have migrated from central Mexico to the Yucatán. Scholars believe the Itzá founded CHICHÉN ITZÁ, abandoned it, returned later, and rebuilt it but abandoned the city again when war broke out between various tribes of Maya. At this time, the Itzá migrated south and built the city of Tayasal near what is now Flores, Guatemala. The Spanish took over Tayasal in 1697. The Itzá were the last of the Maya to fall under Spanish control.

ITZAMNA (YZAMANA, ZAMANA, Lizard House) Yucatán MAYA sky god, perhaps the biggest god—god of heaven and the Sun. Some saw him as lord of all the gods. Itzámna was everywhere, and to accommodate his roles he had many names. Among them were Kin-ich-kak-mo (The Eye of the Day, or Lord of the Sun's Face) when he was considered the Sun and Kabil (He of the Lucky Hand) when he was prayed to to bring a cure. He is considered the LETTER GOD D. The first priest, benevolent Itzámna brought writing and knowledge to the Maya, and because of his association with the heavens, the other gods, and the priests, he was thought to have invented the CALENDAR. Itzámna's sky associations include the constellation PLEIADES, the Sun, Moon, and wind. On Earth his associations were with animals such as the CAIMAN, mussels, and king vulture and plants such as the CEIBA TREE, CACAO, and CORN, which he taught the people how to grow. Itzámna was the god that priests often paid special attention to at the beginning of the new year. The priests prayed to him for protection in years during which they had predicted disasters and to prevent drought. Blood sacrifices were often made in his honor.

According to different interpretations, Itzamna was thought to be the son of the first god, HUNAB-KU; married to IX CHEL, the Lady Rainbow of many aspects; and father of the BACABS. AH KIN may have been Itzamna's younger form. He was portrayed as a toothless, kind old man who had a large nose (sometimes resembling a SERPENT) and hollow cheeks. Although he was very popular before the CONQUEST, worship of Itzamna gradually disappeared afterwards. Some believe he was annoyed by the Spanish and their Christian god and left. More likely his characteristics were melded into Christianity.

ITZLACOLIUHQUI (ITSLI, Carved Flint Knife, Knife) The AZTEC OBSIDIAN knife god, also a god of SACRIFICE. These are other names for the smoking mirror god TEZCATLIPOCA.

Popocatépetl, a volcano known as the Smoking Mountain, is named for the warrior who loved Iztaccihuatl, the daughter of an Aztec emperor. *(Carlos S. Pereyra/DDB Stock)*

ITZPAPALOTL (Obsidian Butterfly)   A NA-HUA goddess with associations to FIRE, the heavens, hunting, and pain as well as pleasure. Itzpapalotl was considered lovely to look at. Although her early aspect was as a JAGUAR, most people thought of her only as the jaguar's claws. According to myth, long ago, Itzpapalotl became angry while visiting Earth; when picking a rose, she got pricked by a thorn and bled. Because of that, she made sure that humans had unhappiness and pain in their lives as well as pleasure.

IX CHEL (IXCHEL, IX CHEBEL, YAX, The Lady Rainbow)   Mayan goddess of water, medicine, weaving, childbirth, and the Moon; sometimes referred to as Goddess I (see LETTER GODS). According to some interpretations, Ix Chel was married to the sun god, ITZAMNA. As a married couple, the pair illustrated DUALITY: Itzamna was benevolent while Ix Chel was destructive. To be fair, Ix Chel also had a good side. She protected weavers and women in childbirth. The destructive side was more pronounced, however. She was responsible for the floods and heavy rains that knocked out crops and often brought death. Ix Chel was said to "personify" the destructive side of water and was generally considered to be an angry old woman. She was usually shown as haggard and clawed, with a SERPENT around her head, crossbones on her skirt, and other symbols of destruction all around her.

According to myth, Ix Chel's grandfather killed her after discovering that she was living with the Sun. She sprang back to life after a host of dragonflies flew around her grave and sang; then she returned to the Sun. But the Sun became jealous and sent her back to Earth when he thought she had become the lover of Venus, the morning star. Later he begged her to return but he soon became jealous again. Ix Chel, tired of his jealous fits, left for good and to this day wanders invisibly through the night, helping women as they give birth to children.

IXCHUP   The young moon goddess of the MAYA, married to AH KIN. Ixchup may be a young version of IX CHEL.

IXCUINA (Four Face)   Another name for TLA-ZOLTEOTL, the AZTEC goddess of vice.

IXTAB The Mayan goddess of suicide. She is usually shown hanging by a noose around her neck from the sky or from a tree, with her eyes closed and her body in a state of decomposition. The MAYA considered suicide by hanging honorable. Those who hanged themselves went straight to paradise where Ixtab guarded their souls.

IXTLILTON (YXTLILTON, The Little Black One) AZTEC god of medicine and healing, feasting, and games. Black jars filled with water were kept in his temple to use for healing. This water was thought to be especially helpful in healing children. Priests, acting as Ixtlilton, brought the water to the house of a sick child. If the child got well, the family gave a feast with music and games in honor of the priest and presented him with rugs or shawls when he left.

IZTACCIHUATL (White Woman) An AZTEC mountain goddess, guardian of animals needed for food; also the name of a 16,000-foot volcanic mountain in Mexico that is thought to look like a resting woman wrapped in a white cloak. Iztaccihuatl was the daughter of an Aztec emperor who did not want her to marry the warrior she loved. When the warrior was sent off to war, her father told Iztaccihuatl that he had died. She was so filled with grief that she wasted away and died. But the warrior was not dead. When he returned, he took her body to the top of a mountain where he lay alongside her and died. The gods pitied them both and covered them with snow. Then they turned the lovers into mountains. She is the Sleeping Woman; he is Popocatépetl, Smoking Mountain, a volcano that still erupts to show his anger and grief.

J

JADE A semiprecious stone made up of jadeite, found primarily in Asia, or nephrite, found in Meso-America. Jadeite can range in color from white to dark green, and also is found in shades of yellow and brown. Nephrite is usually various shades of green and, because of its hard and heavy nature, can be worked well. It is capable of taking a good edge and can be polished to a smooth, waxy finish. In the old Meso-American cultures, jade was more valuable than GOLD. The OLMEC, possibly as early as 1100 B.C., may have been the first to value and use it, carving it into objects and ornaments. They brought it from what is now El Salvador, 500 miles away from their cultural center. The route they took, which became known as the Jade Route, ran along the coast. Olmec influence along this route was strong.

Jade was very highly prized by both the MAYA and AZTEC. The Aztec particularly prized jade that was emerald green. Only high-ranking people wore jade as ornaments. It was also used for decorative objects, in mosaics, and for ornaments used to adorn the images of the gods. The rain god TLALOC, for example, is often shown wielding a jade tomahawk. Skilled artisans cut jade with a copper tool and then cleaned and polished it with sand and water.

JAGUAR A large wild cat (*Panthera onca*) with a range from Mexico south and throughout South America. Today, jaguars are most often found in the forests of Central America and Brazil. They are white to rich yellow in color with black rosettes—several spots in a circle with another in the center. A few jaguars are dark brownish-black and the rosettes, therefore, are difficult to see. Jaguars are the largest of the American cats and are the only one considered a "big" cat, on the order of lions and tigers. On average, they are about seven feet long and two feet high at the shoulder; they weigh about 300 pounds. Although they are respected and feared by humans, attacks on humans are rare. Jaguars are quick whether running, swimming, or climbing trees and they are fierce hunters. The name comes from the Guarani *yaguara*, which means "he who kills with one leap." The jaguar's favorite foods are the capybara, a large rodent, and the peccary, a wild piglike mammal. Jaguars also hunt deer, birds, fish, and CAIMANS.

Scholars are not sure, or at least do not agree whether ancient Americans considered the jaguar a god. The Maya associated jaguars with obsidian—a dark rock used for ornaments and for the cutting edge of spears and knives. They made their day Ix a jaguar's day, the day of obsidian, when "heaven and Earth embraced" (see also CALENDAR). Jaguars appear on so many objects in Meso-America that it might seem that a jaguar god was the most important of all. TEZCATLIPOCA sometimes did take the form of a jaguar, and humans and gods alike could not do better than be associated with the power of this cat. Certainly there were jaguar cults, such as the Aztec warrior order of Jaguar Knights. In South America, many tribes in Bolivia have cult associations with jaguars, but there is no mythology attached. A member of the Mojo who is wounded by a jaguar and lives becomes part of a rank of shamans believed able to tap into jaguar energy and readily transform themselves into the animal. One can also gain power, it is thought, by killing a jaguar. Some believe that eclipses occur because a jaguar has tried to eat the Sun or the Moon.

An Opaye story from central South America tells both how FIRE came to the people and how Jaguar came to eat raw meat: Once, Jaguar's mother possessively kept all the fire. She would not share it even when asked politely. The other animals tried to steal some or trick her into teaching them how to make it

The jaguar was a much-revered animal throughout South and Meso-America. This 13th- or 14th-century jaguar pot is from the Guanacaste-Nicoya region of what is now northwestern Costa Rica. *(Museum of Fine Arts, Houston, Texas/Bridgeman Art Library)*

but without success. Then Prea (an animal like a large guinea pig) came and boldly asked for some. He snatched a burning stick before Jaguar's mother could speak. Jaguar chased after Prea, who tried many tricks to get away, but finally Jaguar caught up. Prea sat down and said he thought fire seemed like a lot of trouble and asked Jaguar why he and his mother did not just eat their meat raw. Jaguar explained the different ways to cook meat and why cooked meat was so good. They talked a long time and the fire went out. But Jaguar showed Prea how to make fire by rubbing sticks together. Then they went off to their own homes. Prea taught everyone he saw how to make fire; Jaguar looked for something to kill so he could have his first taste of raw meat.

JURUPARI (YURUPARI, Crooked Mouth) A chief god, cult god, or an evil spirit of various groups in the tropical forests of the Amazon and Orinoco River regions of South America. Jurupari is considered by some to be a god that only males could worship. He is associated with coming-of-age rituals of boys. So male-oriented are these ceremonies that women risked death if they found out about them. The MAKU, who still practice a *jurupari,* include flute music and the taking of HALLUCINOGENS to induce trances to get in touch with the gods and spirits. Part of the ritual includes a reenactment of the coming of the ancestral anaconda (a giant snake) to the rivers. As a cult god, Jurupari is said to make sure people continue their traditional way of life.

As an evil spirit Jurupari is a jungle demon who takes many animal forms to draw humans toward it. It is said to also appear at night, often to children, gripping their throats just enough to bring on an illness or a bad dream. The first Jurupari was a young boy who was born to the first woman just after the time of creation. When he was born, he had no mouth so he could not eat or talk. One of the first men, Exhaler,

blew wind all around him, which gave the boy nourishment so he grew. One day the creator god, Son of the Bone, asked the boy if he was fish, animal, or human, but with each question, the boy shook his head no. Then the creator god asked if he was a Jurupari. As the boy nodded yes, he suddenly had a mouth, which he opened wide as he sent out a loud roar.

Not long after this, Jurupari watched as some boys from the villages sneaked some fruit their parents had asked them not to eat. Having taken it, of course, the boys knew they would get into trouble. Jurupari opened his mouth wide and the boys, thinking it was a cave, ran in to hide from their parents. Then Jurupari went back to the village and threw up the children.

The Jurupari story comes into modern life in the name of a river fish. The *jurupari* species (native name *juruparipindi*) are what are known as mouthbreeders: After being fertilized, their eggs are somehow brought into the fish's mouth where they are kept in a pouch until they hatch; then they are released. Some varieties keep the eggs in the pouch for only a little while and then lay them in nests in the sand on the river's bottom at some point of their development. But if the eggs are endangered at all, the parent takes them back into its mouth—just as the first Jurupari took in the fruit-eating boys.

KAMINALJUYÚ One of the earliest Mayan centers; today, it is the site of Guatemala City. Kaminaljuyú's peak of influence was 800–300 B.C. There are few remains today. Because there was little local stone, the pyramids and other large buildings were built of clay, which has deteriorated. Skilled artisans in Kaminaljuyú made beautiful decorative pots, and a writing system of glyphs developed that evolved into the Mayan writing.

KARUSAKAHIBY AND RAIRU Father and son creator gods of the Mundurucu in Brazil. They came out of the chaotic beginning of all things. After the son, Rairu, put a bowl on his head from which heaven began to grow, his father, in a jealous rage, wanted to kill him to stop his cleverness. But Rairu explained that there were people within the Earth who would worship them when they came above ground. So they brought people up from the center of the Earth to work for the gods. Lazy people were transformed into butterflies, bats, birds, and pigs.

KASOGONGA The rain goddess of the CHACO of central South America.

KAUYUMARI A trickster god of the HUICHOL in Mexico; also known as Wolf. The Huichol tell many stories about Kauyumari. In some stories, he is part of the creation process—surviving the flood, populating the world, and performing the first funeral. In stories such as the following he is the classic fool, usually taken advantage of by the Moon: One day, Moon asked Kauyumari to do him a favor. Kauyumari was skeptical; he had learned not to trust Moon. But Moon seemed to really need his help and even called him Brother, which had never happened before. Maybe, thought Kauyumari, Moon had begun to respect him just a little. So, Kauyumari agreed and

asked how he could help. Moon explained that he needed a tree cut down. That the tree was filled with honey would be a bonus to Kauyumari. The poor fool cut down the tree, but as the honey poured out of it, it changed into a torrent of smelly, black water and small stones that knocked Kauyumari over and gave Moon a laugh as he moved across the sky.

KERI AND KAME Hero twins of the Bakairi Indians in Brazil, and throughout central South America. Keri and Kame were twin sons of Oka the jaguar. When their jaguar grandmother, Mero, killed their mother, Keri and Kame brought on a great fire to destroy Mero and everything else on Earth. The fire destroyed them as well, but they recreated themselves and then set out to recreate the world. First they separated the heavens from the Earth; they stole balls of feathers from a great vulture and set them in the sky as the Sun and Moon. Then they went down to Earth, taking water from the Great Serpent with them and distributing it as oceans, rivers, and lakes. They caught the spark from a fox's eye and turned it into fire, then tamed wild reeds to create humans. After teaching humans how to live, they parted and led separate lives.

KINICH AHAU (AHAU KIN, AH KIN) The sun god of the Yucatán MAYA. Kinich Ahau was a god of the day, who moved across the sky and became a JAGUAR at night to travel through the UNDERWORLD. He is the daytime ITZAMNA (sky god) and was adopted by rulers and warriors alike. Undoubtedly, these leaders hoped to tap into the power of both the Sun and the jaguar. Kinich Ahau was also the patron of the Mayan city Itzamal, which he visited daily at noontime, flying down from the heavens as a macaw to eat whatever offerings people had set out for him. He is often shown with crosses for eyes, a large hooked nose, and a full beard whose curled ends resemble the rays of the Sun. He has also appeared as a large bird with brightly colored feathers, and because of his solar association, Kinich Ahau was identified with FIRE. The same four-petaled glyph in Mayan writing stands for both Kinich Ahau and the Sun. Kinich Ahau is also known as Ah Xoc Kin, the god of poetry and music.

KOGI   A people of the Sierra Nevada de Santa Marta of northern Colombia. The traditional life, culture, and practices of this mountain people survived the Spanish CONQUEST and colonization and are still practiced today. The Kogi culture is similar to that of the TAIRONA. They may, in fact, be descendants of the Tairona but there are enough differences that some anthropologists believe that the Kogi may be unique.

The Kogi consider themselves Elder Brother to the rest of the world and believe that theirs is the one true religion. They worship a Mother Goddess and believe the world was animated and is kept alive by the Sun. They believe that life depends on a balance of good and evil. They are a deep-thinking, serious people who are very religious and live with the knowledge that one attains wisdom in old age. As a people, their mission is to protect the health of the Earth. In a message to the world, they have said:

> Younger Brother thinks,
> "Yes! Here I am! I know much about
> the universe!"
> But this knowing is learning to destroy
> the world,
> to destroy everything,
> all humanity.
>
> The Earth feels, they take out petrol, it
> feels pain there.
> So the Earth sends out sickness.
> There will be many medicines,
> drugs,
> but in the end the drugs will not be of
> any use.
>
> The Mamas say that this tale must be
> learned
> by the Younger Brother.

In this message, "Younger Brother" refers to those who have come to the Kogi mountain—which they call "The Heart of the World"—for oil and minerals. Their mountain, they believe, is symbolic of the rest of the world: When the mountain is out of balance, the whole world is out of balance.

KON-TIKI   Creator god of the COLLA, who believed that he could walk on water and that he crossed oceans. The similarity between Kon-Tiki and the Easter Island sun god Tiki was part of the reasoning that led the Norwegian explorer Thor Heyerdahl to believe that ancient people from the coast of South America had sailed to the South Pacific and settled there. Heyerdahl built a raft in Peru in a style and from materials that the ancient people would have used, and in 1947 he made the trip to prove it could be done.

KORUPIRA   (KURUPIRA, CURUPIRA, CORUPIRA, Inhabitor of the Woods)   A forest demon of various groups, including the Tupí, in the AMAZON rain forest of Brazil who protects the animals of the forest and treats them when they have been wounded or are sick. He also is a protector of trees. Korupira has two sides. Although he can be kind and helpful, he is also capable of great harm—but he is not considered evil. Particularly angry when a hunter wounds an animal but does not kill it, takes more game than needed, or is otherwise wasteful, Korupira may punish the hunter in various ways. The worst of these punishments is the taking of the hunter's soul. Korupira can take any animal form but most frequently is a frog, brocket deer, or paca, a large rodent; he can also take the form of a human, often a young boy. As a human, he may call out to a hunter by name, appear and taunt him, and then disappear. If the hunter tries to escape, Korupira may trick him into coming closer by switching his feet so they are backwards. The hunter, following tracks to escape to the place from where the Korupira had come, actually heads toward him. Because he lives deep in the forest and because men do most of the hunting, Korupira is most often seen by men.

KUAT   Sun god of the Mamaiurans in the Brazilian Amazon forests; brother of the moon god IAE.

KUKULCAN (KUKULKAN, CUCULCAN, CUCULKAN, The God of Mighty Speech, A Serpent Adorned with Feathers) The supreme god of the Yucatán MAYA, the creator, and the god of RESURRECTION and reincarnation; associated with VENUS. In Mayan history and mythology, Kukulcan appears as a god and as a CULTURE HERO and historic leader. He may be more than one person. *Can* was a well-established family name among the Maya, and *Kukul* could be a first, or personal, name.

Some sources name him the leader of a group, perhaps the TOLTEC, who with the Itzá Maya occupied Chichén Itzá by about A.D. 987. They built several other cities, including Mayapan, which became the capital of the Mayan empire. Kukulcan ruled for many years and then left. In the CHILAM BALAMS, he is also said to be a ruler priest in Mayapan in the 14th century.

As a hero-god, Kukulcan brought peace to Chichén Itzá, created Mayapan, and then went west into the heavens to guard the people and answer their prayers. Other stories have him both originating from and disappearing into the ocean. The Maya showed him with the body of a SERPENT, feathers of the QUETZAL, and the teeth of the JAGUAR, holding a human head in its jaws. As part of his creator-god status, he controlled the four elements—EARTH, FIRE, air, and WATER—which gave him as ASPECTS the ear of CORN, lizard, VULTURE, and fish.

Kukulcan is often described as comparable to the Quiché Maya GUCUMATZ, and the AZTEC QUETZALCOATL. Kukulcan is less a god of the Sun and wind than Quetzalcoatl; he is more a god of the sky, for thunder was very much part of his responsibility.

KURURUMANY ARAWAK creator god of men and goodness. (His wife, Kulimina, the creator goddess, made women.) He was not, however, the supreme god—that was Aluberi, the great spirit.

L

LAKE GUATAVITA Location of the great temple of the SERPENT god of the CHIBCHA Indians of Colombia. Lake Guatavita may also have been where the legendary king EL DORADO washed the gold dust off his body. In 1540, after hearing the story of El Dorado, the Spanish made an expedition to the 130-foot deep lake. They took along hundreds of Indian slaves who were ordered to use gourds to empty the lake. Three months later, the lake had been lowered 10 feet and only a few small pieces of gold had been found. In 1580, Spanish authorities made another attempt to empty the lake by digging a trench. This time, the lake was lowered about 60 feet, and some emeralds and gold pieces were found. In 1912, another group pumped the water out of the lake but the muddy lake bottom dried rock hard before the prospectors found much gold. Then in 1965, when yet another group wanted to try, the Colombian government refused and declared the lake a historic site.

LAKE MACHIRA In stories of the CARIB of the Orinoco region in South America, this lake swallowed the souls of the dead, thus releasing the bodies to paradise.

LAKE TEXCOCO A once-large saltwater lake in the central valley of Mexico that was the site of TENOCHTITLÁN, the cultural center and capital of the AZTEC empire. The Aztec believed that the lake had been created from and was still connected to the sea. To test this, according to legend, they once dropped a sealed gourd in the ocean near a deep cavern along the seacoast. Several days later, the gourd floated to the surface of Lake Texcoco.

There is much salt around the lake, and the Aztec harvested the salt, mounding huge piles of the salty earth during the dry season. They washed the mounds and put the salty solution in large pottery jars. Heating the jars evaporated the water and left the salt, which they packed in blocks or in jars and used for trade. Lake Texcoco was almost completely drained in the early 1800s in hopes that the bottom land could be turned into farmland, but it was too salty.

LAKE TITICACA A 110-mile long, 45-mile wide lake high in the ANDES on the border of Peru and Bolivia. Water from the mountains that surround Lake Titicaca flows into it; from there it flows into Lake Poopó. Over time, the water level of Lake Poopó has dropped enough that it is below the level of the natural outlet, and water leaves the lake only through evaporation.

TIAHUANACO, the cultural center of the COLLA, was located on the shore of Lake Titicaca. According to myth, the sun god sent his children to Earth and placed them on an island (also called Titicaca) in the lake, the place the rays of the Sun first strike Earth. Some legends say the gods chose this island as a sign of hope to the people. It is considered a sacred place and was the location of a temple to the Sun that contained as much GOLD and silver as the main temple to INTI in the Inca capital at Cuzco. It is said that when the Spanish came and began looting Cuzco, the people threw all the gold and silver from the island temple into the lake.

LA LLORONA A legendary figure recognized throughout Meso-America that today is believed to cry out at night for her dead children and to materialize in the woods, dressed all in white, to tempt men and then leave them unconscious. Stories that tell how and why Llorona's children died vary. Some stories say that the NAHUA earth mother CIHUACOATL spirited them away to be sacrificed, but in most stories they were drowned. Llorona is most often heard crying near a lake, river, spring, or the ocean. Some stories say that Llorona killed the children to escape having to mother them. Others explain that she killed them out of revenge or grief at being left by her husband, who either left her or died. In Mexico, Llorona and MALINCHE are considered the same figure; some scholars believe her roots are in the AZTEC creation myth of the giant earth monster TLALTE-CUHTLI who cries out for blood at night.

LANDA, DIEGO DE (1524–79)

A Franciscan priest who in 1562 ordered the destruction of Mayan records and other artifacts. "We found," he wrote, "a great number of books in these letters of theirs, and because they contained nothing but superstition and the devil's falsehoods, we burned them all." Although he felt kindly toward the MAYA, Landa ordered all Mayan religious monuments and books destroyed. Later, perhaps out of shame or regret, he wrote about the customs, religious practices, language, and writing system of the Yucatán Maya. Much of what we know about the Maya is from his writings and, therefore, colored by his perception. But because his writings were thoughtful and observant, they are still valued, and his description of Mayan writing has helped archaeologists translate surviving books and carvings.

LETTER GODS

A system scholars have used to identify the Mayan gods and goddesses that appear in the CODICES and in other writings. Some of the gods have been identified with named gods; others seem to have no names. There was no God J.

God A   God of death; may be AH PUCH.

God B   God of rain and thunder; may be CHAC or KUKULCAN.

God C   God of the North Star; often shown with symbols or signs of other heavenly bodies.

God D   God of the Moon and nighttime sky; may be KUKULCAN or ITZAMNA.

God E   God of corn; may be YUM KAAX.

God F   God of sacrifice and war. Human sacrifices may have been made to honor him.

God G   God of the Sun; the Sun personified.

God H   This may be KUKULCAN as a SERPENT; otherwise, it is an unknown god who is shown having scales.

Goddess I   Goddess of WATER; may be IX CHEL. This is the destructive, not the life-giving, side of water.

God K   God of the wind; may be ITZAMNA.

God L   An unknown god sometimes referred to as "The Old Black God."

God M   God of traveling merchants; may be Ex Chuah.

God N   Sometimes referred to as "God of the End of the Year," an otherwise unknown god. Shown as an old man with the symbol for the Haab year (360 days) on his headdress, he represents the five unlucky days at the end of the solar CALENDAR year. During the festival of this time, the Maya made clay figures of God N and carried them out of the village to symbolically remove bad fortune.

Goddess O   Described both as the goddess of old age for women and the goddess of domestic life. She is a patroness of married women.

God P   Sometimes referred to as "Frog God," a water god associated with agriculture. He is shown with froglike features.

LLAMA

A large mammal that can be white with black and/or brown blotches, all white, or all black; the largest of the camel family in the Western Hemisphere, native to the high altitudes of Bolivia, southern Peru, and northern Argentina. Llamas are smart, fast, and easily domesticated, in part because they are curious. They are critical to the culture and economy of the Andes. Llamas are surefooted, and since earliest times, males have been used as pack animals. They can carry loads of up to 200 pounds and are capable of trekking fully loaded for as long as 12 hours. The females are raised for milk and for meat. Llama hides are used as well and their fur is woven for textiles and spun for rope. Because of their size (they weigh up to 300 pounds) and their native curiosity, llamas are also used to guard flocks of sheep. Because they were valuable the INCA sacrificed them, often at the new Moon. To ask the gods for rain, the Inca kept food from black llamas in October to make them weep (symbolizing rain). Llamas are also considered a

Llamas were, and still are, important pack animals to the people of Peru. This vessel is from the Vicus culture that flourished from about 200 B.C. to A.D. 500 in the coastal deserts of what is now northern Peru. *(The Art Archive/ Museo del Banco Central de Reserva, Lima/Dagli Orti)*

healing animal, a concept still embraced by Peruvian groups today.

LONG COUNT Mayan CALENDAR based on a 360-day year, or *tun*. The Long Count was the exact number of days since a zero date equal to August 13, 3114 B.C. It included all years past and present, and ended with the end of the Fifth Sun (see AZTEC SUNS). This was predicted to be December 24, 2011. Only a select few—historians and priests, for example—used the Long Count, and its use was restricted to telling and recording history.

M

MACHU PICCHU (MACHUPICCHU, Old Peak) The site of Incan ruins high in the ANDES, about 50 miles from the Incan capital at Cuzco. The Spanish never found Machu Picchu; an American archaeologist located the ruins in 1911. The site contains about 150 houses, palaces, temples, gardens, baths, and storage rooms arranged around a large plaza. All these areas were connected with walks and stairways. Scholars are not sure how the INCA used this site, speculating that it may have been a summer resort for nobility, a refuge or training site for the ACLLAS, a military outpost, or a religious ceremonial site. The Intihuatana (Hitching Post of the Sun) is a six-foot-high stone sundial that accurately indicates the time of the winter solstice—the day with the fewest hours of sunlight. The presence of this sundial supports the general acceptance that the site was important for astronomical observations. During the ceremony on the solstice celebrating INTI RAYMI, the Sun—considered a god by the Inca—was symbolically tied to the post to keep it from traveling farther north in the sky, thus making the days shorter. The subsequent lengthening of the days showed the Inca that the gods had accepted their sacrifices and their prayers.

MACONAURA AND ANUANAITU The man and woman considered by the CARIB of the Orinoco in South America to be the father and mother of all. According to Carib mythology, Maconaura was fishing in a river and out of anger killed a CAIMAN who had grabbed the large fish he had just caught. He then saw, sitting farther down the river, a young girl crying. This was Anuanaitu. Maconaura took her home to live with his mother. As she grew up, Anuanaitu grew quite beautiful and Maconaura fell in love with her and married her. He

was happy, but she was not. Anuanaitu eventually killed Maconaura because he had killed her much-loved brother—the caiman.

MACUILXOCHITL (Five Flower) Another name for the AZTEC god of flowers, XOCHIPILLI.

MAKONAIMA (MAKANAIMA, MAKUNA-IMA, One Who Works in the Night) A creator god and Great Spirit of several groups in Guyana, including the Acawoios and the ARAWAK. Makonaima works only in the darkness of night. In one story of the Acawoios, all animals once lived in peace and could speak to one another. Makonaima created a huge tree that bore many kinds of fruits. When his son chopped down the tree, a great rush of water poured out of the stump bringing with it schools and schools of fish. Quickly Makonaima put a large basket over the stump to stop the water from pouring out. But a mischievous MONKEY yanked the basket off the stump and a great flood followed, taking the basket with it. Makonaima gathered up as many of the animals as he could, putting some in caves and some high in trees. When the flood had stopped and the land dried up, the present world had been created— with some animals on land, some under the ground, and some in the trees. In other versions of the story, Makonaima is one of five brothers who cut down the tree, and it is Makonaima who causes the flood by removing the basket that his brother had put over the stump.

As the Great Spirit, Makonaima was viewed as a savior in time of need, and sacrifices were made when asking for his help. Once, when the peaceful people of the Patamona tribe were being harassed by the warlike Carib, the Patamona chief sacrificed himself. He canoed over a high waterfall in hopes that

The Incan city of Machu Picchu is located 7,710 feet above sea level in the Andes in what is now Peru. *(Ali Meyer/ Bridgeman Art Library)*

Makonaima would protect his tribe. The waterfall, the highest one-drop waterfall in the world (742 feet), is now called Kaieteur Falls after Chief Kai.

MAKU An indigenous people living in the Orinoco region of the Amazon state in Brazil. The Maku view the universe as being egg-shaped with three levels. The first level is the world of shadow, inhabited by beings that are out of accord with their life—monsters, JAGUARS, scorpions, white people, and poisonous snakes. The second level is the one they consider their world, the world of the rain forest. The third level is the world of light, a land above the sky that is the home of their ancestors and their creator god, Son of the Bone. The world they inhabit is one of contrast: The dark includes death and the animals they believe have the darkest shadows (which they do not eat); the light includes life and the fruits and leaves that best support life.

The Maku believe that after the previous world ended in fire, Son of the Bone—also known as Idn Kami, Kegn Teh, and Ku Teh—tried to recreate the world but kept making mistakes. Somehow wars, illness, death, and misunderstandings of all kinds sneaked in, and Son of the Bone had a hard time figuring out how to perfect his creation. But before he could get it right, Son of the Bone's brother kidnapped his wife. This so discouraged the god that he gave up trying to right his mistakes and returned to the world of the light.

MALINCHE (ca. 1501–50) A NAHUA woman who was an interpreter for the Spanish explorer and conquistador Hernando Cortés (1485–1547). She might have also served as a diplomat. Born into a noble family, Malinche was traded to the MAYA, perhaps to keep her from succeeding to the throne. She was given to Cortés as a gift from the Maya, most likely because of her status and training as a mediator between the Spanish and the Maya. Stories about Malinche show her as both a strong woman and a traitor for helping the Spanish. The latter depiction, many believe, is unjustified because although she was traded to the Maya as a gift, she would have had to cooperate or risk more problems for the Maya and the Nahua in their dealings with the Spanish. Many scholars believe that the success of the Spanish in Meso-America was in large measure due to the role that Malinche played.

When Cortés returned to Spain, he left without Malinche, who married a Spanish conquistador. According to history or legend, she grieved for Cortés for the rest of her life. Her story may be the root of that of LA LLORONA, a legendary woman who grieves for her dead children. A volcano in Mexico bears Malinche's name, and today she is regarded as a guardian for good harvests. She is also connected to the goddess IZTACCIHUATL, protector of animals taken for food.

MAM   The earthquake god of the Yucatán MAYA. Mam is similar to the Chorti Maya's CHICCANS who live deep in the Earth and cause earthquakes when they turn over in their sleep.

MAMA ALLPA   Earth goddess of the INCA. Mama Allpa was a goddess of the harvest and responsible for providing food for humans.

MAMA COCHA (Mother Sea)   Goddess of rain, WATER, and the sea, and wife of the creator god VIRACOCHA. Mamma Cocha was worshiped by most groups living along the Pacific Coast of South America, including the INCA. The oldest deity, she is worshiped by those who fish and is believed to be the provider of good health. Even those who lived in the ANDES highlands would bring their children to bathe in the ocean, thus ensuring their well-being through Mama Cocha.

MAMA CORA (Mother Corn)   The Peruvian and Incan goddess of CORN.

MAMA OCCLO (MAMA OCLLO, MAMA OELLO, First Mother or First Woman)   To the INCA, the first woman. According to Incan mythology, at the beginning, life was very hard for the people on Earth because they did not know how to spin the wool of the alpaca or grow CORN and potatoes. The great sun god, INTI, worried about his children on Earth, sent down Mama Occlo and MANCO

CAPAC, his children from the sky. He gave them a rod of gold and instructed them to travel the land to find a place where the earth was soft. Once such a place was found, the children were to insert the rod into the ground to begin a city. Inti told his children to be wise and gentle rulers, to care for the people, to teach them how to live, and to always look to him, the father of them all, for guidance. He assured them that if they did as instructed, and if the people followed suit, he would always be there with heat and light.

The sister and brother came onto the land from LAKE TITICACA and walked until they came to a great valley. There, the golden rod easily disappeared into the fertile soil. Manco Capac taught the men how to farm and take care of the animals. Mama Occlo taught the women how to spin the wool and weave cloth.

In another version of the story, Mama Occlo and Manco Capac were two of several brothers and sisters that came to populate the Earth. The smartest of them all, Mama Occlo, discovered the best place to settle. Since the valley was already settled, she killed a man, tore out his lungs, put them in her mouth, and walked through the villages to scare off those living there.

MAMA QUILLA (MAMA KILYA, Mother Moon)   The Incan moon goddess and protector of married women. Mama Quilla was considered both the wife and sister of INTI. She was responsible for the passage of time and the seasons and was therefore also the patron of calendars and feasts. The Peruvians saw the Moon as a great silver disk; the markings on the Moon were the features of Mama Quilla's face. At the Sun Temple (CORICANCHA) at Cuzco, mummies of past Incan queens stand alongside the image of Mama Quilla. This shrine, the most famous to her, was covered in silver to symbolize the Moon in the night sky. The INCA believed lunar eclipses occurred when a SERPENT or mountain lion tried to eat Mama Quilla, so during an eclipse, they made a great racket to scare the animal away.

MANCO CAPAC   The son of the sun god INTI and the first ruler of the INCA. Many versions of his role in the origin of the Inca exist. In one he is sent to Earth with his sister MAMA OCCLO to teach the people how to live in a civilized fashion. In another version, he is the youngest of four brothers who came out of a cave at the beginning of humankind. The oldest of the brothers declared that he alone owned the Earth. This idea so angered Manco Capac that he trapped the brother in a cave and sealed it shut. When Manco Capac pushed the next oldest brother over a cliff, the third oldest escaped with his life, leaving only Manco Capac to settle the land and rule the people.

Although the story itself has many versions, they all end with Manco Capac as the first ruler of the Inca. Historically, it is likely that there were many tribes living in the Cuzco valley, which is considered the center and starting point of what would become the Incan empire. As the first ruler, Manco Capac may have governed several villages in the valley but his rule would not have extended any farther. Therefore, he would not have been a unifying influence. Unification began to happen only with the eighth ruler, Viracocha Inca.

The Inca also believed that Manco Capac was one part of Tahuantin Suyu Kapac, the earth gods of the Inca. Sons of the Sun, these earth gods were Ayar Cachi, who ruled the east; Ayar Ayar, the south; Ayar Manco (also known as Manco Capac), the north; and Ayar Uchu, the west.

MANI   A CULTURE HERO, some say food god, of several groups in Brazil. Mani was said to have taught the people how to live in a civilized manner and predicted they would find the MANIOC plant a year after he died. In some versions of the story, Mani was the son of the Great Spirit and a lovely young woman; he died suddenly of an unknown illness. The people noticed birds eating the fruit of a strange new plant that grew on Mani's grave. They dug into the ground and found the root tubers, which they called *Mani-oka*. In still other versions of the story, Mani lives to be a kind, wise, and generous old man, who demonstrates, through his teaching, how people should live—including how to plant, harvest, and use manioc.

MANIOC   A shrubby bush (*Manihot esculenta*) that grows about 8 feet high and bears roots that are about 3 inches thick and up to 3 feet long. Manioc is native to the tropical areas of Brazil and is a staple food plant to the peoples of South America and the Caribbean. The roots provide starch, flour, and tapioca. A beerlike beverage can be made by fermenting a mixture that includes ground manioc root. There are two varieties of manioc—"sweet" and poisonous. The "sweet" variety is used for animal feed. The poisonous variety can be eaten only after cooking the roots to kill the poison. The plant is known as *manioc* in Brazil, *juca* or *yucca* in other parts of South America, and *cassava* in the Caribbean and the United States.

MANTA (HUECU)   A legendary fish that the ARAUCANIAN in Chile believe lives in deep lakes and causes the lake to boil in great waves when it cries. The manta eats people who go into the lake and mates with animals to create monsters. It can be killed only if caught and thrown onto the spiny branches of the *quisco* bush.

MARS   The fourth planet from the Sun. Mars was tracked closely by the MAYA. Mars has a larger orbit than Earth's. That is why from Earth, it appears as though Mars is moving backward in its orbit. This is called retrograde motion. The Maya were particularly interested in the planets because they changed position in the sky. The Maya described the movements and relationships among the planets and the constellations in murals and stories of the POPUL VUH. (The *Popul Vuh* is the book considered by many to be the bible of the Quiché Maya.)

Because the Maya considered action on Earth to be a reflection of what happened in the sky, the stories of the *Popul Vuh* reflect the movements of the stars and planets. One part of the *Popul Vuh* tells how the brothers One Monkey and One Artisan mistreated their half brothers, the HERO TWINS. The twins did not complain and took their harassment day after day without saying a word. Then one day they told One Monkey and One Artisan that some birds they had killed with their blowguns were stuck high in a tree. After One Monkey and One Artisan climbed the tree, the twins made the tree grow so tall that One Monkey and One Artisan could not get down. Then, the twins turned their half brothers into monkeys. XMUCANE, the first woman, was not happy about this, so the twins allowed One Monkey and One Artisan to come down from the tree after all. But when Xmucane saw them as monkeys, she laughed, and One Monkey and One Artisan ran off to live in the treetops forever. The brief time that One Monkey and One Artisan came back to live in Xmucane's house represents the planet Mars when its movement is considered retrograde.

MASAYA The goddess of the UNDERWORLD to the AZTEC who lived in Nicaragua. Masaya ruled the underworld with the god Mictanteot. She was the receiver of those whose souls had not been absolved of their sins. Masaya also received those who had not died in an honorable manner. For example, if someone died of an illness that was brought on by the gods because they acted against the strict moral code, they would be received by Masaya. Being of the underworld, Masaya was also responsible for causing earthquakes and volcanic eruptions.

MATLALCUEYEH The name used in the Mexican state Tlaxcala for CHALCHIHUITLICUE, the AZTEC water goddess.

MAYA A Native American culture in what is now the Yucatán peninsula and southern Mexico, Belize, Guatemala, and parts of Honduras and El Salvador, that thrived between about A.D. 5 and 1350. One of the most developed civilizations in the Americas before European CONQUEST, it was made up of independent villages and cities loosely bound with a similar culture. Although there was no central ruler, a village or city and its outlying areas were ruled by a chief. Such a position was inherited, and most rulers were male. Large cities, such as Tikal, CHICHÉN ITZÁ, and Mayapan, often controlled adjacent villages. Mayan groups or tribes were often at war with each other.

Villages and cities alike were centers built around temples, palaces, ball courts, and plazas. Temples, especially in the cities, were set atop pyramids in a style probably copied from TEOTIHUACÁN, a city begun in about A.D. 1. There may have been 40 Mayan cities and hundreds of stone pyramids. Only a few of these have been identified, excavated, and studied, even in part. The rest have been long overgrown in the thick, fast-growing forests.

Mayan cities grew rapidly until about 900, at which time people began leaving what is now Guatemala. Why they left and why the culture began to decline are not known. Scientists have found no evidence of a natural catastrophe, such as an earthquake. It is possible that the cause may have been overpopulation, disease, or that the land had become overworked. But the Maya did move into other areas and new cities rose to dominate—first Chichén Itzá, then Mayapan. These were more militaristic, fighting to control larger areas of land. Because of the warfare between Mayan states, the Spanish had little trouble taking control of the region. Some Mayan communities in Mexico, however, remained independent until 1901.

There are several groups of Maya today, including the Yucatec Maya, of the Yucatán peninsula in Mexico and into Belize and Honduras; the Quiché Maya, of the eastern and central regions of Guatemala; and the Huastec, in the Veracruz and San Luis Potosi states in central Mexico.

Mayan Culture The Maya were skilled stone workers, creating both massive stone structures and carved figures. They worked to create ornamental objects from gold and copper, as well as beautiful decorative and functional objects from clay. Farmers raised CORN, beans, squash, MANIOC, cotton, turkeys, and a variety of DOG, which they ate. Cotton was spun, dyed, and woven for clothing. Without any native draft animals, the Maya had no wheeled vehicles, though they had an extensive system of roads and a wide trade network that depended on the roads, rivers, and the sea. Traders reached well into central Mexico, southward to Panama, and possibly into South America.

Mayan Religion and the Calendars The Mayan people were intensely religious, and everything they did was to please their gods. Religion was an integral part of their everyday lives. Most houses displayed a shrine of some kind, and each day began with prayers. The Maya believed that any material rewards they received would be with the gods' help. Daily prayers were usually about immediate concerns: needed rain for the crops, the health of a child, good hunting. These prayers were made to such gods as

HUNAB-KU, the creator god; ITZAMNA, the father of all gods except Hunab-Ku; IX CHEL, the mother of all; YUM CIM, the god of death; KINICH AHAU, the sun god; YUM KAAX, the corn god; GUCUMATZ or KUKULCAN, the feathered serpents; and CHAC, the god of rain. There might have been as many as 166 gods, and all were demanding. To help keep the cosmic forces in balance and chaos at bay, regular offerings were expected. Rulers were considered links between commoners and the gods, and there is some evidence that ceremonies included rituals during which rulers gave blood to feed the gods. Scholars are unsure to what extent blood offerings were made.

At the center of the culture, along with the worship of the gods, were the Mayan CALENDARS. Two of the most widely used calendars were the solar calendar, based on the 365-day orbit of the Earth around the Sun, and a 260-day sacred calendar. The sacred calendar was used for many purposes: to make predictions or foretell the future, to decide on the best time to begin an activity—planting, having a wedding, or waging a war—or to get the gods' perspective on why something happened on a particular day. The Maya also had a LONG COUNT calendar, as well as calendars based on the orbit of Venus and the orbit of the Moon.

We know that the Maya were skilled mathematicians and astronomers because they would have to be to have made such accurate calendars. Their mathematics was a highly developed system that used and incorporated the concept of zero. As astronomers, the Maya closely watched the Sun and planets, for they believed the heavens were the home to the gods and that objects in the sky reflected the actions of the gods. The Maya's skill as both mathematicians and astronomers is evident in the accuracy of their observations. They determined that Venus's trip around the heavens took 584 days and the Moon's took 29.53020 days. Scientists in the 20th century determined that it takes 583.92 days for Venus to orbit the Sun and 29.53059 days for the Moon to orbit the Earth.

Astronomical and historical information, as well as stories about the gods, was recorded in books called CODICES. Only four of these books, written before the Spanish Conquest, have survived. They are in a form of hieroglyphic WRITING developed by the Maya that also survives in inscriptions on monuments, columns, stairways, and murals.

Mayan Stories of Origin   There are several Mayan stories that tell about the origin of humans. One such story begins with the Sun: One day the Sun shot an arrow into a rock, splitting it open. Two small sparrowlike creatures—one male, one female—hopped out of the rock. They had no bodies (just heads and legs) and, after hopping around for a while, they discovered each other. So happy to see another, they kissed and became full-grown people. Together, they began to populate the Earth.

Another story of the origin of humans explains why some people are rich and some are poor. It begins with four lords or gods who set out to make creatures that would live on Earth. The lords first used mud, which dissolved if it got too wet and crumbled if too dry. Next, they tried wood, which burned. The next material they tried was gold, but it was too stiff and silent and produced a hard heart. Finally, one of the

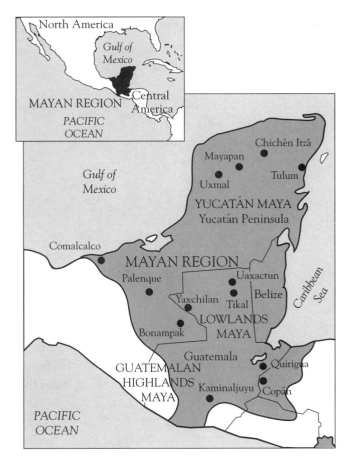

By about A.D. 900, more than 2 million people lived in 40 Mayan cities. *(James Jarvis)*

gods suggested using flesh and chopped off a finger. These flesh people hurried around learning what to eat and how to protect themselves. One day they found the gold people, who were cold and unkind. However, they were hungry, so the flesh people gave them food. They also seemed lonely, so the flesh people took them along. Gradually the gold people softened, bit by bit. One day, the gold people praised the gods and thanked them for what had happened. This surprised the gods, who had been sleeping and not paying a lot of attention to what was happening on Earth. When they saw what the flesh people had done, they were very pleased. So, the gods decided that the gold people would be rich and the flesh people poor. However, the rich always had to watch out for and help the poor, because the only way they could enter heaven was if a poor person led them there.

MAYAHUEL (MAYAUEL) The NAHUA/AZTEC goddess of intoxicants and of childbirth. In one story, Mayahuel was a mortal woman who saw a mouse dancing with joy and abandon. It appeared as if the mouse was not the least bit afraid of her. Mayahuel noticed that the mouse had been gnawing on a maguey plant and decided to collect some of the plant's sap to take home. When she made the sap into a beverage, Mayahuel found that it had an intoxicating effect on her, as it had on the mouse. The gods were so pleased at Mayahuel's discovery that they made her a goddess.

Another myth tells how love and the maguey plant were brought to humankind. The young girl Mayahuel was guarded in the land of the gods by TZITZIMITL, an old woman goddess. The wind god EHECATL, an aspect of the feathered-serpent god QUETZALCOATL, fell in love with Mayahuel, and the two escaped to Earth while Tzitzimitl slept. So great was their love that they became became one and grew into the Precious Tree, each with its own strong branch. Angered that she was tricked, Tzitzimitl came to Earth and broke Mayahuel's branch from the tree. Tzitzimitl's followers, the *TZITZIMIME*, ate the pieces of the branch. When they left, Ehecatl reappeared as the wind god, and as he grieved he buried what was left of Mayahuel. Those pieces immediately grew into the maguey plant.

MAYO Native people of northwestern Mexico, who have settled in small communities called *rancherias*. The Mayo were greatly influenced by the Spanish. The Spanish learned the Mayo language while they were colonizing Mexico. The traditional Mayo gods include Ouraba, god of war, who gave humans bows and arrows; Bamasenna, god of water; Schatoba, god of pleasure; and Cocohuane, god of life and death, who was much feared. The people also worshiped the Sun and Moon and had personal deities, which included animal gods honored to provide for good hunting and fishing. The Mayo also relied on SHAMANS. The shamans were responsible for healing and were feared because they could both help and harm. Shamans received their power from visions and dreams of animals. As the Mayo adapted and converted to Catholicism, they adapted their own gods—the Sun became God the Father, and the Moon, the Virgin Mary.

MESCALINE A hallucinogen used to help create a feeling of joy. Used in South and Meso-America mostly by priests and SHAMANS, it produced trances that helped them to see the gods and to better receive messages from them.

MEZTLI (METZTLI) The AZTEC moon goddess and goddess of the night and darkness; the female form of the god TECCIZTECATL. She (as Tecciztecatl) sacrificed herself so that darkness would end and there would be light during the day. However, because of her initial cowardice, she was made the Moon instead. Meztli is also known as Yohualticitl.

MICTLANCIHUATL (MICLANCIHUATL, MICTECACIHUATL, Dead-land Woman) The goddess of death to the Mexican AZTEC. Mictlancihuatl was married to MICTLANTECUHTLI, the god of the UNDERWORLD.

MICTLANTECUHTLI (MICLANTECUTLI) The god of death and lord of the north to the AZTEC in Mexico. His color was red. Mictlantecuhtli ruled the UNDERWORLD (center of the Earth) where those not destined for heaven were sent to live in eternal boredom. With his wife MICTLANCIHUATL, he lived

Mictlantecuhtli was the Aztec god of death. *(The Art Archive/Museo del Templo Mayor Mexico/Dagli Orti)*

angered at the theft that he sent a flock of quail after Quetzalcoatl, but Quetzalcoatl was too swift and escaped the underworld with the bones.

MILKY WAY The galaxy of which our solar system is a part. It is seen from Earth as a wide band of light across the sky. What we see is only a small part of the Milky Way. The entire galaxy is shaped like a pinwheel and contains more than 200 billion stars. It is visible throughout most of the year in areas where there is not much artificial light. Because it rotates, however, at times it is so low on the horizon that it is barely visible.

The Milky Way was considered by many groups to be a celestial snake, heavenly river, or road of clouds in the heavens. As a road, it was thought to be a path that souls followed into the UNDERWORLD or that the gods used to travel. In parts of Brazil and Peru demons called Kilyikhama are believed to transform themselves into white birds and ride the Milky Way. Then they would come down to Earth to take over the bodies of humans. In the Peruvian ANDES, the QUECHUA people believe that the Vilaconota River is the earthly representation of the Milky Way. They believe that the shadows seen in the Milky Way are "dark cloud" animals—a snake, llama, toad, fox, and birds called tinamous—that watch out for the corresponding animals on Earth. The animals drink water from the Milky Way as it falls below the horizon. Then they take the water into the sky when the Milky Way is visible above the horizon, making the water available as rain. Individually, the animals have additional roles as well. Some of their stories are as follows: The toad and the tinamous race each night, and the slow-hopping toad always reaches the horizon first. The llama drinks water from the sea every night at midnight, which keeps the Earth from being flooded. The serpent is not visible during the dry season but reappears during the rainy weather.

The AZTEC considered the hunting god MIXCOATL to be the god of the Milky Way. He was seen as a shape-changer, a cloud serpent that snaked his way across the heavens. His sons, the 400 sons of the earth goddess COATLICUE that the Aztec supreme god HUITZILOPOCHTLI killed, are the stars of the Milky Way.

in a house and watched out for the souls of the dead. He may be one of the earliest Aztec gods, and some scholars believe he was associated with TEZCATLIPOCA. At the beginning of the Fifth Sun (see AZTEC SUNS), QUETZALCOATL came into the underworld to steal the bones of those that had died at the end of the Fourth Sun. Mictlantecuhtli was so

A story of the MAYA tells the origin of the Milky Way: Long ago the Sun fell in love with a girl living on Earth. He wanted her to be with him, so he captured her with a turtle's shell. The girl's father had built a huge blowgun, but the Sun had sneakily filled the gun with chili pepper. When the father breathed deeply to blow the bullet at the Sun, his mouth filled with chili pepper and he started coughing. This is how the disease whooping cough was brought to humans. The father died before the bullet hit the Sun, but when it did, it so surprised the Sun that he let go of the girl. She fell into the oceans and broke into pieces. The fish put the pieces together and then organized themselves to form a net that could be used to return the girl to the Sun. However, the Sun was too hot, and the fish could not take her all the way there. So they left her in the sky as the Moon, and the fish themselves became the Milky Way.

MILOMAKI

A food god of some groups who live in the AMAZON region of Brazil. Milomaki was a child of the Sun and had a voice that was rich and melodious. One day after listening to him sing, the people ate fish that made them very ill; some even died from it. Believing it was Milomaki's fault, the people killed him and burned his body. A great *paxiuba* palm tree sprang up from Milomaki's ashes. Amazonian men make flutes from this palm, but women or children who play these flutes—or even look at them—will become ill and die.

MIXCOATL

(YEMAXTLI, YOAMAXTLI, Cloud Serpent)   TOLTEC and AZTEC patron god of hunters, god of warriors, and god of the sky. He was also considered the father of QUETZALCOATL. His 400 sons are the stars of the MILKY WAY. The Aztec life centered around their gods and the CALENDAR. Some gods ruled the days, while others ruled the months and years. A period in early November was governed by Mixcoatl. During that period, the Aztec made and repaired weapons for war and made human sacrifices to ensure military success. Once, the sun god and supreme Aztec god TEZCATLIPOCA turned himself into Mixcoatl. He discovered flint and showed people how to use it to make a fire for light and warmth.

Mixcoatl was often depicted with red and white stripes running lengthwise down his body, black eyes or a black mask, and long hair. He wore a crown of plumes on his head and carried a basket of food that he had hunted in one hand and a bow and arrow in the other.

MIXTEC

A civilization in southwestern Mexico, predating the TOLTEC, that reached its height in the ninth to 16th centuries. This was a wealthy civilization that was highly skilled in metal and stonework, mosaics, pottery, and textiles. The Mixtec appeared to have some connection to the MAYA but fiercely opposed the AZTEC and tried to remain independent of them. There was, however, some trade between the two groups, and the Aztec managed to seize some land and slaves from the Mixtec. The Mixtec called themselves Nuudzahui (The People of the Rain). The name *Mixtec* is from the Nahua/Aztec language, and the Mixtec language has its roots in the OLMEC family of languages. The Mixtec were conquered by the Spanish in the 1500s.

The Mixtec used pictographs, or hieroglyphs, to record their history in elaborate CODICES. These have given scholars some idea of what the Mixtec culture was like. The codices indicate that the gods were very much a part of their daily life. The principal gods were COQUI-XEE, the creator god; Dzaui, a rain god; XIPE TOTEC, the god of spring and plants; Cozaana and Huichaana, a deer god and goddess; and MICTLANTECUHTLI, the death god. Other gods include rain gods and a variety of spirits, many linked to natural places considered sacred. Most Mixtec today are Catholic and celebrate Christian festivals and days honoring patron saints.

The Mixtec Creation   The following account of the Mixtec creation story was recorded in the late 1600s by the Spanish priest Francisco de Burgoa. In the beginning, two "magnificent trees, proud and boastful of their branches," fed from a river that began deep in a mountain. The trees loved each other and grew their roots and branches wide enough that they were woven together. From this love was created the first man and woman, the first Mixtec.

In another creation story, after the Earth had been formed, a deer god and deer goddess—in the form of humans—were born. Together they built a beautiful place on a mountain cliff. On top of the mountain, they created the heavens. Eventually they had two sons who could change themselves into several forms—EAGLE, SERPENT, or human. One day, these boys used some tobacco to make a small fire. The smoke from the fire was sent up to the mountaintop as a gift to the gods. The boys continued to live happily, growing food for themselves, offering gifts to the gods, and praying regularly that the world would always be as they knew it—with healthy crops and water pooled in certain places. To make their prayers stronger, they sprinkled their offerings with blood. Nonetheless a great flood came. These two boys were not the only children of the deer gods—the gods had produced other human children as well—but all the children were lost when the great flood covered the land. When the waters receded, the creator god remade the heavens and Earth and put people on Earth to live. The first people he made were the Mixtec.

MOCHICA   An early civilization in the Santa Catalina Valley in Peru that reached its height between 100 B.C. and A.D. 750. Their principal city was Moche, and the culture is sometimes referred to as the Moche. They were a highly skilled people who farmed and fished and used extremely complex engineering to move and regulate water for irrigation and canal systems. Their metalworking, pottery, and painting were unsurpassed and greatly influenced the CHIMÚ and INCA cultures that followed. The Mochica were ruled by warrior-priests who built extensive trade networks that helped expand their territory well outside the valley.

Not much is known about their gods and mythology. The Mochica are believed to have worshiped a thunder god who was god of the heavens. They also worshiped a moon god and a supreme god, PACHACAMAC, who was their creator from whom all things came. Because the Mochica were such skilled artisans, scholars have been able to make links between the Mochica's clay figures and paintings and stories from later cultures in their central Andes area. For example, there is a Mochica vase that shows a two-headed SERPENT that appears to be a RAINBOW that is being held up by a catlike figure. The same scene is reflected in a story from a later culture that tells how a two-headed serpent rainbow helps Grandfather Lightning lift up the sky.

A Mochica stirrup pot probably used for storing and carrying liquids. *(Craig Duncan/DDB Stock)*

MOCTEZUMA I (MOTECUZOMA, MONTEZUMA)   The fifth Head or Speaker of the AZTEC, who ruled from about 1440 to 1469. He was a wise and good ruler who brought order to the expansion that Lord Itzcoatl (1428–40), his predecessor, had begun. See also MOCTEZUMA II.

MOCTEZUMA II (MOTECUZOMA, MONTEZUMA)   The ninth Head or Speaker of the AZTEC, who ruled from 1502 to 1520. He came to power through the military and worked to increase Aztec land holdings and unite the empire. He was strict and is thought to have ruled as more of a dictator than earlier speakers. While Moctezuma II was ruler, the Spanish explorer Hernando Cortés arrived and began his CONQUEST of Mexico.

Monkeys were respected for their intelligence and quickness. This tapestry is from the Chancay culture of the central coast of what is now Peru. *(Jorge Provenza/Museo Amano, Lima, Peru/Art Resource, NY)*

Could Moctezuma II have saved the empire? It is hard to know. Several omens had predicted the end of the Aztec civilization—one when MOCTEZUMA I was chief. Moctezuma I sent magicians to AZTLAN, the first home of the Aztec. The magicians met with the earth goddess COATLICUE, who told them that the empire would end. Moctezuma II believed that Cortés might be the feathered-serpent god-king QUETZAL-COATL, returning to resume his rule. So, Moctezuma II gave Cortés a cloak believed to have belonged to the rain god TLALOC. In any case, Moctezuma II seems to have been unable to use his military skill against the Spanish, either because he was afraid that Cortés was indeed Quetzalcoatl or because the strangeness of the Spanish was so overwhelming.

The Spanish put Moctezuma II in prison, fearing that he would rally his armies for a full-scale attack. He was killed either by the Spanish or by his own army for not taking a stronger position against the Spanish. Today, in plays and historical reenactments, actors portray Moctezuma II as the historical figure he was or in a parody, poking fun at the Spanish invasion and the Catholic Church, in which Moctezuma II wins the confrontation.

MONAN (Ancient One) Creator god of the Tupí-Guaraní of Brazil. Monan created humans and twice tried to destroy what he had made—once by fire, once by flood—because he was displeased with how the people were living. (Some say he tried to destroy the world by fire and the flood saved it.) Maire-Monan, who replaced Monan, was more of a CULTURE HERO, teaching humans how to farm and make laws to live together in a civilized fashion. He was known as the Transformer, because he changed the forms of animals and people. Maire-Monan may also have been the culture hero Maira Ata, who, with help from the spirit world, could predict the future. ARICONTE AND TAMANDONAR were his sons, but he tested them before he would accept them.

MONKEY The spider monkey and the howler monkey are the two most common monkeys in South and Meso-America. Both are tree dwellers, the spider monkey particularly adept at swinging through the treetops. While the spider monkey lives in the tops of trees, the howler lives at any level and usually travels by walking along branches. The name *howler* comes from the male's loud voice, which can be heard as much as a mile away.

Throughout South and Meso-America the monkey is respected. It is quick and smart. In Peru, the monkey is particularly revered for its cunning. One of the most famous line figures on the NAZCA plains is of a monkey, which is believed to be a symbol of hope for sufficient rain. In one story of the Acawoios of Guyana, the mischievous monkey caused a great flood that destroyed the world (see MAKONAIMA).

The monkey was a sacred animal of the MAYA, and the Maya believed monkeys had once been human—stiff wooden figures that did not worship the gods as the gods wanted to be worshiped. When the gods destroyed these wooden people, some escaped, and became monkeys (see GUCUMATZ). The AZTEC too believed that monkeys had once been human. In the Aztec mythology, the people who survived the great wind that destroyed the Second Sun (see AZTEC SUNS) became howler monkeys. Monkey is a day sign in the Aztec CALENDAR.

MOON The natural satellite that revolves around Earth every 29.5 days. Many groups considered the Moon more powerful than the Sun because it could be visible day and night. Mysterious and considered a deity, the Moon served as a reminder that life could be renewed, because it changed shape, disappeared, and came back. The AZTEC attributed the changing shapes of the Moon to their sun god HUITZILOPOCHTLI. They believed he chopped off pieces of his sister, the moon goddess COYOLXAUHQUI whom he had made into the Moon. (See COATLICUE for the story.) The monthly changes, or phases, of the Moon regulated the lives of the people, forming the basis for the earliest CALENDARS. (The Incan moon goddess MAMA QUILLA continues to be associated with the calendar.) But long after calendars were an integral part of Meso-American life, the people continued to associate events with the phases of the Moon:

Phase	Meso-American Interpretation
New Moon	Moon is filled with sap (blood), which makes living things prone to illnesses. This is not a time to cut trees or harvest grain, including corn.
Waxing	Plants, animals, and people are hard, which makes hunting and harvesting crops difficult.
Full Moon	A good time to harvest crops and cut trees.
Waning	A time to finish harvesting in order that the harvest is in before the new Moon.

Because the Moon was thought to fill up with blood or sap and indicate good times to plant, Meso-American moon deities were associated with fertility of all kinds—including human fertility and childbirth. Ancient Meso-Americans often made sacrifices to the moon deities in order to ensure the fertility of females and successful crops. Deities associated with the Moon include the Mayan goddess IX CHEL, who was also the goddess of floods, horrific driving rain, and childbirth; the Aztec goddess Coyolxauhqui, her male form TECCIZTECATL, and the goddess MEZTLI (also goddess of darkness); and the YANOMAMI god Hanuxa.

One truly mysterious aspect of the Moon was the eclipse. Both the Maya and the Inca accurately predicted when eclipses would occur. Not only did eclipses upset the natural order, the ancient people also believed they were a sign that the gods were upset. An eclipse of the Sun was considered a victory for the Moon. Some believed that a fight between the Moon and her husband, the Sun, caused eclipses of the Moon. Others believed that an animal, usually a JAGUAR, was eating the Moon. Either way, people made much noise to stop the Sun from harming the Moon or to chase the jaguar away.

A Myth of the Moon In many creation myths, the Moon worked with the Sun to create the world. In the following story of the Apinaye people of the Brazilian highlands, competition between the two resulted in the Earth as we know it: Long before the Earth was inhabited, Moon slipped down to look around and hunt. When he saw Sun was already there, he hid. But Sun had already seen him and asked why he was hiding in a bush. Moon said he had not known it was the Sun, so he hid. Sun offered to take Moon to his house. Along the way, however, Moon was subjected to much teasing. First Sun ordered Moon to pick up a wasp's nest, which he claimed was a gourd. When Moon did, he was stung all over his face so badly that his eyes swelled shut. Sun, pretending to be helpful, carried Moon on his back. But, while walking under low-hanging branches, Sun "accidentally" knocked Moon into them, which pinched Moon painfully.

Finally, they reached the house, and Sun removed the wasp stingers from Moon's face, gave him some medicine, and offered him half the house. But the tricks continued. Poor Moon had bad luck hunting and got stung by wasps again. Sun stole meat from Moon's roasting fire. Then, as he threw the meat on the ground, it turned into new forms of animal. This inspired Moon to grab meat off Sun's fire, heave it into the air, and turn it into new species of birds. On and on the story went. The new birds that were created became human women that Sun and Moon took for wives. They planted gourds that become more people. Sun caused some of Moon's people to become blind, and Moon caused some of Sun's people to have diseases. They created a village for their children and argued about who would rule (Sun won). So Sun and Moon returned to the sky, Sun to light the days, Moon the nights. And with that, they decided that their children would have to continue on their own.

See TECCIZTECATL for the story of how the Aztec believed the Moon was created.

MOUNT RORAIMA A 9,219 foot flat-topped mountain on the borders of Brazil, Guyana, and Venezuela. Mount Roraima, "the great and ever fruitful mother of streams," is thought by some indigenous groups to be the home of their gods. Others consider it a place of mystery and magic that is guarded by demons.

MUMMY A dead body that has been treated with chemicals or herbs to keep it from decaying. The INCA mummified the bodies of their rulers because they believed them to be direct descendents of their supreme god, INTI, the Sun. Once mummified, the body would be placed in front of the statue to Inti in the CORICANCHA—the Sun Temple in the Inca capital of Cuzco. Sacrifices were made, and the mummy stayed there for the official year of mourning. The body would then be returned to the palace where the ruler had lived. There, slaves and descendants waited on the mummified ruler, much as if he were still alive. Mummies were worshiped as idols, consulted as oracles, and often brought out and paraded through town on special occasions.

MUSIC Throughout Meso-America music was associated with most occasions. Priests or shamans often used music to help bring on trances and to make it easier to receive messages from the gods. The earliest instruments were types of whistles, flutes, and percussion instruments. The OLMEC made the oldest known instruments. In addition to drums, they made instruments out of clay or carved wood. Many of these were decorated with, or in the shape of, animals (such as snakes, frogs, coyotes, birds, or crickets) or made in the images of the gods.

In South America, the INCA used music to accompany plays and the telling of stories about their history and gods. With no written language, the Inca used poetry and song to help keep their stories alive. Their instruments included flutes, panpipes, drums, and trumpets made from conch shells. The Inca also used conch shells to summon the war gods and to prepare themselves for battle.

N

NAHUA Native groups of central Mexico that included the AZTEC, TOLTEC, and ZAPOTEC. Today there are many Nahua communities in central Mexico. The people primarily farm, raise animals, and weave textiles. Although most are Catholic and focus on village saints and the Mexican patron, the VIRGIN OF GUADALUPE, they still have close ties to their ancient gods and goddesses.

NAHUAL (*NAGUAL*) A personal spirit of the NAHUA, including the AZTEC, that protects, guards, and inspires humans. Gods might have a *nahual*, as well. The FEATHERED SERPENT, for example, was the *nahual* of the hero-god QUETZALCOATL; the hummingbird was the *nahual* of HUITZILOPOCHTLI. *Nahuals* were usually birds or animals but could also be natural phenomena, such as lightning or meteors. Sometimes a child was given a *nahual* at birth; it would be linked to the birth date of the child. The child's name might be linked to the *nahual* as well, but often children were not told what their *nahual* was until they were old enough to know how to use the information. Other times, a person would find his or her own *nahual* by going off alone into the forest. The *nahual* would appear to him or her in a dream or might be present when the person woke up from a sleep. Today a *nahual* might be the first animal that comes near a baby after it is born. To be sure of what it is, some parents sprinkle ashes or powder around the house to record an animal's footprints.

Nahuals are powerful. They will travel while a person sleeps to gather information and report back in a dream. They can be sent off to carry out difficult tasks, such as confronting someone or helping someone who does not want to be helped. According to tradition, some people can transform themselves into their *nahual*, as one woman did in El Salvador. Her *nahual* was a pig, and she could change into a pig by standing on a particular rock and turning around two times. She did this regularly to steal from people as they came from the market. One night a man watched as the woman transformed herself into the pig. When she left, he moved the rock. Try as she could, the woman could not transform herself back without the rock, and she stayed a pig.

NANAUTZIN (NANAHUATZIN) The AZTEC god of self-sacrifice, courage and bravery, and light. Nanautzin was considered the father of the Sun. Long ago, when the gods were creating the world and had not yet given it light, the slight, shy Nanautzin threw himself into the fire when the more outgoing—and arrogant—TECCIZTECATL was too afraid to do so.

NAZCA A people in the valleys along the southern coast of Peru. The early Nazca culture flourished between 200 B.C. and A.D. 600. They were a farming society that used complex irrigation systems to bring water to the naturally dry valley. The Nazca carved images and designs into the plains. The Nazca Lines cover an area of about 200 square miles and the immense designs are visible only from the air. The monkey, for example, is 210 feet long, and the pelican is 935 feet. Although scholars at one time assumed these designs were related to an astronomical calendar, no direct relationship among the figures, the lines, and the constellations or sky movements has consistently been found. It is now believed they were made to please the mountain gods, whom the Nazca thought controlled the weather and watched out for the people living in the valleys. The figures include birds, believed to show the people's reverence to the gods; monkeys and lizards, to show hope for sufficient WATER; spiders and other insects, to ask for rain; and whales, to request luck in fishing. The spiral patterns are thought to represent the ocean and ocean shells, while the zigzags may represent lightning and rivers. Today, straight lines on the Nazca plain are still used to bring water from the mountains. Many lines are part of ceremonial rituals that revolve around water or rain. Other plains or pampas along the coast of Peru and in northern Chile have similar "lines" but not as extensive as those at Nazca.

The word *Nazca* is related to the Quechua word for pain. According to legend, the people first exhibited pain whenever drought hit their valley, which was frequently. Once, the people met together at the base of Cerro Blanco, the great white dune that

This spider is one of the Nazca Lines carved into the coastal plains of Peru. *(James D. Nations/DDB Stock)*

stands at one end of the valley. There, they pleaded for rain. The great god VIRACOCHA began to cry when he heard his people suffering so. His tears poured out of Cerro Blanco and formed canals, thus teaching the people how to channel the water from the mountains to irrigate the land below. Other deities of the Nazca include the mountain spirits, WAMANIS; the all-powerful god INKARRI, a rain god that threw thunderbolts and may also have been a warrior; and the feline spirit CCOA.

NEMTEREQUETEBA A hero-god of the CHIBCHA of Colombia, also known as BOCHICA.

NEW FIRE CEREMONY An AZTEC ceremony held every 52 years to ensure that the Sun would rise for another 52 years and that the world would be safe; also known as the Binding of the Years. The ceremony was held when the 260-day sacred and 365-day solar CALENDARS ended on the same day and coincided with the beginning of the dry season, and when the constellation PLEIADES began to rise. In preparation, houses were cleaned, pots were smashed, and all fires were put out. Priests and other religious officials waited on a mountaintop near the Aztec capital of TENOCHTITLÁN and watched the sky. At midnight, if the path of the Pleiades—which the Aztec called Tianquiztli (Market)—was directly overhead, a new FIRE was built in the chest of someone who had been sacrificed and whose heart had been removed and offered to the gods. A runner then lit a torch with the new fire and brought it to all the temples. Then each household received new fire from these temples. If the priests could not build a new fire on the mountain, the Aztec believed, the Sun would not rise, and in the darkness, the much-feared star demons, the TZITZIM-IME, would come down to Earth to eat all humans.

The New Fire Ceremony included a bird dance called *voladores* (flyers). A high pole stood in the center of a plaza. One dancer sat on top of the pole while four others, tied to the pole with long ropes attached to their waists, "flew" around the pole with their heads down and arms out wide. The dancers dressed in costumes that represented birds of the Sun—eagles and macaws. Each of the four dancers

These pages from the Nahua Codex Borbonicus show priests obtaining fire from the temples (right) and distributing it to the people (left). *(Bibliotheque de l'Assemblee Nationale, Paris, France/Foto Marburg/ Art Resource, NY)*

attempted to fly around the pole 13 times to represent the 52 years. If they were successful, the Aztec believed that the Sun would continue to shine. A version of *voladores* is still performed in parts of Mexico and Guatemala. Four dancers start from a platform at the top of the pole. When they launch themselves off the platform they try to circle the pole 13 times before landing on their feet on the ground.

NOHOCHACYUM   A creator god known as Grandfather to the Yucatán MAYA in Mexico. Nohochacyum was the god of creation, the supreme god, and was served by the spirits of the east and the constellations. As the chief god, Nohochacyum spent his time battling the evil god and great SERPENT Hapikern. At the end of all time, Hapikern will wrap itself around Nohochacyum and bring him all the humans to eat.

NUMBERS   Throughout Meso-America the people used a system of numbers and counting that was based on the number 20. The MIXTEC, AZTEC, and other groups used dots to represent each item, with other symbols to represent larger numbers. The

Aztec, for example, used a banner to represent 20 and a feather to represent 400. To show 40, they would use two banners attached together. The Aztec considered the numbers 3, 7, and 10 through 13 to be lucky, while 2, 4, 5, 6, 8, and 9 were considered unlucky. The number 1 was viewed as a neutral number and stood for the beginning.

The MAYA used a dot and bar system, with each bar equaling five dots. The system also included a shell, which equaled zero. The Maya were the first group in Meso-America to have a representation for zero. Numbers also represented the gods. The patrons of the numbers were the HERO TWINS. Xbalanque, one of the twins, was the number 9. The number 4 was the sun god KINICH AHAU, the number 8 was YUM KAAX, the CORN god.

The early South American cultures had no written language. The people of the ANDES, including the INCA, kept numerical records with quipus—bright-colored knotted strings attached to a base cord. Quipus may also have been used to keep historical records, and the implements are still used in the highlands of the Andes.

OBSIDIAN A volcanic lava that cools quickly to become very hard and shiny, like glass. Obsidian is usually black and was considered by Meso-Americans to be precious and valuable. Knives (used for sacrifices) and spearheads were made out of obsidian because it could be shaped to a sharp edge. The glass, used for making pots and other objects, was also polished to make mirrors. AZTEC magicians looked into obsidian mirrors to glimpse the future. This use of the mirror represents the power and spirit of the magician god TEZCATLIPOCA (Smoking Mirror).

OKONOROTE A CULTURE HERO who the Warau of Guyana believe was the first man on Earth. Long ago when the people lived only in the sky, a young hunter, Okonorote, saw a beautiful bird. He followed the bird for several days and finally shot it with his spear. When he tried to find where the bird dropped, all he saw was a huge hole. Looking over the edge of the hole, Okonorote thought he would see the bird at the bottom. Instead, he saw a whole wondrous world below. Okonorote made a long rope and climbed down into the hole and landed on Earth. There were birds, flowers, plants, and trees, and more kinds of animals than he could have imagined. After making several trips down to explore, he convinced other Warau to climb down as well. When a very large woman got stuck in the hole, the people who had already climbed down could not return to the sky and remained on Earth.

OLMEC The first of the great pre-Colombian Meso-American civilizations, and considered mother to other groups in Meso-America. The Olmec center was on the southern Gulf coast of what is now Mexico at Veracruz, and the civilization was most influential between 1100 and 800 B.C. The society was disciplined and class structured, and based on physical strength and technical skill. The Olmec built extensive trade networks and created the first calendar in Meso-America. They also were thought to have been the first in North America to make sculptures and buildings of stone. Some of the most monumental buildings were temples. Such creations were a remarkable feat given that the Olmec used stone from the Tuxtla Mountains, nearly 100 miles away. Like other pre-Conquest groups in Meso-America, the

This Olmec stone carving is about 10 feet high and may be of a ruler. *(Anthropology Museum, Veracruz, Jalapa, Mexico/Werner Forman/Art Resource, NY)*

Olmec had no draft animals and used no wheeled vehicles to move the stones.

Early scholars believed that a "were-JAGUAR"—half human, half jaguar—was a rain god and the primary god of the Olmec. But it is now believed they may have worshiped 10 major gods, including the were-jaguar, FIRE and rain gods, EARTH and CORN gods, a dragon sky god, a shark god thought to be a deity of the sea, and a FEATHERED SERPENT believed to be the forerunner of the Mayan KUKULCAN and the Toltec-Aztec QUETZALCOATL. The Olmec viewed the universe as having three layers: heaven, which was the home of the gods; Earth; and a watery UNDERWORLD.

OMACATL (Two Reeds)   AZTEC god of joy, feasts, and other festivities, particularly worshiped by the wealthy. Omacatl was an ASPECT of TEZCATLIPOCA—the "Smoking Mirror" magician god. Large and generous gifts, such as CORN, were made to Omacatl.

OMETECUHTLI AND OMECIHUATL (Lord and Lady of Duality)   The male and female aspects of the TOLTEC and AZTEC creator god OMETEOTL. These dual lords were considered the parents of all humans on Earth (see also DUALITY). They sent a soul to Earth each time a new child was born.

OMETEOTL (Dual God)   The supreme being of the TOLTEC and AZTEC. Ometeotl created himself and was therefore outside of space and time. He lived in Omeyocan, the Place of Duality. This was the highest of the 13 levels of heaven. Below him lived his male and female aspects, OMETECUHTLI AND OMECIHUATL. The Aztec built no temples to him and rarely made any images.

ONA   A people of Tierra del Fuego, an archipelago off the southern coast of South America. The Ona were nomadic hunter-gatherers who lived in bands of 40 to 120 and traveled only on foot. Their language relates them to the YAMANA and the ARAUCANIAN. The Ona had a supreme being, Temaukel, who was thought to be outside of creation—a spirit, an essence, that had always been and would always be. He was kind but invisible, and the people prayed

to him, occasionally making nonreligious offerings. When a person died, his or her soul returned to live with Temaukel. Kenos—the first man and culture hero of the Ona—was father to all and taught his children how to live. The Ona also had forest spirits and a hunter hero, Kwanyip. He fought many battles with evil, first in the guise of an evil spirit, Chenuke, then against an invisible giant. The Ona's mythology included stories of ancestors who had turned into the mountains, lakes, and rivers.

OPOCHTLI (The Left-Handed)   The AZTEC god of fishing and snaring birds, and the inventor of the fishing rod and harpoon.

OPOSSUM   A grayish-white mammal (*Didelphis marsupialis*) about the size of a house cat with a long hairless tail. Opossums eat both plants and insects, live primarily in and around trees, and are most active at night. Females carry their young in a pouch when they are first born. In many South American cultures, the opossum is considered a trickster. In a Tupínamba story, for example, the opossum tricks a woman who is pregnant with the son of the god Maira to share a hammock with him. While she sleeps alongside the opossum she becomes pregnant with a second child.

Throughout Meso-America, the opossum was often associated with old age and sometimes with childbirth. Opossums were frequently shown in ZAPOTEC art as small figurines or in painted decorations. The MIXTEC associated the opossum with the new year, crossroads, and the ceremonial BALL GAME. QUETZALCOATL and the opossum were often connected because they had so many similarities—both stole FIRE, discovered CORN, brought rain and the dawn, and both sometimes appeared as an old man. The MAYA said the opossum was responsible for the colored sky at sunrise. The story goes that the opossum painted the sky with colors while the HERO TWINS were competing with the UNDERWORLD lords in the ball game. In some versions of the story, the colors distracted the lords and thus slowed down the game. These colors also came to represent the coming of the Sun that, according to the *POPUL VUH*, the sacred book of Quiché Mayan history, had not yet been seen. Thus began the first 365-day solar year.

According to Cora legend, when Iguana stole fire from Earth and took it to the sky, only Opossum was successful in bringing it back for humans to use. In another version from Mexico, Opossum asked the old woman who kept all the fire to herself if he could warm up next to the fire. She was so surprised that he didn't demand fire outright that she let him get close to it. Eventually, he worked his way next to the flames and his tail caught fire. (That is why opossums have no hair on their tails.) Opossum ran away, taking the fire with him. He gave the fire to the humans in exchange for their promise to never eat an opossum. There are many variations on this story. In some modern versions, the opossum gets its pouch because she took fire to Mary and the baby Jesus. In others, the opossum's tail is hairless because it used its tail to carry the fire to Mary and Jesus in Bethlehem.

A myth of the Barasana people of Colombia reflects the opossum's association with rain: Once when a man spirited away Opossum's wife, Opossum chased after him to get her back. When he caught up with the man, Opossum began to fight him. Opossum was killed, and immediately it began to rain. The Barasana say that Opossum has died when the rainy season begins every year.

ORACLE A command or message from a god, often delivered through a human priest who acts as a messenger. South American scholars believe there was an oracle at the Chavín ceremonial center at CHAVÍN DE HUÁNTAR. There, a priest would have lain in a small room above the statue known as the SMILING GOD and replied through a pipe connected to the statue. In Meso-America, many oracles were thought to exist, including one of the MAYA in the statue of the IX CHEL, the goddess of the Moon, in Cozumel. The statue was hollow and life-size. Priests were said to enter it through a small door at the back and speak through the statue to relay messages from the gods. Since the widespread conversion to Catholicism, many in Meso-America believe that religious images, saints, and crosses, as well as house spirits, can speak. A SHAMAN, or someone else, speaks for each of these "Talking Crosses," stones, or images.

OREHU To the ARAWAK of Guyana, a generous water spirit similar to a mermaid and sometimes referred to as Water-Mama. In one myth, a good and kind chief was saddened by the evil spirits and the way they had infected his people, causing pain, illness, and bad luck. As the chief stood on a riverbank and cried, an *orehu* came out of the water and asked him what was wrong. After he told her his troubles, she gave him a branch and told him to plant it. She also instructed him to return to the riverbank when the plant had born a large round fruit. So the chief planted the branch and watched it as it grew and produced calabash, a large hard-shelled fruit. When the chief returned to the river with the fruit, the *orehu* was there waiting for him. She showed him how to make a rattle from the fruit, which would help scare away the evil spirits. She also gave him tobacco. From then on, the chief's people lived well and only occasionally were bothered by the evil spirits.

The wood of the calabash tree (*Crescentia cujete*) is not useable, but the shells of the fruit are very hard when dried and are used for bowls, spoons, pipes, and other household objects.

ORIGIN MYTHS Stories of how humans, cultures, and things in the natural world came to be. These stories can take different forms and reflect the beliefs of the people. Some origins came directly from the gods: In an AZTEC story, for example, humans were created, at the beginning of the Fifth Sun, from the blood of the feathered-serpent god QUETZAL-COATL and the ground bones of the people who had lived before (see CIHUACOATL). In one story of the MAYA, the Sun struck a rock to release the first beings. In one version of the origin of the INCA, MANCO CAPAC and MAMA QUILLA, children of the Sun, were sent to Earth to teach people how to live and become the first Inca. Still other origins were the result of an action by a CULTURE HERO: In a story from Peru, APOCATEQUIL killed the UNDERWORLD people, making it easier to bring the people up into the land. And finally, the Warau people of Guyana believed they originated in the sky (see OKONOROTE).

OWL Any of several mostly nocturnal birds with a large head and large eyes that face forward. Most owls are predatory—they hunt and eat other animals, mostly small mammals such as mice, voles, and rabbits, but they also eat fish, and large insects. Because they are active at night, owls are associated with death and the UNDERWORLD. However, they were also considered healers and are used to fight witchcraft, even today. Owls were thought to be a harbinger of death, certainly, but were considered too to be capable of carrying messages between humans and the gods. The AZTEC were quite fearful of owls. Besides the association that owls had with death, the Aztec considered them untrustworthy because they could change shape. The MAYA, on the other hand, linked owls to death but as messengers of their underworld gods and also to fertility. The screech owl, for example, gave the Earth rain and corn.

OXOMOCO In AZTEC mythology, the first human man, who was created, along with his wife, Cipactonal, by the first four gods. Oxomoco and Cipactonal had one son who married a young woman created from the hair of XOCHIQUETZAL, the goddess of flowers and love.

P

PABID To the Tupí in Brazil, the spirit of the dead, created when the eyes of a dead person left the body. After the *pabid* entered the land of the dead, worms would bore into its stomach, eat the intestines, and then take the *pabid* to the head magician, Patobkia, who restored the *pabid's* sight with pepper juice.

PACHACAMAC (Earthquake, He Who Gives Life to the Universe) The creator and supreme god of the early coastal people of Peru; son of the Sun. Pachacamac was thought to be an ORACLE and exerted great influence over the people. His influence was so great, in fact, that after the INCA conquered the people who worshiped him, they added him to their PANTHEON of gods. They also built a temple to INTI alongside the one to Pachacamac. He has been identified with VIRACOCHA, the creator and supreme god of the Inca. They may have had the same roots.

Pachacamac was considered awesome and was held in such reverence that the people did not speak his name. Instead, they made gestures—kissing the air, raising their eyes toward the sky and then down to Earth, bowing their heads. Pachacamac was worshiped only at one temple. Regular pilgrimages were made to the site, where priests led the worship, gifts were given, and human and animal sacrifices were made. As the writer Garcilaso de la Vega (1539–1616), son of a Spanish conquistador and an Incan princess, wrote, "If I were asked today what is the name of God in [my] language, I would reply 'Pachacamac' for in the general language of Peru, there is no other word which so well expresses the concept of God."

Although a creator god, Pachacamac did make mistakes. When he created the world and the first man and woman, he did not supply any food. As a result, the man died of starvation. Bitterly angry, the woman blamed the Sun, believing it had been done deliberately. Pachacamac then made the woman able to bear children. After she had two sons, Pachacamac killed one, cutting him into pieces that he strewed around the Earth. These grew into fruits and vegetables of all kinds. Pachacamac tried to kill the second son, but he escaped and hid. But when the great god killed his mother, the second son returned and chased Pachacamac off into the sea.

PACHAMAMA (MAMAPACHA, AMARA, Mother Earth) The mostly kind earth goddess of the INCA and earlier people in Peru, who believed she *was* the Earth. Viewed variously as an earth-monster, wife of the creator god PACHACAMAC, and wife of INTI, the sun god, Pachamama was viewed as the generous provider of all crops and food. The Inca made regular sacrifices and daily offerings to her, walking the fields to sprinkle ground corn on the Earth as they whispered their prayers. Peruvians still worship Pachamama today and sometimes link her to the Virgin Mary.

PANTHEON All the deities, or gods and goddesses, of a particular religion or group. The deities in the pantheons of some of the groups mentioned in this book are as follows:

Arawak deities

AIOMUN KONDI	The highest god
KURURUMANY	Creator god
MAKONAIMA	A creator god and Great Spirit

Aztec deities

APIZTETL	God of famine
ATLACAMANC	A storm god
ATLAUA	A god of water and identified with arrows

(Aztec deities)

CAMAXTLI	God of fate, war, and the hunt
CE ACATL	A warrior aspect of Quetzalcoatl
CHALCHIHUITLICUE	Goddess of rivers, lakes, oceans, storms, and whirlpools; considered by some to be the sister or wife of Tlaloc
CHALCHIUHCIHUATL	A corn goddess; an adult form of the young corn goddess Xilonen
CHICOMECOATL	A corn goddess; an adult form of Xilonen
CIHUACOATL	A goddess considered the earth mother
CINTEOTL	God of corn
COATLICUE	An earth goddess, ruler both of life and of death, mother of Huitzilopochtli
COYOLXAUHQUI	The moon goddess
EHECATL	God of wind god; an aspect of Quetzalcoatl
HUEHUETEOTL	God of fire
HUEMAC	God of earthquakes
HUITZILOPOCHTLI	God of war and the Sun
ILAMATECUHTLI	A corn goddess; an adult form of Xilonen
ITZLACOLIUHQUI	God of sacrifice; possibly an aspect of Texcatliopoca
IXTLILTON	God of medicine and healing, feasting, and games
IZTACCIHUATL	Mountain goddess and guardian of animals needed for food
MASAYA	Goddess of the underworld
MAYAHUEL	Goddess of intoxicants and childbirth
MEZTLI	Goddess of the Moon, night, and darkness; the female form of Tecciztecal
MICTLANCIHUATL	Goddess of death; wife of Mictlantecuhtli
MICTLANTECUHTLI	God of death and the underworld
MIXCOATL	God of the sky and of warriors; patron god of hunters; considered by some to be a father to Quetzalcoatl
NANAUTZIN	God of self-sacrifice, courage and bravery, and light

(Aztec deities)

OMACATL	God of joy, feasts, and other festivities; an aspect of Tezcatlipoca
Omecihuatl	Female aspect of the creator god Ometeotl; mother of all humans; possibly the same as Tonacacihuatl
OMETECUHTLI	Male aspect of the creator god Ometeotl; father of all humans; possibly the same as Tonacateucti
OMETEOTL	Supreme being regarded as having two aspects: Ometecuhtli and Omecihuatl
OPOCHTLI	God of fishing and snaring birds
PATECATL	God of PULQUE; patron of medicine; possibly the son of Cinteotl and husband of Mayahuel
QUETZALCOATL	A supreme god and deity of many parts of everyday life, including medicine, fertility, agriculture, the air and clouds, the planet Venus as the morning star, thieves, and gambling; in his Ehecatl aspect, the god of wind; son of Omecihuatl and Ometecuhtli
TECCIZTECATL	God of the Moon
TETEO INNAN	Earth goddess and great-grandmother of all
TEZCATLIPOCA	An ever-present god with many aspects and responsibilities, including a sun god, a creator god, god of the north and of the cold, god of darkness, patron of war and warriors; capable of seeing into the future; husband of Xilonen
TLALOC	God of rain, thunder, and the mountains; sometimes said to be the wife or sister of Chalchiuhtlicue, sometimes considered the brother of Xochiquetzal and Uixtocihuatl
TLAZOLTEOTL	Goddess of vice; a goddess of the Moon, Earth, and curing; forgiver of sins; considered the mother of Cinteotl and Xochiquetzal

(Aztec deities)

TLOQUENAHUAQUE	A high god and creator god, possibly another name for Ometeotl; Tonacateucti and Tonacacihuatl are the male and female forms
TONANTZIN	An earth goddess; possibly the same as Cihuacoatl, Coatlicue, and/or Teteo Innan
TONATIUH	Sun god
TZITZIMITL	Goddess of inertia
UEUECOYOTL	God of unnecessary enjoyment and chaos
UIXTOCIHUATL	Goddess of salt; sister of Tlaloc
VITZILOPUCHTL	A war god
XILONEN	Young corn goddess; wife of Tezcatlipoca
XIPE TOTEC	God of planting, flowers, sun-sets, springs, and rebirth; patron of jewelers and combat; son of Omecihuatl and Omete-cuhtli; brother of Quetzalcoatl, Huitzilopchtli, and Tezcatlipoca
XIUHTECUHTLI	God of fire
XOCHIPILLI	God of flowers, love, beauty, songs, feasts, and dances; possibly the twin and/or husband of Xochiquetzal
XOCHIQUETZAL	Goddess of gaiety, love, and flowers; daughter of Tlazolteotl; possibly the twin and/or wife of Xochipilli
XOLOTL	God of the planet Venus as the evening star; a lightning god
YACATECUTLI	Lord of travelers and god of merchants

Carib deities

Anuanaitu	First mother; mother of all Carib
Auhinoin	A star god
Couroumon	A star god
Icheiri	A household goddess
MACONAURA	First father; father of all Carib
Mama Nono	The earth mother

Chibcha deities

BACHUE	Mother goddess
BOCHICA	Sun god and founder god

(Chibcha deities)

CHIA	Goddess of the Moon
CHIBCACHUM	God of work
CHIMINIGAGUA	Creator god
CUCHAVIVA	Goddess of the rainbow; wife of Bochica
HUITACA	Goddess of excess and drunkenness and of joy in life

Huarochiri deities

CONIRAYA	Creator god
PARIACACA	Hero god

Incan deities

CATEQUIL	God of thunder and lightning
CUICHU	God of the rainbow
ILLAPA	God of rain, lightning, thunder, and storms
INTI	Sun god
MAMA ALLPA	Earth goddess
MAMA COCHA	Goddess of rain, water, and the sea; wife of Viracocha
MAMA CORA	Goddess of corn
MAMA OCCLO	First woman; a daughter of Inti
MAMA QUILLA	Goddess of the Moon, protector of married women; patron of calendars and feasts
MANCO CAPAC	First man; son of Inti; first ruler of the Inca
PACHAMAMA	Earth goddess
PARIACACA	A creator god, adopted from the Huarochiri
THUNUPA	A culture hero, considered by some to actually be the creator god Viracocha
URCAGUAY	God of the underground
VIRACOCHA	Supreme god and creator of the people

Mayan deities

AB KIN XOC	God of poetry
AH PUCH	A god of death
AH RAXA LAC	An earth god
AH RAXA TZEL	A sky god
AHTOLTECAT	A silversmith god
AHULANE	A god who governed the course of arrows
Alom	A creator god

(Mayan deities)

BACABS	Gods that stand at the four corners of the world and hold up the heavens; also associated with beekeeping
BALAM	Everyday gods that protected the people
Bitol	A creator god
CAMAZOTZ	The bat god
CHAC	God of rain, thunder, lightning, wind, and fertility
EK BALAM	The jaguar god
EK CHUAH	God of war, cacao, and traveling merchants
GUCUMATZ	A culture hero and creator god
HACAVITZ	A mountain god
HEX CHUN CHAN	A war god and demon spirit
HOMSHUK	The corn spirit
HUNAB-KU	Supreme god
HURAKAN	Creator god; also considered the god of fire, water, thunder, lightning, and heavy rain
ITZAMNA	God of heaven and the Sun
IX CHEL	Goddess of water, medicine, weaving, childbirth, the Moon
IXCHUP	A young moon goddess
IXTAB	Goddess of suicide
KINICH AHAU	God of the Sun
KUKULCAN	Supreme god (Yucatán Maya)
MAM	God of earthquakes
NOHOCHACYUM	Creator god (Yucatán Maya)
PAUAHTUN	God of thunder, lightning, mountains, and the middle of the Earth (early Maya)
Qaholom	A creator god
TEPEU	A creator god
TOHIL	God of fire and sacrifice
Tzacol	A creator god
VOTAN	An old earth god
Xamaniqinqu	God of the north, guide of merchants
XMUCANE	Mother of all Quiché Maya
Xpiyacoc	Father of all Quiché Maya
YUM KAAX	God of corn, coca, and crops

Mayo deities

Bamasenna	God of water
Cocohuane	God of life and death

(Mayo deities)

Ouraba	God of war
Schatoba	God of pleasure

Mixtec deities

COQUI-XEE	The creator god
EHECATL	God of wind; an aspect of Quetzalcoatl
TONATIUH	Sun god

Ona deities

CHENUKE	An evil spirit
Kenos	First man and culture hero; father of all
Kwanyip	Hunter hero
Temaukel	Supreme being

Orinoco deities

CACHIMANA	A great benevolent spirit
Iolokiamo	An evil spirit; opposite of Cachimana
JURUPARI	A chief god and protector

Panamanian deities

CHIPIRIPA	God of rain
DABAIBA	Goddess of water and mother of creation

Toltec deities

AHTOLTECAT	God of silversmiths; patron of the Toltec
CIHUACOATL	An earth mother
ILAMATECUHTLI	A corn goddess
MIXCOATL	God of the sky and of warriors; patron god of hunters; considered the father of Quetzalcoatl
OMECIHUATL	Female aspect of the creator god Ometeotl; mother of all humans; possibly the same as Tonacacihuatl
OMETECUHTLI	Male aspect of the creator god Ometeotl; father of humans; possibly the same asTonacateucti
OMETEOTL	Supreme being regarded as having two aspects: Ometecuhtli and Omecihuatl
QUETZALCOATL	A supreme god and deity of many parts of everyday life,

(Toltec deities)

	including medicine, fertility, agriculture, the air and clouds, the planet Venus as the morning star, thieves, and gambling; son of Omecihuatl and Ometecuhtli
TLALOC	God of rain, thunder, and the mountains
TLOQUENAHUAQUE	A high god and creator god, possibly another name for Ometeotl
XOCHIQUETZAL	Goddess of gaiety, love, and flowers
XOLOTL	God of the planet Venus as the evening star; a lightning god

Tupí-Guaraní deities

ARICONTE	The god of night
MONAN	The creator god
Tamondonar	The god of day

Zapotec deities

COCIJO	A rain god, also the god of lightning
Coquihani	God of light
Copichja	God of the Sun
ITZPAPALOTL	Goddess of the afterlife
Piyetao	Creator god
Tepeyollotl	God of earthquakes; lord of the night
XIPE TOTEC	God of planting, flowers, sunsets, spring, and rebirth; patron of jewelers and combat

PARIACACA (PARYACACA)   The hero god of the Huarochiri (or Warachiri) and other groups along the coast of Peru. Pariacaca was considered a creator god by the INCA, who adopted him. Pariacaca was considered the god of waters and the personification of a huge mountain that produces rain and running streams. The Inca believed he hatched out of a falcon egg along with four others who became the winds. Pariacaca was god of rain, flood, and thunder, and at one point he flooded the Earth when humans displeased him.

PATECATL   AZTEC patron of medicines and the god of PULQUE, an alcoholic drink made from the agave plant. Some scholars consider Patecatl the son of the corn god CINTEOTL. He has also been portrayed as the husband of the pulque goddess MAYAHUEL in some stories.

PAUAHTUN   A god of the ancient MAYA with four parts that held up the four corners of the sky, bearing the same function as the BACABS. Pauahtun was also thought to be the god of thunder, lightning, mountains, and the middle of the Earth. He was shown to be a very old man. As a LETTER GOD, he is known as God N.

PAYNAL (PAYNALTON, He Who Hastens)   An associate god, a messenger, who called men to go off to fight. This is also the name given to the person who stood in for HUITZILOPOCHTLI, the war god, in AZTEC ceremonies.

PEK   Also known as Nahua Xolotl, the MAYA dog-god of death. Pek was thought to announce death's arrival. He was also thought to be the one who brought lightning; some say he was a god of lightning.

PILLARS OF HEAVEN   A common thread in mythology is that a great flood once destroyed the world. When the world was recreated, heaven, or the realm of the gods, was put above the Earth to protect it from another deluge and to separate it from the mortal Earth. To keep it there, it had to have supports. The MAYA believed the heavens were supported by the four BACABS who held them on their upturned arms. The AZTEC believed that the heavens were supported by the DUALITY of pain and beauty (represented by THORNY FLOWERS), by rebirth and RESURRECTION, by SACRIFICE (represented by the SERPENT OF OBSIDIAN KNIVES), and by the interplay between the power of the gods and the way humans on Earth demonstrate that power (represented by the FALLING EAGLE).

PLEIADES   An open cluster of about 400 stars also known as the Seven Sisters and constellation

M45. Six, or sometimes seven, of these stars can be seen without a telescope. The name *Pleiades* comes from a Greek myth of the seven daughters of Atlas who were being chased by the hunter Orion and escaped to the sky.

In South America The Abipone people in what is now Paraguay worshiped the Pleiades as their ancestors. The INCA called the constellation *Collca*, which means "The Seed Sower," referring to a place where seeds are kept. This reflects the return of the Pleiades to the sky in the spring when crops are planted. The Inca regarded the constellation so highly that they built a shrine in its honor within the CORICANCHA, the great temple to their sun god INTI. The return of the Pleiades to the sky also signals the beginning of the rainy season.

In Meso-America Some Mayan groups saw the constellation as the rattle of a great cosmic rattlesnake whose head was the Sun. They kept a close eye on the constellation and studied its movements carefully along with those of VENUS. In their round observatory, the Caracol at CHICHÉN ITZÁ, the windows were aligned to mark the appearance of the Pleiades in the sky. For the Maya, the appearance of the Pleiades also signifies the beginning of the growing season. The Mayan name for the constellation is *motz*, which means "fistful" and refers to a hand filled with seeds to sow.

A story from the Quiché Maya sacred book, the *POPUL VUH*, tells how *motz* came into the sky: Before all time, the HERO TWINS killed VUKUB-CAKIX, an arrogant giant who claimed he was the Sun and the Moon—he was not, of course, he just bragged that he was. The twins, with the help of two old gods, XMUCANE AND XPIYACOC, killed the giant and his wife, leaving only one son, who was very strong. One day 400 young men came along struggling to carry a large tree. The son, ZIPACNA, offered to help them carry the tree, which he did all by himself. The youths were so upset that he could easily do what had been so difficult for all of them that they tried to bury him in a pit. Zipacna tricked them and escaped, but the youths claimed they had actually won the conflict. As they boasted among themselves, Zipacna returned and killed most of them. The youngest of them escaped to the sky and became the Pleiades.

The Pleiades served a different purpose for the AZTEC. Because it is directly overhead in late October and early November, they used its appearance to make the periodic adjustments for their solar calendar. In a similar way, every 52 years during the NEW FIRE CEREMONY, the priests relit the new fire when the constellation was directly overhead at midnight.

POCHTECAS Followers of QUETZALCOATL, the FEATHERED SERPENT hero-god of the AZTEC. The *pochtecas* may have been a guild or linked to specific arts, but they were primarily traders and messengers of the "ethical principles" of the Aztec. Their routes took them at least as far as Mayan territory.

POK-A-TOK See BALL GAME.

POPUL VUH (Council Book) The sacred book of the Quiché MAYA, written in the 1550s. It may have been translated from a Mayan pictoglyph book. It begins (as translated by Dennis Tedlock):

> This is the beginning of the ancient word, here in this place called Quiché. Here we shall inscribe, we shall implant the Ancient Word, the potential and source for everything done in the citadel of Quiché, in the nation of Quiché people.

The *Popul Vuh* was discovered in the early 1700s. Francisco Ximenez (1666–1729), a Spanish priest, translated it into Spanish. The *Popul Vuh* includes myths about the creation of the world, the origin of the Maya, and the gods. Through these stories much has been learned about the everyday life of the Maya. For stories from the *Popul Vuh*, see DEER, GUCUMATZ, HERO TWINS, MONKEY, OPOSSUM, PLEIADES, VUKUB-CAKIX, and ZIPACNA.

PREDESTINATION The belief that a god or gods has determined in advance what will occur and that nothing can be done to change the outcome. Throughout Meso-America the 260-day CALENDAR was seen as a guide to what the gods had already determined. It was up to the PRIESTS who kept and interpreted the calendar to put the clues together to know what would happen. Clues came from the gods

Pyramids helped connect the people on Earth to the gods. This pyramid at Chichén Itzá was built to honor Kukulcan, the Mayan god of creation. *(Erich Lessing/Art Resource, NY)*

associated with each section of time, along with any numbers associated with them. It was believed, for example, that the day on which one was born determined one's fate. However, if a child was born on what was considered a bad day, he or she could be renamed on a better day, giving the child a chance at a better destiny.

PRIEST   For the most part, throughout South and Meso-America the priest was highly regarded but below the nobility in the CLASS STRUCTURE. Early societies and small groups, however, may have had ruler-priests. Priests were different from SHAMANS, who more frequently used hallucinogens to go into trances or to assume a supernatural spirit. Priests, who often lived apart, were teachers, scholars, and interpreters of messages from the gods.

The MAYA, for example, had a priestly hierarchy. Head priests were called Ah Kin. Below them were the *nacom*, who led sacrificial ceremonies. Then there were the *chilan*, who were soothsayers and mediums, and *chacs*, who were elders and assisted the *nacom*. At the bottom were the *ah men*, who carried the messages of the priests into the villages, offered specific prayers for people, and helped cure the sick. The *ah men* had the most contact with the people.

The AZTEC had a similar hierarchy: The high priests to the supreme god HUITZILOPOCHTLI and the rain god TLALOC were at the top. Priests in charge of the rituals of the major cities assisted the high priests. Next were the specialists in ritual practices. They assumed more administrative roles, which ranged from running the temples to training boys to become priests.

Although priests in South and Meso-America were highly respected, their lives were not easy. They fasted often, prayed several times a day, and were ultimately responsible for making sure the gods were satisfied. As guardians and interpreters of the calendars, they were also the official timekeepers (see also CALENDAR).

PULQUE   A thick alcoholic drink made from the sap of the maguey cactus. The people of Central Mexico, where the maguey grows, believed the gods gave them pulque to make them happy because they did not yet have music. Pulque was ritually used during important occasions, sacrifices, and marriages.

The beverage, however, was rationed and only certain people could indulge in it—sacrificial victims, for example, before their deaths. The AZTEC had many pulque deities, including MAYAHUEL and PATECATL, which were collectively referred to as Centzon Totochtin (The Four Hundred Rabbits). These were the gods of drunkenness and immoral behavior. According to some stories, these gods were thrown off the Earth onto the Moon, which is one explanation for why there is the shape of a rabbit on the Moon.

Pulque was not the only use for the maguey cactus. Its leaves were used for the roofs of houses; the fibers from the trunk were woven into baskets and ropes; and the leaves and roots, rich in vitamins, were eaten.

PYRAMIDS The earliest pyramids in the Western Hemisphere were believed to have been built by the OLMEC at La Venta in about 800 B.C. Scholars are not sure for what reason the pyramids were built, although they do believe early Meso-Americans built temple pyramids to honor the Sun or the Moon. Later cultures built them as bases for the temples to the major gods or as centers for ancestor worship.

Possibly as many as 100,000 pyramids were constructed in Mexico alone, with large numbers also in Central America. A structure in the shape of a pyramid was a very wise choice because earthquakes are frequent in Meso-America. The pyramid provided a stable base.

Pyramids were symbolic mountains that connected humans on Earth to the gods and other spirits in the sky. In some cases they were built to represent specific mountains, especially those the people considered sacred. In Tenochtitlán, for example, the Aztec built the massive Templo Mayor (Great Temple), which honors both the rain god TLALOC and the supreme god HUITZILOPOCHTLI. The temple was built to resemble the mountain Coatepec, which they considered to be the birthplace of Huitzilopochtli.

The Aztec built over existing pyramids and thought that they should be rebuilt every 52 years (see also CALENDAR). The Maya also built pyramids over other structures, but theirs were built more often to honor the dead. A pyramid might be built over the tomb of a dead ruler, for example, and used for worship as well as for other ceremonies, such as celebrating a new ruler or a victorious battle.

Q

QUECHUA The language of the INCA, still spoken throughout the ANDES highlands; also a people of the Andes who occupied land west of the Inca capital of Cuzco and gradually became part of the Incan empire. The Quechua came under Incan rule by the end of the 1400s and then Spanish rule when the Spanish took over the Incan empire in 1532. Today Quechua still live in the Andes from Ecuador to Bolivia. They primarily farm and raise llama and alpaca for wool. Their religion is a combination of Roman Catholicism and traditional beliefs. The Quechua language is the most widely spoken Native American language.

QUETZAL A colorful but shy bird (*Pharomachrus mocinno*) native to the mountain rain forests of Mexico and Bolivia. The quetzal has a goldish-green breast, a bright yellow belly, and brightly colored feathers. The rest of its body, including its tail, is an iridescent blue-green. The 12 long tail feathers can be as long as 36 inches. The quetzal is not a common bird and was thought to be a symbol of hope. It was also thought to be capable of helping humans rid themselves of the burden of time and of the CALENDAR-driven life that was so controlled by the gods. The feathers of the quetzal were worn in headdresses of only the ruling classes and were considered more valuable than gold or jade, which Meso-Americans believed to be the most precious stone. (Other upper-class people used feathers from different birds along with cloth woven or painted with patterns, woven cornstalks, animal fur, and bones.) To collect the feathers, hunters did not kill the birds. Instead, they used a blowgun to stun the birds, removed their tail feathers, and then released them.

The Nahuatl word for *quetzal* is *quetzalli* and its reverence is seen in the name of the AZTEC great feathered-serpent god QUETZALCOATL. The MAYA called the quetzal *kuk*, a word that was part of the name of several Mayan kings as well as part of the Mayan great feathered-serpent god KUKULCAN. Today the quetzal is still an important symbol in Guatemala. It is the central image on the national flag, and the word *quetzal* is used to denote the Guatemalan unit of currency.

QUETZALCOATL (Feathered Serpent) An important and ever-present god of the NAHUA (this includes the AZTEC, TOLTEC, and ZAPOTEC) who considered him a supreme deity of many aspects of everyday life—medicine, fertility, agriculture, the air and clouds, Venus as the morning star, thieves, and gambling. He was thought to have invented the CALENDAR, books, and writing, and according to some stories he was one of the four creator gods. As EHECATL, he was the god of wind. Although there was virtually no aspect of daily life that he did not touch, he was not considered the most powerful god.

Early scholars believe Quetzalcoatl, who is an old god, to have been an agricultural or rain god before the Toltec made him god of the morning star, Venus. He is the son of the creator couple OMETECUHTLI AND OMECIHUATL. In one series of stories, the creator god OMETEOTL sent Quetzalcoatl to Earth to lead the people. Quetzalcoatl proved an able king until the smoking mirror god, TEZCATLIPOCA, held up his mirror. Quetzalcoatl was so horrified at the sight of his face that Tezcatlipoca offered to paint it. After painting Quetzalcoatl's face, Tezcatlipoca dressed him in QUETZAL feathers and a turquoise mask and teased him into drinking a magic potion. No good came of this, of course. Quetzalcoatl became involved in a drunken orgy and slept with his sister. When he sobered up, he was so disgusted at how he was dressed

The ever-present god Quetzalcoatl was important to the Aztec. This carving of him is part of the temple built in his honor at Teotihuacán and was originally painted with bright colors. *(J. P. Courau/DDB Stock)*

and what he had done that he threw himself into a fire. Then he rested in a stone casket for a week as he traveled to the UNDERWORLD. His heart rose to the heavens and became the morning star Venus. Some versions of the story say that instead of sacrificing himself into the fire, he left, sailing off toward the east. The rising Sun set fire to Quetzalcoatl and his raft, and his heart came out of his body and became part of the Sun.

This story links to actual history on two fronts. First, there were several Toltec leaders who were called Quetzalcoatl, following the first whom the Toltec believed was sent to Earth by Ometeotl to rule. The second link came in 1521 with the Spanish conquistadores, under the leadership of Hernando Cortés (1485–1547). The Aztec believed Quetzalcoatl would return from the east over the ocean. So when the Spanish arrived, the Aztec believed that Hernando Cortés and his soldiers were the returning god Quetzalcoatl and his attendants. Thus, the Aztec welcomed them.

After the Spanish arrived and forced Meso-Americans to convert to Christianity, Quetzalcoatl became linked with Saint Thomas and gradually became more of a culture hero or god than a historical figure. In the early 20th century, Quetzalcoatl became popular during the Mexican Revolution. Since then, he has been frequently depicted in art and is used by Mexicans to represent their heritage as a country founded by a strong, proud Indian people. (For Quetzalcoatl's role in creating the world, see AZTEC. For a story of how he brought corn to the people, see CORN.)

QUILAZTLI Another name for the AZTEC earth goddess CIHUACOATL.

QUINCUNX A decorative symbol often used in Mayan art—four objects are arranged in a square with a fifth one in the center. It forms a cross that indicates constant movement out from the center. It also relates to the belief that a CEIBA TREE stands in the center of the world, from which all life comes, and BACABS stand guard at the four corners of the world and hold up the sky.

R

RABBIT The rabbit (*Sylvilagus* spp.) is often hunted in Meso-America and appears frequently in art and writing. When the rabbit is depicted in a curled up position, it is thought to symbolize uncertainty. The rabbit is also associated with the Moon—Meso-Americans see a rabbit on the Moon, not a person's face. According to one AZTEC story, the Moon is TECCIZTECATL, and a rabbit was thrown at him so he would not shine as brightly as the Sun. A rabbit also is said to help the young moon goddess (her name is not known) when she was in trouble, and a rabbit is often shown with a picture of any moon goddess. The rabbit is also associated with the alcoholic beverage PULQUE. The collective name of the pulque gods is Centzon Totochtin (400 Rabbits).

In the Quiché MAYA account of the BALL GAME of the HERO TWINS in the UNDERWORLD (found in the *POPUL VUH*), a rabbit stole the ball to distract the underworld lords. After the Spanish invasion and CONQUEST, Rabbit began appearing in stories as a folk hero, often as a trickster battling Coyote or as a mediator. Symbolically, Rabbit, as trickster and mediator, was the native people of Meso-America—smart and wise and able to overcome the foolishness of Coyote, who represented the Spanish or any other invader. In the following Mayan story, Rabbit bests Coyote twice: Coyote always followed Rabbit around, so one day when Rabbit was tired of this shadow he hopped ahead of Coyote, then leaned against a huge rock to wait for him. When Coyote appeared, Rabbit said the heavens were falling down but because Coyote was strong, he could hold them up by pushing against the rock until Rabbit could find a big enough stick to prop the rock up again. Rabbit ran off, and did not return of course. Coyote pushed and pushed until he was dizzy from tiredness and staggered off, tumbling right into a canyon. Coyote learned noth-

ing from this experience and soon was following Rabbit again. When he caught up with him, Rabbit was drinking water from a large pond. He stopped for a moment and told Coyote there was cheese at the bottom of the pond. Being the poor small rabbit that he was, he knew he could not drink all the water to get to the cheese, but he said that surely Coyote was big enough to do it. So Coyote started drinking and was so distracted by his greed for the cheese, he did not notice that Rabbit had run off. In fact, he was so distracted, he did not notice that the water level of the pond was not lowering, and he did not realize how

This rabbit is from a 16th-century Aztec manuscript. *(The Art Archive/Mireille Vautier)*

much his stomach hurt from all the water until he was very, very sick.

RAINBOW The curved bands of COLORS—from outside in: red, orange, yellow, green, blue, indigo, violet—that arc across the sky when the SUN shines on a light rain or mist. The rainbow is seen as a SERPENT, a road, or a multicolored rope and is an object of magic and mystery to many peoples. Those living in South and Meso-America are no exception. In a creation story of the MAYA, one world ended in a great fire that showered the heavens and Earth with fine ash. As the sky began to clear, the survivors of the destruction saw a rainbow, which gave them hope and the knowledge that a new world was beginning. The Maya considered IX CHEL the rainbow goddess.

Many groups in the highlands of the ANDES consider the rainbow to be the husband of the moon goddess. The rainbow is often associated with agricultural gods because the people rely on rain for the successful growing of crops. The Incan rainbow god was CUICHU, and one of the most important HUACAS, the mountain Huanacauri, was associated with the rainbow. The INCA believed rainbows were two-headed serpents—capable of moving and causing trouble—whose heads were buried in springs deep in the Earth. Sometimes they entered humans, women in particular, and caused disease. The disease could be cured if the person unraveled a multicolored ball of yarn. According to tradition, some boys once tried to find the end of a rainbow but could not. This made the boys angry and they threw rocks at the rainbow, which is one reason why the rainbow does not often show itself to humans. Another reason is that it considers humans too cheerful.

REBIRTH AND RENEWAL To Meso-Americans, life was seen as a continual process of birth and rebirth that was played out in everyday life by the planting and harvesting of crops and the rising and setting of the Sun. It was a balance of sorts between the gods and humans—what happens in the heavens is reflected by life on Earth. It was a balance, not a partnership, because the gods always had the upper hand.

For example, after the AZTEC gods had created all and set the Sun and Moon in the sky, the wind god EHECATL blew on the Sun to start it moving across the sky. However, it took the continual "wind" from humans in the form of work, prayer, and sacrifice, to keep it going. Humans had a 52-year period to keep everything moving properly. At the end of the 52 years, when the solar and sacred CALENDAR cycles ended together, the people learned if they had kept the balance. If the constellation PLEIADES passed directly overhead at midnight, it signaled that the correct order had been maintained and that the Sun would continue to rise for another 52 years (see NEW FIRE CEREMONY). If the gods were not satisfied, the Sun would not rise and the world would be destroyed.

For life to make sense, the Meso-Americans needed their gods to be constant, but they had to keep their ideas about the gods flexible to account for what they learned as they watched the movements of the heavenly bodies. This is comparable to our own "information age" scientific view of the universe and how it works, which changes as scientists make new discoveries. Throughout Meso-America, renewal was constant and came in part through the retelling and adjusting of the stories. The renewal process also depended on pilgrimages, rituals, and the ongoing history of war and new rulers. This may be one reason there are so many stories, gods, and names and ASPECTS in the Meso-American traditions. The renewal process for the traditional Meso-American religions still depends on storytelling, pilgrimages, and rituals.

RESURRECTION One of the four ideals the AZTEC believed humans must live by to support the gods. Resurrection is the rising from the dead or the return to life—rebirth. The Aztec referred to these ideals as the PILLARS OF HEAVEN. The other pillars were FALLING EAGLE, SERPENT OF OBSIDIAN KNIVES, and THORNY FLOWERS. See also REBIRTH AND RENEWAL.

S

SACRIFICE The offering of something valuable to a god. Any object or action could be sacrificed or made as an offering—a favored or significant object, food, abstaining from a pleasurable activity, animals, blood, human life. Sacrifices were made often, even daily. Pleasing the gods was important, for all life depended on the gods' being satisfied. The giving of gifts is one way humans have always shown their appreciation and gratitude.

Because most of what we know about the early civilizations of South and Meso-America is influenced by the Spanish and early European colonists' perspective, scholars do not know how often blood sacrifices were made. What has appeared to some as being a regular—even frequent—occurrence, may in fact have evolved from an exaggeration or distortion from the Spanish and other European colonists' viewpoint. Taking these qualifications into consideration, some scholars have said that blood or human sacrifices might have begun when food and object offerings did not appear to satisfy the gods, such as when a natural catastrophe occurred: an earthquake, a volcanic eruption, or a severe drought. Human blood, or the life of a human, would have been the ultimate gift humans could give. If blood and human sacrifices were made at all, it appears that Meso-Americans offered them more often than the INCA.

For the AZTEC, the idea of making blood or human sacrifices came from the gods. In one story of the creation, NANAUTZIN, the god of light, and TEC-CIZTECATL, the moon god, both made sacrifices in the form of prayer and fasts to prepare for a self-sacrifice in which they would throw themselves into a fire. The feathered-serpent god QUETZALCOATL also sacrificed himself. Depending on the version of the story, he either threw himself into a fire or left his homeland and sailed into the Sun. The making of offerings and blood sacrifices also appears in the creation story of the MIXTEC.

SERI A native people of Sonora state in Mexico who were largely nomadic until the mid 1800s. Since that time, they have maintained an independence from most outside influences, including conversion to Catholicism. There has been, however, some influence from evangelical Protestantism. The Seri rely on hunting, fishing, and gathering wild plants, buying very few items. A few Seri stories have been recorded, such as one describing how the marks came to be on the Moon. In it, Coyote springs to pounce on a flock of ducks. They fly off, and Coyote lands on the Moon. Another recorded story explains the origin of FIRE. It tells how Fly made fire by rubbing his hands together. Little is known, however, about their gods, except for the story of He Who Builds Fires. The Seri believe that giants once inhabited the world and that the road to the underworld is a long one guarded by a dog. This has led some scholars to believe the Seri mythology is related to that of other cultures in Meso-America. Shamans are used as intermediaries with the spirits for healing.

He Who Builds Fires Long ago a great teacher, He Who Builds Fires, came by boat from the west. The people at that time lived in disharmony—always fighting, always hungry and cold. He Who Builds Fires taught the people how to start a fire and keep it going. He taught them how to hunt, which animals were best to kill, how to use animals for more than food, and how to use fire to cook. With his help, the people learned how to build shelters and live together as a family. They learned to settle their differences and to work together. When He Who Builds Fires saw that the people were living peacefully, he went into the heavens and became the Sun.

The serpent characteristics of Quetzalcoatl are clear in this carving from the temple honoring him at Xochicalco, Mexico. *(Ian Mursell/Mexicolore/Bridgeman Art Library)*

SERPENT Snakes and serpents have been feared and revered by many peoples, including the people of South and Meso-America. Because these reptiles are cold-blooded and slither along the ground, they are often associated with darkness and the underworld. The power of the snake is believed by many peoples to have come from a time before the Earth was inhabited.

Throughout South and Meso-America the serpents or snakes that held the most powerful spirit were the large poisonous snakes—boa constrictors, rattlesnakes, and anacondas. They were magical and mysterious creatures. Many of these serpents were as much at home in the water as on land, and they could move and strike swiftly. Like the gods, serpents and snakes can remain hidden, making their actions unpredictable. Snakes eat their prey whole and periodically shed their skins. This corresponds with the Meso-Americans' belief in REBIRTH AND RENEWAL. Serpents and snakes were often used symbolically on monuments, in warriors' headdresses, and on decorative objects.

Many of the Meso-American deities had close associations with serpents and snakes, and serpent gods were part of Meso-American cultures from the earliest times. The feathered-serpent deity that evolved into QUETZALCOATL first appeared with the OLMEC. In fact, the only figure the Olmec showed more often than a serpent was a JAGUAR. The TOLTEC and AZTEC rain god TLALOC and the Mayan CHAC were usually depicted with snakes surrounding them. Often, the snakes would be configured to resemble a bolt of lightning, perhaps because snakes, like lightning, can strike quickly. The Nahuatl word for serpent is *coatl*, which shows up not only in *Quetzalcoatl*, but also in COATLICUE (the Aztec earth mother goddess, known as The Serpent Lady) and *MIXCOATL* (the god of war, known as Cloud Serpent).

In South America, the people of the ANDES see the RAINBOW as a two-headed serpent. In the AMAZON basin, the great serpent, or *cobra grande*, lives in the great holes it digs in the bottom of rivers, lakes, and channels but not in the creeks and small streams of the rain forests. It is a powerful spirit that is smelly, noisy (with a muffled explosive rumbling), and active primarily at night when it lures people into the water or pulls boats toward it with a magnetic force. The origin of the *cobra grande* is unknown. Some say it is a boa constrictor, anaconda, or some other type of snake that grew too large to live on land. Others believe it had human origins. The people of the Itacaiumas River areas, for example, say it came from a young pregnant girl who was so ashamed that she had gotten pregnant that she threw her baby into the river when it was born.

SERPENT OF OBSIDIAN KNIVES   One of the four PILLARS OF HEAVEN the AZTEC believed supported heaven—that is, supported the ideals of the gods and the manner in which humans on Earth played them out. The other pillars were FALLING EAGLE, RESURRECTION, and THORNY FLOWERS. The Serpent of Obsidian Knives was SACRIFICE, which the Aztec felt was needed for the continuance of the REBIRTH AND RENEWAL cycle.

SHAMAN   An intermediary between humans and spirits who performed duties that included curing, healing, interpreting messages from the gods, guiding souls after death, and performing sorcery. Shamans were, and still are, both revered and feared because of their power. Some are thought to transform themselves into spirits, particularly animal spirits. In some societies shamans are also judges and interpreters of moral codes. They obtain their insights from dreams, trances, and vision quests, and they often use hallucinogens. Many wear JAGUAR skins, headdresses, or necklaces of jaguar teeth, and some are thought to change into jaguars after death.

SI   The CHIMÚ moon deity, shown as both a god and a goddess. Si was the supreme god and ruled the weather and agriculture and punished thieves. When depicted, he was usually shown wearing a headdress of feathers and being attended by a quarter moon.

SIBU   In South and Meso-American mythology there are two gods named Sibu. Both are creator gods—one of the Bribri in southern Costa Rica and northern Panama, and the other of several groups of the ANDES in Peru.

Sibu of the Bribri   Sibu is the god of creation, and everything that exists is within his house. A Bribri myth explains that as Sibu was building his house, he realized he needed strong vines to attach the logs and thatch the roof. The house had to be very tall because it needed to reach to the constellation PLEIADES, the center of Sibu's universe. Ordinary forest vines would not be strong enough to hold the thatch together, so Sibu used a whisker from a SERPENT that lived in the ocean waters. This worked perfectly—it was so long and thick that Sibu needed only to cut it lengthwise to make all the rope he needed. When the house was finished, he asked all the village people to come and see it. They refused to go inside because the Sun was setting and the only light was the little bit that came from the Moon. But Sibu urged them to come, and when they did they found light came from the knots of the serpent's whisker. The Bribri know this light as the stars of the nighttime sky. The traditional house of the Bribri is patterned after Sibu's house—round and tall with a thatched roof.

Sibu of the Andes   As the world was being created, the BAT left guano on rocks that Sibu had created. All kinds of plants, flowers, and trees grew from these rocks. The bat then flew into the UNDERWORLD and began sucking the blood from the Earth. This infuriated the people of the underworld so much that they wove a net to trap the bat, and then chopped it in two. Sibu did not want the bat destroyed, so he sewed it back together. However, the only way he could guarantee that the bat's intestines would be in their correct place was to sew the bat's head on in a way that caused it to hang down slightly, which it does today. (For another story that includes Sibu, see SURA.)

SMILING GOD   Also known as The Great Image, a statue found at CHAVÍN DE HUÁNTAR, the cultural center of the CHAVÍN. The statue is carved granite, stands about 15 feet high, and weighs two tons. It is believed to be the oldest ceremonial object in the Americas still in its original setting. Scholars believe the Smiling God is a representation of the Chavín's primary deity. It is half human, half feline with two large fangs that protrude from a mouth that appears to be smiling. The figure has snakelike hair and clawed feet. ORACLES may have been delivered through the statue. The Smiling God is believed to be one of the few surviving statues of the Chavín; the TELLO OBELISK and the STAFF GOD are two others.

This 19th-century engraving shows the details of a stela that is part of a Mayan temple in what is now Honduras. *(private collection/Bridgeman Art Library)*

SNAIL To Meso-Americans, the sea snail was a symbol of REBIRTH and joy. Its whirled shape represented the continuous cycle of life and death.

SPANISH CONQUEST See CONQUEST.

STAFF GOD One of the three remaining statues of the CHAVÍN, found at CHAVÍN DE HUÁNTAR, and believed to be an image of a rain god. The statue has a human face with an unsmiling, down-turned mouth. It holds a staff, or stick, in each hand. The other two remaining statues are the SMILING GOD and the TELLO OBELISK.

STELA A slablike monument carved of stone and erected by Meso-Americans, particularly those in the east. Many stelae were pillars that stood as tall as 30 feet high. Stelae were first made by the OLMEC and were carved with likenesses of rulers. They included dates and symbols relating to events of a ruler. Initially, the MAYA erected stelae every 20 years. Then in the sixth and seventh centuries they began building them every five years. In the beginning, the carvings were primarily historical records, but the Maya gradually included more mythic elements. Later stelae in the Yucatán were almost entirely of images of the gods and other supernatural figures. Scholars believe they were not used as objects of worship but as a way of recording information about the gods, as they had of the rulers. The stelae may also have helped to keep the gods foremost in the people's minds. Stone is permanent and reflected the lasting power of the spiritual world.

SUN The Sun is likely the single most important object in the mythology of most of the peoples of South and Meso-America, for it was the object most central to their lives. Its presence in the sky meant that life would be sustained, that there would be warmth, light, and plants to gather or harvest for food. The daily lives and activities of the people were regulated by the Sun's schedule of rising and setting. Many groups believed the Sun was created by a creator god as part of the cosmos. Others regarded the Sun as a bad child who was sent to live in the sky. Still others believed another god created the Sun—the ZAPOTEC, for example, believed the lightning god COCIJO created the Sun from a bolt of lightning.

The Sun in Meso-America The OLMEC considered the Sun to be a birdlike monster of the sky that ruled everything. The MAYA, who considered *Sun* and *day* synonymous, used the same glyph or symbol, *kin*, to stand for both. To both the Maya and NAHUA, including the AZTEC, the Sun had two faces. To the Maya, the Sun was their god KINICH AHAU during the day, but at night, it turned into a JAGUAR to prowl the UNDERWORLD. The Nahua believed the Sun rose as an eagle and set as a jaguar. Likewise, the Sun itself had two sides. It brought needed light and warmth but also caused excessive heat and drought. The Sun was also at the heart of the cycle of death and REBIRTH—it was seen to die each night and be reborn the next morning.

For the Aztec, the Sun was so important they aligned their cities east-west to replicate the path of the Sun across the sky. Their mythology was told in eras called Suns, and in each the Sun died and was reborn. (See AZTEC for the stories of the Suns.) The present era is called the Fifth Sun. In order for the Sun to survive throughout each era, humans had to try to obtain wisdom and liberation through sacrifice (spiritual and material). They also had to keep the gods alive by searching for those gods that greatly honored the creator. The Aztec did not take any chances. They kept the gods of earlier civilizations, as well as those of the people they conquered, active. Daily sacrifices were made to nourish and give strength to the Sun. Every 52 years, when the 365-day solar and 260-day sacred calendars ended at the same time, the Aztec held a NEW FIRE CEREMONY (see also CALENDAR). The purpose of the ceremony was to renew the Sun and guarantee its presence for another 52 years. According to some Aztec accounts, the Sun is the father of their feathered-serpent god QUETZALCOATL. The Sun came to be in the sky because of the self-sacrifice of NANAUTZIN, the god of light, at the time of creation. HUITZILOPOCHTLI, the Aztec god of war, was associated with the Sun, but the primary Sun god was TONATIUH.

In one Mayan story, the Sun and the Moon were the first dwellers on Earth. They lived as husband and wife in harmony, until they moved to the sky. Then, the Sun believed the Moon was unfaithful, so he took out one of her eyes to make her less attractive and shine less brightly. Eclipses were thought to be part of the ongoing argument between the two. Many Maya considered the Sun to be the doorway to heaven. Their principal Sun god was KINICH AHAU.

For other Meso-American stories that involve the Sun, see COCOPA, EHECATL, HUICHOL, and IX CHEL.

The Sun in South America   The Inca believed they were literally children of the Sun, that their rulers were direct descendants of the sun god INTI, and that he watched over and protected them. According to some stories, Inti sent his son and daughter, MANCO CAPAC and MAMA OCCLO, to Earth to teach humans how to live. In other stories they are the first couple from whom all Inca were born. The Inca's attitude toward Inti and the Sun are legendary as reflected in their reverence for GOLD, which they considered the sweat of the Sun. The Sun Temple, CORICANCHA, for example, was literally lined with gold and contained golden images of Inti.

In other parts of South America, the Sun was an accepted part of the universe, not to be taken lightly of course, but with a less regal bearing. In one story from the Pehuenche ARAUCANIAN, the Sun got involved in the eternal struggle between men and women. Long ago, the men stayed home and the women went out to hunt. The men grumbled that the women mistreated them. They felt that the women, who went out, had all the fun while the men had to stay home and work hard—cleaning up after the women, dressing the game, fixing the food, and turning hides into clothes. In short, they felt that they were slaves, and they banded together and killed all the women. The Sun, however, despaired over what men had done. So together with his wife, the Moon, the Sun hid under a large rock so as not to provide any light for the men. And so the world stayed dark until two CONDORS discovered the Sun and Moon and carried them back to their rightful places in the sky.

For other South American stories about the Sun, see BOCHICA, COLLA, IAE, MOON, VIRACOCHA, and YAMANA.

SUN STONE   A circular stone slab, with a 12-foot diameter, also known as the Calendar Stone. It is thought to have been created around 1479 and is dedicated to the sun god TONATIUH. The Sun Stone is not considered a calendar, but a solar disk that some believe may have been used for sacrifices to the Sun. Scholars, however, generally consider it to be a symbolic representation of the four eras, or Suns, of Aztec mythology and of how the Fifth Sun was created (see AZTEC and AZTEC SUNS). The present Sun is ruled by Tonatiuh and is based on the cycle of death and rebirth. Tonatiuh and the other gods, the Aztec believed, would be sustained only through regular offerings and sacrifice.

Tonatiuh appears in the center of the Sun Stone. He is holding an obsidian sacrificial knife in his mouth and human hearts in each hand. Surrounding him in the first ring are symbols of the five Suns. Symbols for the 20 named days of the Aztec month

This 12-foot Sun Stone shows the history of the Aztec's mythological ages. *(D. Donne Bryant/DDB Stock)*

appear in the second ring. This third ring has symbols for the rays of the Sun, for CHALCHIHUITLICUE, the Aztec goddess of water, and for blood. Among the symbols in the outer ring are two SERPENTS. They appear face-to-face at the bottom of the ring with their tails joined at the top. The symbol for 13 Reed, the day considered to be the beginning of the Fifth Sun, is also depicted.

SUPAY (CUPAY) An evil spirit of the INCA. According to some sources, Supay was so intent on influencing everyday life that children were sacrificed in order to keep him happy. Other sources, however, report that he was of little or no concern. Supay is also a name used to refer to all the evil spirits of the ANDES highlands, including the ANCHANCHO. Supay has been linked to the Christian devil, and some consider it to be a god of death and the lord of the UNDERWORLD.

SURA A creator god of the Andean people of Peru. One of his greatest achievements was making sure there were enough seeds so humans would have enough to eat. According to the myth, long ago the great god SIBU gave Sura the power to create animals from seeds. After burying the seeds, Sura left to tend to other things. While he was away, the evil trickster god Jaburu dug up and stole all the seeds. When Sura came back and saw what had happened, Jaburu attacked him, cut his throat, and buried him. Some time later Jaburu walked through this same place and saw CACAO and calabash trees growing where he had buried Sura. Standing there among the trees was the great god Sibu, who asked Jaburu to make him a drink of cacao. Jaburu did as he was asked while Sibu watched closely. When the drink was ready, Jaburu handed it to Sibu who told him to drink some first. Jaburu drank greedily. His belly got so big that it exploded and thousands of cacao seeds came out. Sibu collected them all. Then he brought Sura back to life and gave him the seeds. Forevermore, Sura plants cacao, calabash, and all the world's important plants where they are needed.

T

TAIRONA A native people of northern Colombia in the Sierra Nevada de Santa Marta mountains. The Tairona are considered the foremost engineers and craftsmen of the pre-Columbian period. They lived in self-sufficient interdependent villages that practiced highly ecological farming—terraced gardens that supported a large population with seemingly no ill effect on the environment. There was no central government, and through guerrilla warfare the Tairona managed to hold off the Spanish for more than 100 years. The Spanish eventually defeated them, destroyed their villages, and killed many of the people.

The spirit god primary to the lives of the Tairona was the Gaulcovang, the Great Mother and the creator of all. Other deities helped keep the environmental balance in harmony. They included Abu Se, a spiritual parent who was more a concept than an actual figure. He was responsible for all thought and spirit. The other parents were Zaku Se, Ade Se, Kaku Se, Jawa Se, and Jate Se. Alauhuiku was lord of FIRE, the dry season, and animals. He was the youngest and wisest of the Great Mother's sons and was associated with the four directions. Bunkua-se, another son of the Great Mother, was the lord of the universe. He personified an ethical way of life, symbolizing light and justice. Se was the force that kept everything in motion and working harmoniously. Se was neither a person nor a god, but a collective energy. Archaeologists have also found remains of what they believe are ceremonial houses dedicated to a JAGUAR god or spirit.

See also KOGI.

TARAHUMARA Seminomadic hunter gatherers of the Sierra Madre mountains in the southwestern part of the Mexican state of Chihuahua who do practice some farming. There is no Tarahumara written language. The Tarahumara came easily under Spanish rule. While they merged their traditional religious practices into Catholicism, they took on only those things that tied to their way of life. For example, their supreme god Onoruame (He Who Is Father) became the Christian God and their moon goddess Yeruami (Mother Moon) became the Virgin Mary. They adopted the use of incense for rituals and healing and have traditional fiestas for Easter, Christmas, and Epiphany. They make food offerings to God in ceremonies for crops, rain, and to help prevent natural disasters, such as drought and earthquakes. Such ceremonies are conducted by SHAMANS, who are believed to get their power from dreams. Shamans play a large role in the everyday lives of the people, who depend on shamans both in this life and the next. Dreamtime is important to everyone—it is considered a time when the mind and body communicate with the soul.

TECCIZTECATL (TECCUCIZTECATL) Moon god of the AZTEC. Also known as MEZTLI, Tecciztecatl is the Moon personified. He is often shown as an old man with a white shell on his back and with wings like a butterfly's. At the time of creation, Tecciztecatl had a chance to become the Sun, but he hesitated. This is what happened:

At the beginning of the Fifth Sun, the humble god NANAUTZIN was chosen to bring light to the world. Tecciztecatl, the cocky old seashell god, volunteered for the job as well. So they both fasted and made offerings in preparation. Tecciztecatl's offerings were very pleasing to the gods. Then the time came when they were to throw themselves into a fire as a sacrifice to create the Sun. Tecciztecatl was given the first chance, but he was afraid. Four times he made an attempt but turned back. Then Nanautzin quietly walked into the fire and disappeared. Shamed, Tecciztecatl ran in after him. The two gods soon appeared in the sky as two shining objects, Nanautzin the Sun, Tecciztecatl the Moon. The other gods thought that Tecciztecatl was such a braggart that he should not shine as brightly as the Sun. They decided to throw a RABBIT across his face, which dimmed the light. The shape of the rabbit is still visible on the face of the Moon. In Aztec mythology Tecciztecatl was eventually replaced by the moon goddess COYOLXAUHQUI.

TELLO OBELISK A tall granite pillar, about 8 feet high and 1 foot wide, that is one of three surviving statues of the CHAVÍN at CHAVÍN DE HUÁNTAR. The monument is richly carved with elaborate symbols that include a CAIMAN-like god, possibly a dual god of the underworld and sky. It is believed to have been an object of worship. The other surviving statues are the SMILING GOD and the STAFF GOD.

TEMPLO MAYOR (Great Temple) The pyramid and dual shrines to the god of war, HUITZILOPOCHTLI, and the rain god, TLALOC, at the AZTEC capital at TENOCHTITLÁN. Its sacred name was Coatepec (Serpent Mountain). This great temple was the central feature of the temple precinct in Tenochtitlán. The pyramid's base was about 80 by 100 yards square and it rose about 90 feet high. It was built as a symbolic mountain with two staircases on the front (west) side. These staircases led to the top of the pyramid where temples to the two primary gods stood. On the north was Tlaloc, symbolizing the rainy season—a time to plant and harvest crops. On the south, Huitzilopochtli, symbolizing the dry season—a time for war, to expand the Aztec territory and bring in more people for soldiers, and to obtain victims for sacrifices to nourish the gods. The Templo Mayor is now an archaeological site in the center of Mexico City. It is undergoing exploration and excavation.

TENOCHTITLÁN (Land of the Prickly Pear Cactus) The AZTEC island city in LAKE TEXCOCO and center of worship of the war god HUITZILO-POCHTLI. When the Aztec migrated from AZTLAN,

their land of origin, their great god Huitzilopochtli led them. He told the Aztec to stop only when they saw a great EAGLE holding a SERPENT and sitting on a cactus. There, the god said, they should build their home and begin a great empire. And that is exactly what they did, beginning with a few reed huts and a small temple to Huitzilopochtli on an island in a swampy lake. Eventually, the Aztec filled in much of the swamplands surrounding the island. They built great temples, floating gardens, aqueducts to supply the city with fresh water, and dams to control the level of the lake during the rainy season. They also connected the island to the mainland by building two wide causeways. The city was divided into quarters—the Moyotlan, or "mosquito place"; Cuepopan, "place of blooming flowers"; Atzacoalco, "place of the herons"; and Teopen, "place of the gods." Teopen included the Great Temple (TEMPLO MAYOR); temples to QUETZALCOATL, TEZCATLIPOCA, and the SUN; a ball court; schools; and a place for combat between gladiators. In 1521, the Spanish completely destroyed Tenochtitlán. They rebuilt a city, which became Mexico City, on the same site.

TEN-TEN AND CAI-CAI Mythological SERPENTS of the ARAUCANIAN in Chile. Long ago the two serpents Ten-ten and Cai-cai, good and evil, battled so hard they caused the sea waters to rise up and flood the land. When Ten-ten saw what was happening, he stopped fighting, but Cai-cai persisted. Ten-ten raised mountains out of the land so the people and animals would be saved, but as he raised the mountains, Cai-cai kept raising the level of the water. Eventually, Ten-ten changed some of the people into birds so they could fly ever higher to escape the water, leaving room at the very tops of the mountains for the people who remained. When the waters receded, some of the people had turned to stone, but the others came down the mountain and repopulated the land.

The people of Chiloé Island off the Chilean coast believe the battle between Ten-ten and Cai-cai lasted through many ages and was responsible for the way their island, and those around it, became separated from the mainland. At one time they were connected to the mainland, but the long years of floods by

Cai-cai and the mountain building by Ten-ten created the valleys, channels, mountains and hills that form the landscape of their home.

TEOTIHUACÁN (TEOTIHUCÁN, City of the Gods)
A pre-Columbian city in central Mexico, about 30 miles northwest of what is now Mexico City. It was the largest city in the Americas, and one of the largest in the world, before the Spanish arrived. At one time, it had a population of as many as 200,000 people and covered an area of about 80 square miles. Teotihuacán was first settled about 400 B.C. by people of unknown origin. What was known about them is that they had a wide trade network and exerted a strong cultural influence throughout northern Meso-America. A great religious and ceremonial center, Teotihuacán had massive pyramids to the Sun and Moon. Although the city burned in about 700 B.C., the AZTEC were well acquainted with it and regarded it as a sacred place; they still do. They consider it the place the gods met to create the world of the Fifth Sun and call it the City of the Gods. Carvings on buildings and monuments have images of the gods the Aztec assumed into their pantheon and worshiped. Some of these include the feathered-serpent god QUETZALCOATL, the rain god TLALOC, the goddess of water CHALCHIHUITLICUE, and the god of spring and REBIRTH XIPE TOTEC. Teotihuacán is a site of ongoing archaeological excavations and a tourist destination.

TEOTL
Nahuatl word for *god*. Many of the names of the NAHUA's gods are compound words, some ending with *teotl*. For example, OMETEOTL, "two god" or "dual god."

TEPEHUAN
A people of the southern part of the Mexican state of Chihuahua; related to the AZTEC. Their name is possibly from the Aztec *tepetl*, meaning "mountain." Their principal gods were a creator god, Diusuroga (God Our Father); a deer god, Ku'kuduli; a spirit of the afterlife, Ugai; and a mountain spirit, Ku'kuvuli. Catholicism is well blended with the Tepehuan traditional spiritual practices.

Today most ceremonies and festivals follow the Christian calendar—festivals at Easter, Christmas, and Epiphany. The principal religious figures for the Southern Tepehuan are Dios Padre, identified with the Sun; Jesus Nazareno, sometimes identified with the Moon; Madre Maria, the morning star; and Ixcaitiung, a CULTURE HERO. Ixcaitiung redeemed himself for his wicked life by dancing the first *mitote*—a dance or ritual of celebration usually done as a group—and thus going to heaven. Many Tepehuan returned to the practices of their traditional culture after a young Southern Tepehuan woman saw the Mexican patron VIRGIN OF GUADALUPE at Cerro Amarillo (Yellow Hill) in 1956. They wear traditional dress and continue to dance the *mitote* for redemption. Healing of physical and spiritual wounds is achieved through prayer with the help of SHAMANS, whom the gods visit and give whatever specific knowledge is needed.

TEPEU
One of the seven creator gods of the MAYA, who along with GUCUMATZ created the Earth and water and created humans from wood. The other five creator gods are Alom, Bitol, HURAKAN, Qaholom, and Tzacol.

TETEO INNAN (Mother of the Gods)
An AZTEC earth goddess; a great grandmother, full of powerful healing capabilities. During ceremonies honoring Teteo Innan, all those connected to medicine and healing practices danced with their arms filled with flowers. Sometimes the dancing continued for several days with participants in a trance-like state for much of the time. Teteo Innan was also known as Toci, and some scholars believe these are other names for the moon and earth goddess TLAZOLTEOTL. Teteo Innan is also associated with the earth goddess TONANTZIN and with the VIRGIN OF GUADALUPE, the patroness of Mexico.

TEZCATLIPOCA (Mirror That Smokes)
The AZTEC and TOLTEC god considered QUETZALCOATL's opposite. He was everywhere and in everything—a supreme god, a creator god, the sun god, god of the north and of the cold, god of darkness, the source or provider of both good and bad luck, and the patron of war and warriors and of those considered courageous. He is thought by some scholars to be a true god—an

all-powerful, all-present deity—because he had so many forms and so much power. He could look into his OBSIDIAN mirror and see the future. He knew everything humans were up to, and he judged their actions, often sternly. Still, Tezcatlipoca was a trickster, capable of changing shape, and impulsive.

According to some stories, Tezcatlipoca was a son of the great god OMETEOTL in his first pair of ASPECTS, OMETECUHTLI AND OMECIHUATL, along with the feathered-serpent god Quetzalcoatl, the god of war HUITZILOPOCHTLI, and the god of REBIRTH AND RENEWAL, XIPE TOTEC. As a creator god he ruled the First Sun. The creation and destruction of the four Suns or ages of Aztec mythology (see also AZTEC SUNS) are based on the ongoing struggle between Tezcatlipoca and Quetzalcoatl.

In one story of the Toltec, Tezcatlipoca tried to conquer Quetzalcoatl so he could rule. Capable of changing shape and taking on many disguises, Tezcatlipoca tricked Quetzalcoatl into drinking a lot of wine. While Quetzalcoatl was drunk, Tezcatlipoca slept with his daughter and overtook the Toltec armies. He then lulled the people into great sleepiness with music. Next he took a puppet figure of Quetzalcoatl and, while the people laughed at the puppet, turned around and stoned it. The stones turned into waste that polluted the land. Next, Tezcatlipoca caused a great volcano to erupt and over its last burning coals roasted corn. After so much devastation, the remaining Toltec came out of hiding when they smelled the roasting corn. But it was another trick. As soon as they had come to claim the food, Tezcatlipoca killed them all, hoping still to get Quetzalcoatl as well. By this time Quetzalcoatl had awakened and was grieving deeply, but he eluded Tezcatlipoca and prevailed, sailing to eternity on a raft of serpents. (See QUETZALCOATL for another version of the story; see TLALTECUHTLI for an Aztec story of how Tezcatlipoca and Quetzalcoatl worked together to create the Earth from a great earth monster.)

When the Spanish arrived and began to force Meso-Americans to convert to Catholicism, they connected Tezcatlipoca to the devil and worked to rid him entirely from the native mythology and suppress his identify as a god. Gradually Tezcatlipoca became unimportant in the everyday lives of the people.

Today his name is mentioned only as a literary figure, a character in the old stories.

THORNY FLOWERS One of the four PILLARS OF HEAVEN the AZTEC believed supported the ideals of the gods and how humans acted upon them. Thorny Flowers symbolizes the DUALITY of pain with beauty in life. (See ITZPAPALOTL for a story that explains how humans were brought both beauty and pain.) The other pillars are FALLING EAGLE, SERPENT OF OBSIDIAN KNIVES, and RESURRECTION.

THUNUPA (TONAPA, TAAPAC) A CULTURE HERO of the central Andean people, including the COLLA, Aymara, and INCA. Thunupa was said to have come from the north with five disciples or attendants. Although he was an old man with long white hair who dressed simply, Thunupa was impressive and commanded one's attention. He preached, speaking out strongly against war, drinking, and the worship of idols, and he was believed capable of miraculously healing the sick. Although the priests supported him, Thunupa's teachings angered a chief named Makuri who called him a fraud and forced him to leave. At another village Thunupa's virtuousness so angered the people that they burned down his house. Thunupa escaped and returned to Chief Makuri's village, but he found no peace there. The chief's daughter had become a follower, so when Thunupa returned, Makuri killed all the disciples in revenge and left Thunupa dying. His supporters put Thunupa's body on a raft and set it adrift on LAKE TITICACA. Some stories imply that he was gentle and kind, while others suggest that he was harsh, turning those who would not listen to him into stones. The ending varies as well. In one, Thunupa disappears into the mountains as mysteriously as he had arrived. In another, he floats on his cloak across the lake toward the rising Sun and disappears into the Sun.

Thunupa is regarded by some as the great Andean creator god VIRACOCHA, moving among the people in disguise. There is some evidence of a cult of Thunupa around Lake Titicaca. Since the arrival of the Spanish, stories about Thunupa have told of him carrying a huge cross to the top of a mountain. Some pictures of him now have him carrying a cross on his back.

TIAHUANACO (TIWANAKU, TIWANACU)

An ancient city on the southern shore of LAKE TITI-CACA in Bolivia, thought to have been created by ancestors of the Aymara people of the ANDES. Although most scholars believe Tiahuanaco was first settled around 200 B.C., there is evidence suggesting it might have been settled as far back as 17,000 years ago. It is considered by some to be the oldest capital in the world, with a population of as many as 35,000 and serving as a cultural and ceremonial center for a wide area. The city's three primary ruins include the Akapana, a ceremonial stepped pyramid aligned exactly to the cardinal directions, which may have been carved from a hill; the Kalasasaya, a low ceremonial platform; and the Gateway to the Sun, a huge partially carved single piece of granite weighing more than 10 tons. In the central position at the top of the Gateway is a carved figure similar to the STAFF GOD of the Chavín. This may be a sun god, and the Gateway may have served for tracking the movement of the Sun during a year. Some scholars believe that VIRACOCHA was the primary god of the pre-INCA people at Tiahuanaco, and the city is included in stories that tell where Viracocha traveled as he moved around the land bringing culture to the people.

TIME

Every moment that has ever been or ever will be—the past, present, and future. To the native people of the Americas, time is not a straight road. Instead, it has dimension—the past and future mingle with the present. Every moment that ever was or ever will be is wrapped up in the present. Change—by births and deaths of all kinds—is evidence of time passed. However, change proves only that time exists, not that any distance has been traveled. Time itself is seen as a cycle—of the solar year, a human life, planting and harvesting crops, a ruler's reign. To the AZTEC, time is the cycle of renewing the Sun and the fires every 52 years (see NEW FIRE CEREMONY). With a cycle, time is circular, coming back and beginning again always in the same place. To many groups in Central and South America, such as the MAYA, this meant that the rulers simply repeated the actions of their ancestors and that all action repeated the activities of the gods. To be released from time, as the Meso-Americans believed could happen after death, meant that one was free of these cycles in a paradise that was blissful, harmonious, and without change. In other words, one would be immortal.

TLACHTLI   See BALL GAME.

TLALOC (TECUTLI, TLALOQUE, Inside the Earth, He Who Makes Things Grow)

The AZTEC and TOLTEC god of rain, thunder, and the mountains who, along with the water goddess CHALCHI-HUITLICUE, controlled all water. According to some stories, Chalchihuitlicue is Tlaloc's wife. Other stories say she is his sister. The following is a description of Tlaloc from the Florentine Codex, the account of Aztec life written from interviews in the mid 1500s by the Spanish priest Bernardino Sahagún (1499?–1590).

Tlaloc received daily offerings in hopes that he would provide rain. (collection of Philip Goldman, London/ Werner Forman/Art Resource, NY)

Tlaloc the priest. To him was attributed the rain; for he made it, he caused it to come down, he scattered the rain like seed, and also the hail. He caused to sprout, to blossom, to leaf out, to bloom, to ripen, the trees, the plants, our food. And also by him were made floods of water and thunder-bolts.

And he was thus decorated: his face was thickly painted black, his face was painted with liquid rubber; it was anointed with black; his face was [spotted] with [a paste of] amaranth seeds. He had a sleeveless cloud-jacket of netted fabric; he had a crown of heron feathers; he had a necklace of green stone jewels. He had foam sandals, and also rattles. He had a plaited-reed banner.

Tlaloc was an important god, with a temple often next to HUITZILOPOCHTLI as with the TEMPLO MAYOR in what is now Mexico City. One of the oldest gods, and associated with mountaintops, Tlaloc's main temple was on Mount Tlaloc. It symbolized his actual home in TLALOCAN, the layer of heaven he ruled. Humans were sacrificed on Mount Tlaloc to feed the water rocks in the temple. Lesser rain gods, known as Tlaloques (some say old men, some say Tlalocs' sons), kept rain in four jars—one with good rain, one with frost, one with drought, and one with contaminated water. The Tlaloques broke the jars to send water to Earth. The Aztec made sacrifices and prayers to Tlaloc to invoke the Tlaloques to break the jar with good rain. Sacrifices in the form of offerings were made to Tlaloc year round. These offerings were often in the form of giving Tlaloc part of a meal to ask for good rain during the rainy season or to prevent floods or inopportune frosts or disease from harming the crops. Tlaloc was considered to be a son of the first couple, OMETECUHTLI AND OMECIHUATL. In some stories he is a husband of XOCHIQUETZAL, the goddess of flowers.

TLALOCAN The level of heaven ruled by the AZTEC rain god TLALOC, and the home of CHALCHI-HUITLICUE. It was a peaceful, flower-filled land of plenty with much singing, dancing, and game playing. Tlalocan was inhabited by the souls of people with physical disabilities, dwarfs, and those who had died in a water- or weather-related incident (such as drowning or being hit by lightning). Souls that reached Tlalocan stayed for four years before returning to Earth. Most of these souls spent eternity moving back and forth between this level and Earth.

TLALTECUHTLI A giant crocodilelike monster that the AZTEC believed *was* the Earth. According to one Aztec myth, after the fourth age, or Sun, when everything was covered by water, Tlaltecuhtli swam in the cosmic waters, reportedly looking for human flesh to eat. The brother gods and often adversaries—the feathered-serpent god QUETZAL-COATL and the smoking mirror god TEZCATLIPOCA—saw Tlaltecuhtli and grabbed her by her legs. They wrestled long and hard until the monster was so tired she gave up. Quetzalcoatl and Tezcatlipoca cut Tlaltecuhtli in two. The lower half became the heavens and stars, and the upper half became the Earth. The other gods were so unhappy about what Quetzalcoatl and Tezcatlipoca had done that they came down and turned Tlaltecuhtli's hair into grass and trees, her eye cavities into caves, wells, and springs, her nose into mountains, her skin into flowers, and her mouth into rivers and caves. This, however, did not appease Tlaltecuhtli, who still occasionally screamed out in pain at night, demanding the blood and hearts of humans.

Tlaltecuhtli was also associated with midwives and women giving birth. Prayers were made to her asking for strength for the mother during an especially difficult birth. She was often depicted with a grinning deathlike face, with a skull at the back and claws at her elbows and knees.

TLAZOLTEOTL (TLACOLTEUTL, Filth Eater, Lady of Witches) The AZTEC/NAHUA goddess of vice; also a goddess of the Moon, Earth, and curing, and the forgiver of sins. Some also consider Tlazolteotl as the mother of the corn god CINTEOTL and the goddess of flowers XOCHIQUETZAL. The Aztec believed that Tlazolteotl held and controlled all the magic in the universe. Tlazolteotl had four aspects, or sides, all witches who rode on broomsticks through the night and visited places where roads or paths crossed. They also visited humans when they were making important decisions, usually involving a choice that could have a good or unfortunate or evil outcome. When an Aztec was about to die, he or she made sacrifices and confessed to a PRIEST all the wrongs committed during his or her lifetime. These wrongs might include not acting in accordance with the gods, making inappropriate sacrifices, or acting cowardly during war. If the priest believed the confession to be honest, he would offer absolution. The sins would be eaten by Tlazolteotl and the person's soul would become pure again.

TLILIPAN (TLILLAN-TLAPALLAN) An AZTEC heaven known as "The Bright Land." The Aztec believed heaven was made up of 13 layers. Tlilipan was above TLALOCAN, which was ruled by the rain god TLALOC, but not as high as TONATIUHICÁN, the house of the SUN. Tlilipan was the heaven of those who had learned well the wisdom imparted by the model of the feathered-serpent god QUETZALCOATL: One's life should be honorable, and honor comes through hard work, personal cleanliness, and behavior that is polite, gracious, and dignified. The Aztec believed that when one truly knew the wisdom of Quetzalcoatl, one shed one's need to return to Earth and live as a human.

TLOQUENAHUAQUE (TLOQUE NAHUAQUE, Lord of All Existence) A high god and creator to the AZTEC and TOLTEC. Some scholars believe Tloquenahuaque is another name for OMETEOTL, the supreme Aztec god. Not much is known about him, although some stories say he ruled during the first age, or Sun, of Aztec mythology.

TOCI Another name for TLAZOLTEOTL, the AZTEC goddess of vice, to whom the Aztec confessed their sins as they were dying.

TOHIL (Obsidian) The one-legged fire god and god of sacrifice of the Quiché MAYA. Tohil was one of the first Mayan gods. According to the *POPUL VUH*, the sacred book of the Quiché, when the people received FIRE, they accepted the concept of human sacrifice. In the beginning, there was no fire and the people were cold. Only Tohil was capable of making fire, which he made by drilling with his one leg. Only those people who followed him had fire. When other peoples asked Tohil for fire, he gave it to them declaring that he was their one and only god. In exchange for getting the fire, the people always agreed to this. But then a fierce hailstorm came and put out all the fires. Again the people asked for fire and Tohil gave it to them. However, this time in exchange he asked them to give themselves to him. Again they readily agreed, unaware that Tohil had asked a trick question. The fact was that Tohil meant that the people promise to literally sacrifice themselves to him when the time came. Thus, some believe, originated the Mayan practice of human sacrifice.

TOLLAN (Place of Reeds) The capital city of the Toltec, thought to be near the present-day Mexican city of Tula. It is believed that after the early city center at TEOTIHUACÁN collapsed, the TOLTEC migrated into central Mexico, built the city of Tollan, and from there controlled central Mexico. Included in the remains of the presumed site are three pyramid temples, the largest of which honored QUETZALCOATL. Tollan is thought to have been a wealthy and cultured city. Since much of the history of Meso-America has been pieced together from fragments of many historical accounts, the exact nature of Tollan and the Toltec is not clear. In some accounts Tollan is described as a paradise where the Toltec lived an easy and abundant life.

TOLTEC (Reed People, Cultured People) An important, possibly legendary, civilization that came after the OLMEC and exerted great influence throughout the Valley of Mexico. Some scholars believe that after TEOTIHUACÁN collapsed, the Toltec moved into the central valley of Mexico. They became a highly militaristic people, building a great city at TOLLAN and honoring primarily the feathered-serpent god QUETZALCOATL. According to legend, the Toltec were led by Quetzalcoatl and controlled the valley until about A.D. 1000. Quetzalcoatl and his followers were driven out—legend says by the war god TEZCATLIPOCA and his followers—and took over the Mayan city CHICHÉN ITZÁ. It is believed that they gradually merged with the MAYA. The Toltec who remained at Tollan followed Tezcatlipoca and continued to have an important influence in the central valley until about A.D. 1200, when the Toltec empire began to decline. Eventually the AZTEC became dominant.

The Toltec had a highly developed culture, a contrast to the "rougher," more warlike Chichimec who moved into the valley from the north. Once in contact with the Toltec, many groups, including the Aztec, appeared to have learned from them, developing their own cultures more quickly. Some scholars believe that the Aztec view of themselves as warrior-priests was modeled directly from the Toltec. The name *Toltec* may have evolved from the Nahuatl (the language of the NAHUA) word *totecatlt,* meaning "master artist."

Many of the Toltec gods and stories have merged with those of the Aztec. The principal Toltec gods were Quetzalcoatl and Tezcatlipoca, the CORN god CINTEOTL, the earthquake god HUEMAC, the flower goddess XOCHIQUETZAL, and the supreme gods OMETEOTL and TLOQUENAHUAQUE and their dual male and female aspects. In addition, the Toltec revered Chimalmatl, the Earth-born mother of Quetzalcoatl in one of his guises. In one purely Toltec story Yappan, a human, so wanted to please the gods that he lived as a hermit on top of a great rock. Suspicious of his intent, the gods sent one beautiful woman after another to tempt him. Yappan always refused their attention until the flower goddess Xochiquetzal came. Yappan fell in love with her and was seduced. Disappointed in him, the gods turned Yappan into a scorpion, forced to spend his life living under rocks.

TONACATECUTLI (Lord of Our Existence)
AZTEC god, both male and female; also considered, in individual forms as the creator couple, Tonacateucti and Tonacacihuatl, who some say are the male and female forms of the supreme god TLOQUENAHUAQUE or OMETEOTL. Tonacatecutli is a creator god and giver of food and is believed to have separated the primordial waters from the heavens.

TONALMATL
The 260-day sacred almanac or CALENDAR of the AZTEC; also called the Count of the Days. It was formed by combining 20 named days, each ruled by a god, with the numbers 1 through 13, also influenced by the deities. For example: 1 alligator, 2 flower, 3 rain, and so on. (See CALENDAR for a chart of all 20 named days and the gods that ruled them.) Priests used the *tonalmatl* to determine fate and to make prophecies, such as determining the best day to begin a battle or what the fate might be for a child born on a certain day. This divination process was complicated and was determined by more than the day sign and number. Other important parts of the process included consideration of each hour of the day and night, as well as weeks and solar years. These considerations were ruled by gods who would exert an influence over the future. For example, using the day 10 Ocelot, the god TEZCATLIPOCA, who represents eternal youth, ruled the number 10; Ocelot is protected by TLAZOLTEOTL, an earth goddess considered to be the confessor of sins. The day 10 Ocelot would be good for going to war, for it was powerful and warriors would be fearless in battle.

TONANTZIN (HUEYTONANTZIN, Our Honorable Mother)
An AZTEC earth goddess associated with CIHUACOATL, COATLICUE, and TETEO INNAN. She later became associated with the patroness of Mexico, the VIRGIN OF GUADALUPE, who first appeared in 1531 on ground considered sacred to Tonantzin. In Aztec times, she was particularly celebrated at the winter solstice in December. A masked

These images from the Aztec Codex Borbonicus are part of the *tonalmatl. (Bibliotheque de l'Assemblee Nationale, Paris/Archives Charmet/Bridgeman Art Library)*

woman, garbed in a long white cloak decorated with feathers and shells, sang and wept as she paraded through the village with a priest always at her side. According to some accounts, at the end of the solstice celebration, the PRIEST removed the woman's mask and sacrificed her to Tonantzin. To help bring life back to the Earth as the winter turned to spring, men threw small bags filled with green pepper at the women on the day following the celebration.

Tonantzin was also considered the mother of the lords of the four directions who sacrificed her to the Sun daily. Her sons were Hueytecpatl, Nanactltzatzi, Ixcyub, and Tentmic.

TONATIUH (Age)

The AZTEC and MIXTEC sun god. Tonatiuh was seen as all-powerful and the primary source of life—the supreme ruler of the current age, or Sun. Each day, Tonatiuh traveled across the sky, dying as he sank into the west, and then renewing himself the next day. This daily journey was so difficult that the people believed he needed human blood and flesh to survive. Aside from the human sacrifices made, the Aztec believed that Tonatiuh was nourished by their daily sacrifices. Living a moral and virtuous life, living honorably through hard work, showing courage during war, and acting always in a dignified and gracious manner were some of these daily sacrifices.

In some versions of the beginning of this age, known as the Fifth Sun in Aztec mythology (see AZTEC SUNS), NANAUTZIN sacrificed himself into the fire to become the Sun, but Tonatiuh did not appear. So, the feathered-serpent god Quetzalcoatl took the hearts of the hundreds of gods who sacrificed themselves to provide nourishment for the Sun. As a result, Tonatiuh did rise, but he stayed stationary in the sky until EHECATL, the wind god, blew on him to get him moving. On his daily journey, Tonatiuh was thought to rise as an eagle and was helped along by warriors. As he descended in the afternoon, the spirits of women who had died in childbirth provided their help.

TONATIUHICÁN (House of the Sun)

The highest heaven that the AZTEC believed human souls could reach. It was ruled by TONATIUH and considered a place of the gods. Only the souls of humans who had reached a high level of spiritual enlightenment reached Tonatiuhicán, a land of eternal bliss.

TOTEM See NAHUAL.

TREE

Trees were important in the daily lives of people. They provided wood for fuel and for building homes, boats, and household objects. Because of their importance, trees became part of a mythology. To the INCA, a tree might be a sacred place, a HUACA, or the place from which a group of people emerged at the time of creation. In Meso-America, trees might also have a sacred spirit and serve as a NAHUAL, or personal guardian or spirit. The MAYA believed that a great CEIBA TREE stood at the center of the world and served as a road that the gods and souls traveled along between the underworld and the heavens. The Chacomoco of the CHACO region in South America believed that at one time humans could climb a great tree to get to heaven to hunt—that is, until an angry woman chopped the tree down.

In one story of the Guaraní of Paraguay and northern Argentina, the beautiful daughter of a chief fell in love with the young chief of another tribe and left home to be with him. Her father followed her, stopping often to put his ear to the ground to hear her footsteps and know where she was. Eventually he was so exhausted that he fell asleep while listening. He slept for so long that his ear became rooted and grew into the beautiful Timbo tree (species *Clathrotropis*), from which the Guaraní got wood for their boats. The fruit of the Timbo is black and ear shaped, and the tree is often called "Black Ear."

TUPARI

A people of the Rio Branco in Brazil who live traditionally. The Tupari are a small group whose mythology is similar to many other groups in South America in that it reflects their belief in magic and the supernatural. One story explains that the world was once just rock. There were no people and no gods, but eventually a beautiful female rock split open and two men emerged. First came VALEDJÁD and then Vab, both magicians. They cut trees and carved wives from the wood. Then another group of magicians called *vamoa-pod* emerged from the Earth and waters, and they began to populate the Earth. Valedjád was wicked, however, and when he became angry he brought rain. Once he brought so much rain that a flood killed many *vamoa-pod* and nearly destroyed the Earth. The survivors decided to end Valedjád's wickedness by covering him with wax.

The Tupari had another evil magician, Aunyain-a, who had a hand in creating reptiles. Aunyain-a roamed the villages eating children. Parents had a hard time keeping him away from their children, so they sent them into the trees to hide. Aunyain-a knew the children had not completely disappeared, but when he could not find them he asked a parrot where they were. The parrot sent Aunyain-a to a river, but along the way he discovered the children and climbed a tree to get at them. The parrot chewed the trunk of the tree causing Aunyain-a to fall and break into pieces as he hit the ground. (The children were protected because they were in the branches and leaves.) CAIMANS and iguanas grew from the pieces of Aunyain-a's fingers, and lizards from his toes. Vultures gobbled up the rest of him, and Aunyain-a was never seen again.

TZITZIMIME Nonhuman followers of the AZTEC demon-goddess TZITZIMITL, or of her clones. The *tzitzimime* were often called star demons because they had hundreds of eyes staring down at Earth each night. They watched for a time when they could swoop down and wipe out everything on Earth. They were especially dangerous during solar eclipses, when they were attacking the Sun. Some scholars believe the *tzitzimime* were also thought to be the spirits of women who had died while giving birth who returned to Earth to frighten those still alive.

TZITZIMITL (Air Demon) The AZTEC goddess of inertia. Tzitzimitl was an old woman demon-goddess who guarded MAYAHUEL, the goddess of intoxicants and of childbirth. She was thought to have come from the stars and is the only Aztec deity that did not have a good side. She either had nonhuman followers called TZITZIMIME or was capable of cloning herself.

U

UEUECOYOTL (The Old, Old Coyote) The AZTEC god of unnecessary enjoyment who was said to cause chaos and to distract people from their ongoing wars waged to increase the empire and secure victims for SACRIFICE. Ueuecoyotl is called a trickster by some scholars, although others believe that the only true trickster in Mexico was KAUYUMARI of the HUICHOL people. True tricksters, they believe, regulate the universe through the pranks they play.

The Aztec are generally considered a serious-minded people. During the height of the empire, their focus was on preparing for war, waging war, and pleasing the gods. They worked hard and were thought to be extremely polite and possibly a bit grave—they were not given often to gaiety and humor. An appearance by Ueuecoyotl in their lives was not welcome. Some scholars have suggested that the Aztec actually feared him because of his disruptive influences.

UIXTOCIHUATL The AZTEC goddess of salt. Uixtocihuatl is the sister of the rain god TLALOC and by association a sister to all the rain gods. During her festival (Tecuilhuitontli, on June 2) Aztec women and girls wore flowers in their hair and danced in her honor, and according to some accounts, a woman was sacrificed at the temple of Tlaloc. Salt was an important commodity for trade and was collected from the shores around LAKE TEXCOCO.

UNDERWORLD The center of the Earth, which many believe is where unhappy or evil souls go after death. The underworld is often thought to be dank, foul smelling, and generally unpleasant.

In South America, the INCA believed that the underworld was where sinners went after death. The Inca did not believe in rebirth per se but did think that life continued in some way. In Meso-America, however, the underworld was especially integral to the mythologies. The OLMEC believed a great dragon floated on a cosmic sea, with the Earth making up its back and the dead residing in its innards. The early MAYA saw the world as a SERPENT with the dead living inside. The way in was through the mouth, and the underworld was made up of caves, passages, and the rooms or homes of the underworld lords. It was here that the HERO TWINS met and tricked the lords so they could escape. The Hero Twins were called

This Mayan temple at Tikal has nine steps that represent the levels of the underworld. *(Ken Walsh/Bridgeman Art Library)*

into the underworld because they were playing ball, and the BALL GAME court is sometimes seen as a way into the underworld.

The AZTEC underworld was multilayered, with nine levels. Most Aztec went into the underworld, where they were tested at each of eight levels before arriving at Mictlan, the lowest level and the land of the death god MICTLANTECUHTLI. Those who committed suicide or died in war, while giving birth, or from a water-related cause, went directly to a paradise. Although Mictlan was the lowest level, it was not considered a hell. Rather, it was a place where not much occurred—where, some say, the dead experienced extreme boredom. Generally, it was where people who had had no interest in gaining wisdom or spiritual enlightenment went. The tests for getting there included crossing a wide river of rough water, which could be done only with the help of a yellow DOG, and traveling a valley between two mountains that alternately moved inward, clapping against each other, and outward. From there, the soul climbed a cliff of polished OBSIDIAN before it crossed along an open area where a strong biting wind blew knives through the air. In the next tests, the dead had to first find their way through a land of billowing fabric and then find their way through one where arrows came from all directions. Moving through a land of monsters that ate only human hearts was the next test. To pass the final test to get into Mictlan, the dead had to climb a steep, narrow, rocky trail. The trip took four years, and at the end, the soul disintegrated. During this four-year period, to help the soul on its travels, relatives of the dead made regular offerings where the person had been buried.

The Spanish are responsible for the idea that the underworld was the land of the devil. Some indigenous people have adopted this belief, although many have adjusted it to include a four-part underworld—a hell for sinners, a place for those who were never baptized, a place where people go to confess and earn forgiveness for their sins while alive, and a place where people wait until Christ frees their spirits. Some NAHUA continue to believe a soul must travel through many lands before it rests in the underworld and that there are deities that help the soul as it makes the journey.

Many groups believe that caves are entrances into the underworld, viewing the underworld as a wet place that is the source of much disease. They also believe it is a place where most of their dead ancestors are located. Others believe the underworld directly reflects life on Earth as if viewed as a reflection on a calm lake—an upside-down mirror image. However, some things may occur in the underworld that are forbidden on Earth, for example, eating certain foods or eating any food that has started to decay.

See also AFTERLIFE; DEATH.

URCAGUAY A serpent-god of the INCA; the god of the underground. Urcaguay was said to live in the cave from which MANCO CAPAC, the first ruler of the Inca, and his brothers emerged. His head is said to be like that of a red deer's and his tail made up of woven gold chains. Urcaguay is said to keep watch over underground treasure.

URUBUTSIN The king of birds who, according to a myth of the Mamaiuran people of the Brazilian Amazon, was forced by IAE and KUAT to share daylight with humans. According to Mamaiuran legend, the wings of all the birds covered the Sun so no light reached the Earth. The people had difficulty living in the darkness: They could not see food to gather or the wild animals that preyed upon them. Taking pity on the people, Iae and Kuat set out decaying meat to attract Urubutsin and waited for him. When he showed up, Iae and Kuat grabbed his legs and held him until he promised to let sunlight through for part of the day, thus giving the people day and night.

V

VALEDJÁD An evil sorcerer in the mythology of several Tupí-Guaraní groups in Brazil. He was the first man, and after he emerged from a rock that had split open, the gods sealed his eyes, nose, and fingers with wax to prevent him from doing evil. He was carried away by a vulture and lives in a rock house and is believed to cause rain whenever he is angry.

VENUS The second planet from the SUN. While the stars stayed relatively fixed and moved as units across the sky, the planets were independent. They seemed to wander, but in cycles. Venus was a heavenly object that was particularly watched. After the Sun and the Moon, it is the brightest object in the sky. To the INCA, the stars and planets were children of the Sun and Moon. Venus was the page CHASCA that served the Sun as it traveled across the sky. In daytime, it helped the Sun on its journey, and when it rose as an evening star, it helped defeat nighttime's darkness. The YAMANA of Tierra del Fuego believed Venus was an old Sun.

In Meso-America, Venus was thought to be dangerous. It was the Mayan patron planet of war and hunters to whom warriors made offerings. The MAYA believed harm could come from Venus's light, so they plugged their chimneys and covered windows and doors to prevent it from entering their home. At the Mayan city of Uxmal, buildings were aligned so the Maya could sight and track the planet through the doors and windows. By tracking the planet, the Maya were able to determine that it took 584 days for the planet to complete a cycle. Twentieth-century astronomers calculated the time to be 583.92 days. One Mayan CALENDAR, used by priests for planning and foretelling future events, was based on the cycle of Venus and its dual nature as both a morning and an evening star.

A Quiché Mayan story from their sacred book, the *POPUL VUH*, tells of the HERO TWINS in the UNDERWORLD and directly reflects the movement of Venus. The Maya believed that in addition to its 584-day cycle, Venus also had a cycle of five periods that took eight solar years to complete. In the *Popul Vuh*, this is represented by the five tests the Hero Twins undergo in the underworld, the last of which is the BALL GAME they play against the underworld lords. It is only when this fifth test has been completed that the universe is prepared for the Sun to rise for the first time. According to different versions of the story, the twins rise from the underworld as the Sun and Moon; one rises in the morning to prepare the second to rise as the Sun; or the twins are the morning and evening stars that are, in fact, Venus.

For the AZTEC, Venus as the morning star was their feathered-serpent deity QUETZALCOATL. XOLOTL, who is sometimes considered to be Quetzalcoatl's twin, was perceived as the evening star.

VIRACOCHA (HURACOCHA, WIRAKOCHA, Foam of the Sea) The supreme god and creator of the people of the Peruvian ANDES; also adopted by the INCA. Viracocha created the Sun, giving it part of his own godliness and power, and placed the Moon to guard the waters. He then made the winds, the planet VENUS, the stars, and all of humankind. Although some believe the Sun created him, more commonly Viracocha is thought to have come from the sea and to have lived in LAKE TITICACA. Although he was perhaps greater than the sun god INTI, Viracocha was seen as remote and bigger than life. Thus he had less influence on everyday life and no temples were built to him.

Stories about Viracocha are varied. In one cycle of stories, he is said to have created five worlds. Vira-

The Caracol, an astronomical observatory in Chichén Itzá, was built by the Maya in the 1100s. It may have been built specifically to observe Venus. *(D. Donne Bryant/DDB Stock)*

cocha ruled the first, a world of the gods, by himself. The second world was inhabited by giants who worshiped Viracocha as a great god. In the third world, humans lived in darkness on Earth with little culture. The fourth world was the world of the early civilizations in the Andes. And the last world—the world of the Inca—ended when the Spanish came and Viracocha escaped over the water.

A more frequently told story of the Inca creation has Viracocha making two worlds. The first was created when Viracocha came out of Lake Titicaca and formed the heavens, the Earth, and humans to live on the Earth. All went well until he was so angered by the way the people lived and treated one another that he came out of the lake again and changed them all to stone. Then he began again. This time he gave the world a Sun and Moon and made from wood a model for each kind of people. He then set his sons to carry and distribute the models throughout the land, bringing many different people to the Earth. Viracocha, too, walked the land calling people forth and teaching them. Eventually he met his sons on the eastern seacoast, and they walked across the water and disap-

peared. Just as the AZTEC believed that Hernando Cortés (1485–1547) was their feathered-serpent deity QUETZALCOATL returning to them, some in South America thought that the Europeans were Viracocha or his messengers who had returned. Many scholars believe that the culture-hero gods CONIRAYA and THUNUPA are aspects of Viracocha, returning under cover to watch over and teach the people he created.

The Spanish gave the name Viracocha (Foam of the Sea) to this great spirit, because the Inca had no word for him. Today, the word *viracocha* is still used by the QUECHUA in Peru to show respect.

VIRGIN OF GUADALUPE Patron of the Mexican people; also known as Our Lady of Guadalupe. The Virgin of Guadalupe first appeared on December 9, 1531, to Juan Diego, an AZTEC who had already converted to Catholicism. She appeared at a place considered sacred to the earth mother TETEO INNAN, usually called in this context TONANTZIN. The first time, she appeared in the form of a white light surrounded by music. The second time, she appeared as a woman who identified herself

This illustration of the Virgin and Juan Diego is located in Mexico City. *(D. Donne Bryant/DDB Stock)*

as the mother of Jesus Christ and said she wanted a shrine built to her at that site. Juan Diego took the request to the bishop who wanted proof of her presence. Afraid of the bishop and not sure what to do, Juan Diego did nothing. Three days later, he crossed the same site on his way to summon a priest for his dying uncle, and again the Virgin appeared. This time, she was seen in the midst of fresh rose petals that covered the ground. Juan Diego took the rose petals to the bishop, who accepted them as proof of the Virgin's appearance, since the hillside where she was seen was rocky and barren and roses would not have been blooming in December. The bishop ordered a small shrine built at that site. In a historical irony, this same bishop had once ordered that a shrine honoring the Aztec earth goddess be destroyed.

The Virgin of Guadalupe is honored yearly on December 12 at churches and shrines throughout Meso-America. In Mexico, she is celebrated with parades, fireworks, and spirit dances. Some consider her the link between the traditional indigenous culture and the culture of the Spanish invaders. The shrine in Tepeyac Hill, where Juan Diego saw the Virgin, is the destination of millions of people every year, making pilgrimages to honor her and show their gratitude. As the Aztec goddess had once been, the Virgin of Guadalupe is considered a healer and bringer of life. Her image served as a unifying force when they fought Spain for their independence in 1810.

VITZILOPUCHTL (Sorcerer) An AZTEC war god with the ability to change shape. In Spanish accounts he is described as a sorcerer-warrior of great strength who was named a god after he died. He was often associated with a dragon. The Aztec may have sacrificed slaves in his honor.

VOTAN (VOTON, The Heart) An old Mayan hero-god sent by the supreme god to divide the Earth into different races and give each their own language. Some scholars refer to him as an earth god. In some accounts, Votan simply appears on Earth, dispensing knowledge, teaching the people how to write, creating sculptures, and planting CORN. When his work is finished, he disappears underground. Other accounts have him emerging out of a genie and traveling underground until he came to the roots of the great CEIBA TREE, where he made his way into the sky.

Instructor gods appear in the mythologies of many people. Besides Votan, the MAYA also considered their great god KUKULCAN to be a teacher. Other teacher gods include the AZTEC feathered-serpent god QUETZALCOATL, the INCA creator god VIRACOCHA, WATAVINEWA of the Yamana people of Tierra del Fuego, and Zume of the Tupí-Guaraní people of Brazil, who taught them how to hunt, fish, and live in a civilized manner.

VUKUB-CAKIX (VUCUN CAQUIX, VACUB-CAQUIZ, Seven Macaw) An evil giant in the stories of the Quiché MAYA. The Quiché sacred book the *POPUL VUH* tells how the god HURAKAN was angry at what Vukub-Cakix and his two sons had done on

Earth. (For example, Vukub-Cakix claimed he was the Sun and the Moon.) So Hurakan sent the HERO TWINS to confront them. The twins tracked down Vukub-Cakix at the top of a great tree where he was eating lunch. They shot him with an arrow, causing him to fall out of the tree. Vukub-Cakix did not die, but his jaw and teeth hurt so much that he could not eat. One day, an old couple came along, and the twins told Vukub-Cakix that the couple were healers, especially good at fixing teeth. Vukub-Cakix asked the old couple to fix his teeth. They did, by removing his teeth entirely, which distorted his face. Unable to eat and ashamed by his appearance, Vukub-Cakix disappeared into the sky. He is still there today as the stars of the constellation we know as the Great Bear. A shadow of Vukub-Cakix did remain on Earth, however, in the form of the scarlet macaw (*Ara macao*), a mostly bright red–feathered member of the parrot family, now on the endangered species list. The scarlet macaw, symbolizing daylight and the rising Sun, was considered powerful by the Maya. Many people took the word *macaw* as a family name to assume power from the bird.

VULTURE   The king vulture (*Sarcoramphus papa)* is the predominant vulture in South and Meso-American mythology. It is a large bird with a wingspread of nearly five and a half feet. Its head and neck are red, yellow, and bluish white; its body is light tan and white with a gray ruff around its neck. The king vulture is a scavenger that eats garbage and dead animals but will occasionally catch a small live animal. Vultures, who nest on mountainside cliffs and sometimes in trees, spend hours soaring on air currents.

In mythology, a vulture is often a sign of impending death. A vulture, for example, tells the AZTEC feathered-serpent god QUETZALCOATL that his father will die, giving Quetzalcoatl a chance to recover his father's bones. In a TUPARI story, when the magician VALEDJÁD falls out of a tree and dies, a vulture eats his body after his fingers and toes become reptiles. The big bird plays other roles as well. Some groups in Brazil believe that the vulture first held fire. In some stories, a hero pretends to be dead, which draws the vultures that bring FIRE, and then steals an ember. In other stories, the hero puts decaying flesh out in the open to attract the vultures and then hides until they appear. In a story from the CHACO region of South America, the vulture outsmarts the FOX, who freezes from sitting in a tree all night.

W

WAMANIS Powerful mountain spirits of the ANDES. The *wamanis* control the weather and the fertility of animals and plants. They also cause landslides and earthquakes. They are considered more accessible than the supreme god Inkarri—or the Catholic God—and are connected to the everyday activities of the QUECHUA people. *Wamanis* can take any form but are rarely seen.

WATAVINEWA (The Most Ancient One) A benevolent but not always forgiving god of the Yamana people of Tierra del Fuego. Watavinewa supported life but was not a creator god. Considered a teacher of how to live—how to plant, hunt, build houses, make clothes, and live communally—he was a supreme being who lived in the heavens and punished people who were not ethical and honest.

WATER In all its forms—rivers, streams, deep wells in the Earth, rain—water has shaped societies and cultures. In the Yucatán, people settled near springs and natural wells because the local ground, rich in limestone, would not hold water. The TAIRONA and KOGI, in what is now Colombia, had highly sophisticated water conservation practices. These included not only irrigation but supplying fresh water and channeling off waste and excess rainwater so it did not erode the land. The AZTEC filled and drained swampy land to create gardens and islands for their capital, TENOCHTITLÁN. The people of the ANDES, including the INCA and NAZCA, built terraced gardens and irrigated extensively. Besides its role as a necessary part of life, water was also used ritually to purify those who had behaved in an immoral or "unclean" manner. Purification could take place through a ritual bathing or a sprinkling of water, much as the late MAYA and the Mexican Aztec did when they sprinkled water and washed newborn babies to help ward off evil. A sprinkling of water was also part of the Aztec marriage ceremony.

In South and Meso-America, water was often considered sacred. The ONA, for example, believed that their ancestors had become lakes and rivers, and the Maya made regular sacrifices by throwing sacrificial objects into deep naturally occurring wells called *cenotes*. TLALOC, the Meso-American rain god, was once considered the supreme god. He remained supreme as shown by his sharing the Great Temple (TEMPLO MAYOR) of the Aztec with the war god HUITZILOPOCHTLI. Water, it was believed, connected heaven and Earth. Other rain deities include the Mayan god CHAC, the ZAPOTEC god COCIJO, the goddess DABAIBA of the Panama Indians, and the Inca god ILLAPA.

In the mid 1500s, the Spanish priest Bernardino Sahagún (1499?–1590) used interviews with the Aztec to write an account of Aztec life called the Florentine Codex (see also CODICES). The following is an excerpt from a prayer to the Aztec rain god Tlaloc from the Florentine Codex.

> Oh master, O our lord, . . . O lord of Tlalocan . . . verily, now, the gods, the Tlamacazque, the lords of rubber, the lords of incense, the lords of copal—have taken refuge. . . . And the common folk, the vassals, here already perish; the eyelids are swollen; they become dry-mouthed; . . . And there are none at all who are passed over; already all the little creatures suffer. The troupial, the roseate spoonbill just drag [their wings]; they are up-ended, tumbled headfirst; they open and close their bills [from thirst]. And the animals, the four-footed ones of the lord of the near, of the nigh, just go here and there; they can scarcely rise; to no purpose is the ground licked; and they go crazed for water. . . . I call out, I cry out to ye who

occupy the four quarters, . . . Come back; come console the common folk. Water the Earth, for the Earth, the living creatures, the herbs, the stalks remain watching, remain crying out, for all remain trusting. Be diligent, O gods, O our lords.

Among the earliest gods in any developing mythology are rain or water gods. Water, of course, can be totally destructive, and the mythologies of many cultures include a great flood that destroys the world. The Aztec Fourth Sun, or age, for example, ended when CHALCHIHUITLICUE, the goddess of running water, sent a flood that destroyed the world; likewise, VIRACOCHA, supreme god of the Peruvian Andes, used water to destroy one world he had created because he was angry at the people. On the other hand, some stories tell how water helped create the world. The ARAUCANIAN believe the islands off the coast of South America got their geographic features from the sea serpents TEN-TEN AND CAI-CAI battling it out—one raised floodwaters while the other raised mountains to save the inhabitants of Earth. And in many mythologies, creation began when there was nothing but a primordial sea, such as when QUETZALCOATL and TEZCATLIPOCA jump into the sea to destroy the monster TLALTECUHTLI and create the heavens and Earth.

Water and the deities of water also figure importantly in many stories other than creation myths. In one ARAWAK story, a great chief sacrifices himself by going over a waterfall to save his people (see MAKON-AIMA). In another, a helpful tree frog that changed himself into a human to help the people is changed back to a tree frog when his wife sprinkles water on him. Water stories of the Araucanian show the helpful and harmful sides of water: One tells of the phantom ship EL CALEUCHE, which guards the well-being of the sea, on which the people depend for their livelihood; another tells of the great sea monster CAMAHUETO, who destroys boats.

WRITING Writing systems developed in Meso-America some time before 600 B.C. People wrote by carving symbols into stone, painting them on pottery, or brushing them onto paper. Writing, like everything else in Meso-American life, was thought to have come from the gods. The Meso-Americans used writ-

These Mayan glyphs were carved into a temple doorway. *(Werner Forman/Art Resource, NY)*

ing to record their histories, which included the stories of the deities, in CODICES. The writing on monuments known as STELAE is thought by many to be historical accounts of the rulers rather than stories about the gods. They may actually have been a form of propaganda, for the monuments were in full display where they could easily be seen.

The writing system of the MAYA was made up of over 800 glyphs, or signs, that represented words or syllables. Many were representational. The glyph for JAGUAR, for example, was the head of the cat. Words or ideas that did not have an easily pictured symbol were usually represented by a picture for a word that, when spoken, sounded the same as or similar to the intended word (a homonym). So readers could tell the difference, another symbol, a complement, was added to the picture for the homonym. That way, when the picture appeared by itself, readers knew it stood for its actual meaning, and when the picture appeared with the symbol, it stood for the homonym of the word. The glyphs were arranged into a block, now called a cartouche, that represented a complete thought. This system for writing a word is similar to the way we use sentences. The Mayan pictogram writing system is not easy to understand and read. Few Maya, primarily priests and high nobility, were literate.

Somewhat easier to comprehend was the AZTEC system, also made up of pictograms. Each symbol looked like the object the word stood for. The pictogram for the Aztec city of TENOCHTITLÁN, for example, was a rock from which a cactus sprouted. This was the sign the great god HUITZILOPOCHTLI told the people to look for as they migrated to the Valley of Mexico from their original home at AZTLAN. Just as the Maya did, the Aztec used a picture to represent the sound of a word if no easy symbol was available. Color was also used to help distinguish a symbol; for example, turquoise was considered a color of the nobility and used in pictograms of a ruler or other high-ranking noble. An Aztec pictogram could be quite detailed and contain many elements of an object. For instance, the fire god XIUHTECUHTLI, also lord of turquoise, was shown covered with turquoise and with a fire serpent on his back.

When the Spanish arrived, the INCA and other South American groups had no formal system of writing. They did, however, keep numerical accounts and some historical accounts on a system of colored and knotted cords called quipus. These are still used today in the ANDES to keep numerical accounts. The Inca also had a series of painted boards, kept in the great temple to the Sun CORICANCHA, which showed the history of the people. The mythology of the Andes, including the Inca, was also passed along orally through poems and songs and woven into textiles.

X

XAMANIQINQU (XAMAN EK) The Mayan god of the north who guided merchants as they traveled; also known as LETTER GOD C. Travelers made offerings and burned incense to him at shrines along roads to guarantee a safe and successful journey.

XBALANQUE Another name for the HERO TWIN HUNAHPU of the Yucatán MAYA.

XIBALBA According to the MAYA, the land of the dead. In some accounts, Xibalba is a place where only evil demons live as they plot to confront the gods of the heavens. It can be reached only by traveling a treacherous rocky road. In other accounts, it is the destination of mortal souls after death and is reached on the back of the sky monster.

XILONEN The young CORN goddess of the AZTEC. As an adult she is known as CHICOMECOATL or CHALCHIUHCIHUATL; her mature form is ILAMATECUHTLI. Xilonen was thought to be a beautiful young woman married to TEZCATLIPOCA. The Aztec made regular offerings to her to ensure a good corn crop. Most households kept a ceremonial basket with five ears of corn in her honor. The Aztec celebrated Xilonen throughout the year but particularly in July, when corn ripens and is ready for harvest.

XIPE TOTEC (Flayed Lord) AZTEC and ZAPOTEC god of planting, flowers, sunsets, spring, and rebirth; patron of jewelers and combat. He was a son of the first parents, OMETECUHTLI AND OMECIHUATL, and a brother to the feathered-serpent god QUETZALCOATL, the god of war HUITZILOPOCHTLI, and the smoking mirror god TEZCATLIPOCA. As the source of all rebirth, he played an important role in Aztec life. At the beginning of creation, Xipe Totec sacrificed himself by tearing out his own eyes and skinning himself alive so CORN could be grown and humans would have food. (This skinning is symbolic of the skin of the seed as it germinates and of the skinning of an ear of corn when it is shucked before eating.) To honor his sacrifice, the gods then gave Xipe Totec a pure spirit, symbolized by a golden cloak. As the Mexican symbol of rebirth, he is seen by the gods as the ultimate example of sacrifice to benefit humankind.

Some accounts of the primary festival in March honoring Xipe Totec have told that sacrificial victims were skinned and their flesh was given to priests to wear. The victims may have been warriors who were captured in battle and kept until the festival. Those who captured the warrior might have worn the victim's skin. Xipe Totec is usually shown either wearing someone else's skin or wearing his own, which was pockmarked.

XIUHCOATL A flaming SERPENT that the AZTEC supreme god HUITZILOPOCHTLI used to behead his sister COYOLXAUHQUI when she threatened to kill their mother, the Earth goddess COATLICUE. The Xiuhcoatl was also used to symbolize an extreme drought and was associated with turquoise, an element of XIUHTECUHTLI, the fire god. Huitzilopochtli's use of the Xiuhcoatl to kill Coyolxauhqui symbolized the triumph of light over darkness.

XIUHTECUHTLI (XIUHTECUTLI, Turquoise Lord, Precious Lord) The AZTEC god of FIRE and Lord of the Year; considered the center of all things and the force behind all life. Xiuhtecuhtli's home was in Mictlan, the UNDERWORLD. Unlike the fire god HUEHUETEOTL, who was considered an old man, Xiuhtecuhtli was thought to be the embodiment of a strong young warrior. He was usually shown with the

Xochiquetzal was the Aztec/Toltec goddess of beauty and love. *(The Art Archive/Album/Joseph Martin)*

fire serpent XIUHCOATL, a good representation of his role as the ruler of the Fifth—and present—Sun, or age. The Lord of the Year concept came from the Aztec belief that Xiuhtecuhtli was the North Star—the star around which the other stars seem to move. Because he did not move, Xiuhtecuhtli was thought to control time and the CALENDAR. In the Aztec calendar, he is protector of day Alt (water), which is considered a good day for waging battle, not a good day to rest. Xiuhtecuhtli was celebrated often but especially at the end of every 52-year period. This was the time when the 365-day solar and 260-day sacred calendars ended on the same day and all life and the Aztec celebrated the Binding of the Years with the NEW FIRE CEREMONY.

XMUCANE AND XPIYACOC The mother and father of the Quiché MAYA, who believed that Xmucane was responsible for the birth of all children and Xpiyacoc arranged all marriages.

According to the Quiché sacred book, the *POPUL VUH*, the creator gods knew what they wanted humans to be like—walking, talking, worshiping creatures who would follow the sacred CALENDAR of the heavens. After failing in their first two attempts to create humans, the gods consulted Xmucane and Xpiyacoc, who were older than the creator gods, asking this old couple if wood would be a good choice. Xmucane and Xpiyacoc consulted the calendar before agreeing that wood might work. The wooden humans, unfortunately, were not quite right—they walked and talked but they did not follow the sacred calendar and they did not worship the gods. So the gods wiped them out with a great flood. Eventually, Xmucane finely ground white and yellow CORN and washed her hands, saving the water to mix with the ground corn. From that mixture she created four sons who were the first of the human forms on Earth.

Xmucane and Xpiyacoc are also considered day keepers, which they needed to be in their roles as midwife and matchmaker. The Maya consulted the sacred calendar to determine the fate of their children based on the date of birth and to arrange auspicious days to hold marriages.

XOCHIPILLI (Flower Prince) The AZTEC god of flowers, love, beauty, song, feasts, and dances; also associated with excess—overdoing a good thing. He is also associated with the CORN god CINTEOTL and was celebrated in the spring when corn was planted. Xochipilli was thought to be the twin and husband (some say only the husband) of the flower goddess XOCHIQUETZAL.

XOCHIQUETZAL (Lady Precious Flower, Beautiful Rose) The eternally young AZTEC and TOLTEC goddess of gaiety, love, and flowers, which symbolize enlightenment. She watched over childbirth, guarded new mothers, and was the patron of weavers, silversmiths, painters, and anyone who used art to recreate nature. She was always depicted with butterflies and birds surrounding her. Marigolds are offered in her honor on the DAY OF THE DEAD and anytime she is honored.

Xochiquetzal is the daughter of TLAZOLTEOTL, the goddess of the Moon and eater of all sins. Some say she was married to her twin, the flower prince XOCHIPILLI, but most accounts name her as the wife of the rain god TLALOC. One myth tells how Xochiquetzal and Tlaloc were the sole survivors of the great flood that ended the Fourth Sun, or age, in Aztec mythology. All their children were born unable to speak. A dove finally arrived on the mountain, Colhuacan, where they lived and gave the children speech. However, each child was given a different language. Eventually, the sun god TEZCATLIPOCA fell in love with Xochiquetzal and came to the mountain to take her away.

XOLAS (Star)   The supreme god of the Alacaluf of Tierra del Fuego. This is a pure spirit, one that existed before the creation of anything else, including the heavens and Earth. Therefore the Alacaluf believe he has no form. Xolas is believed to give babies their souls when they are born and to take them back when they die.

XOLOTL (XOLOTL HUETZI)   The lord of the evening star, VENUS, and a lightning god of the AZTEC and TOLTEC. As the evening star, he rises before the Sun sets, nudging the Sun into the UNDERWORLD, then guarding the nighttime sky with his light. He was also said to bring bad luck and may have had some evil associations, although some scholars believe that he simply displayed traits of a DOG. Xolotl is sometimes referred to as the twin of the feathered-serpent god QUETZALCOATL. This reflects the idea that Quetzalcoatl, as the morning and daytime version of Venus, would have a "dark" twin who rises in the evening (see also DUALITY). Xolotl has also been called the *NAHUAL*, or guardian and protector, of Quetzalcoatl, going with him to the underworld to gather bones to create humans at the beginning of the Fifth Sun, or age, of Aztec mythology. (See CIHUACOATL.) Xolotl was also associated with sickness and physical deformities. In creation accounts, when the gods sacrifice themselves so the Sun will rise, Xolotl has been shown both as the one who sacrifices the other gods and as the only one who tries to escape being sacrificed. He is usually shown as a skeleton or a man with a dog's head and torn ear.

Y

YACATECUTLI (He Who Goes Before) The AZTEC lord of travelers and god of merchants. Not much is known about his origin or what he was like, but it is not surprising that merchants had a god of their own. In the Aztec world, merchants were not only traders dealing with goods, they were also ambassadors in their dealings with other groups, as well as missionaries, spreading the word of the Aztec empire and viewpoint. Under the guise of trade, they also served as spies, going undercover and changing their manner of dress to match the area they investigated. Because of the role they played in Aztec society, merchants were highly regarded, well honored by the government, and often quite wealthy. Still, they most often lived simply so as not to draw attention to themselves. The walking stick, or staff, was the symbol of merchants.

YAMANA (YAHGAN) A hunting-gathering people who once inhabited the islands off Cape Horn. They had one benevolent god, WATAVINEWA, who created life, provided well, and acted as a judge. The Yamana believed their ancestors were an old and a young Sun and the Moon and her husband, Rainbow. Women reigned supreme and were led by the Moon. One day Young Sun, who was Rainbow's brother, gathered all the men together to try to control the women. They killed all the women except the Moon, who escaped to the sky. (Her scars from the attack are still visible on her face.) She was so angry she leapt first into the sea, sending a great wave over all the land and destroying everything, including the men. Young Sun followed her to the sky and became the heavenly Sun. Old Sun became the planet VENUS, and Rainbow could not make up his mind what to do. So, he spends half his time in the sky and the other half on Earth.

Watavinewa was thought to have taught people how to live, but indirectly. He taught or helped the Yoaloh brothers, CULTURE HEROES of the Yamana, who then told the rest of the people. The Yoaloh brothers started FIRE quite by chance. The older brother, considered something of a fool, was picking up rocks, striking them sharply on each other, and listening to the sounds they made. As two rocks struck each other it caused a spark. He tried it again, this time over a small pile of dried grass that caught fire and burned, so he kept adding wood. This brother wanted to keep the fire going and bring all the other people around to show them, but the younger brother, considered to have a great deal of common sense, thought that would be too easy; he felt that fire was too valuable to be gotten so easily. So, the brothers let the fire go out and made sure there were no hot coals left. Then they showed the people which rocks to use to create the sparks to start fire.

YANOMAMI An indigenous people in the Orinoco River basin of southern Venezuela. They are primarily farmers who grow crops for their own use. They also hunt and grow crops such as tobacco and cotton to sell. There are four groups of Yanomami, and they are continually at war with one another. The Yanomami say they were born when the blood of Periboriwa, the moon spirit, was spread over the ground, which gave it the qualities of warrior. More peaceful people were born later. Everything, they believe, comes from Omam, a kind creation god. The universe, the Yanomami believe, has three layers. Once there were just two—the third was created when part of the second layer shed off. The god Omam was one of two men on this new layer. While fishing, he pulled a woman from the river and together they created the people that became the

The Yanomami prepare for a ceremony for the dead. (© *CORBIS SYGMA*)

Yanomami. A large bird created all other races from the mist of the river.

YAOTL Another name for the AZTEC smoking mirror god TEZCATLIPOCA.

YAQUI (Chief River) A people of Sonora, Mexico, and southwestern Arizona. They were originally from Mexico but fled north in the late 1800s. Scholars believe the Yaqui may be Clovis Indians who migrated to Mexico more than 11,000 years ago. In spite of being a generally peaceful people, the Yaqui resisted the Spanish with great force. They have a sacred relationship with their land and believe that supernatural power comes through visions from animal spirits. They honor the Virgin Mary, whom they call ITOM AE (Our Mother); animal spirits of the deer, horned toad, and SERPENT; and Jesus, whom they call Itom Achai (Our Father). Plant medicines and prayers to Jesus and Mary, whom the Yaqui consider

gods, can help heal diseases and other problems that have natural causes.

One Yaqui myth tells how the Yaqui came to have festivals. Long ago, before the people knew about drums, the Father heard a drum beat that filled him with joy—but he did not know what the sound was or who was making it. So, he sent his twin sons named Yomumulin (they both had the same name) to find it. After they had been gone awhile, they heard the sound too, and were amazed. As they looked around, however, they saw only a rat sitting under a cactus. They asked the rat about the sound, and the rat showed them the drum—and a flute as well. The twins headed home to tell their Father what they had seen. Several days later, the Great Mother visited them and told them to have a festival. It had to have music, and the devil must come and dance. The rat agreed to come and bring his flute and drum. The devil would not come, however, and he sent his son with strict instructions to spy but absolutely *not* to participate. The son went and had so much fun that he did participate, which banished the devil from all festivals forever.

YARA   A WATER spirit of various groups in the Brazilian AMAZON forests who spends half her time as a snake living in the mud at the bottom of rivers. The *yara* is a siren—a beautiful young woman who charms young men—drawing them in, sometimes to their death. In one story, a *yara* appears in front of a much-loved young hunter. He is spellbound and tells his mother about her. She warns him not to return to the place he saw her but he cannot stay away, and he is drawn to her and disappears.

Another story of a *yara* evolved after Europeans had arrived in South America, as it includes cows and milk, which had not been known to South America before: One day a *yara* rose out of the water as a young man was fishing and told him to bring her milk from a black cow. When the man brought the milk, however, a great snake had taken the place of the beautiful woman. He was so offended that he threw the milk at the snake and chopped off its head. With that, the snake turned into the woman he had first seen. She came out of the river and explained that the milk had broken the spell and she was forever released from the river.

YUM CIM (YUM CIMIL)   Another name for AH PUCH, the god of death of the MAYA.

YUM KAAX (YUM CAAX)   To the MAYA, the god of CORN; also the god of COCA and crop-growing and lord of the woods. As corn, Yum Kaax was not an aggressive god. He was seen as passive, a god who was

Yum Cim, also called Ah Puch, was the Mayan god of death. *(The Art Archive/National Anthropological Museum Mexico/Dagli Orti)*

often attacked by insects and rodents. He was also dependent on the rain god CHAC and on humans, who gave him life and provided for him (by bringing water if needed, weeding, and working to discourage insect and rodent pests). But Yum Kaax gave as well as he got. In return for all this care, he provided life for humans through his food.

Z

ZAKIGOXOL (ZAQUICOXOL, He Who Strikes from Flint) To the Cakchiquel MAYA, an evil demon that lives in the forests. He also is associated with the destructive side of fire.

ZAPOTEC A Meso-American empire that thrived in the Oaxaca region of Mexico from around 1500 B.C. to A.D. 750. The capital of the Zapotec empire was Monte Albán, a terraced city of palaces, pyramids, temples, and observatories on a mountaintop. This was a wealthy empire, which was reflected in the city's elaborately carved monuments and public buildings. The Zapotec were the first people in Meso-America to make written texts and the first who knew and followed the movements of the planets Mercury, VENUS, and Mars (and possibly Jupiter and Saturn as well), which they believed ruled certain times. The PRIESTS made and consulted the CALENDARS to determine good and bad days for planting and harvesting crops and conducting marriages, battles, and other important activities.

The Zapotec worshiped many gods, including Coquihani, the god of light; Copichja, the sun god, usually symbolized by a macaw; COCIJO, the god of rain; ITZPAPALOTL, the goddess of the paradise of the AFTERLIFE; Piyetao, a creator god; Tepeyollotl, god of earthquakes and lord of the night who as a JAGUAR eats the setting Sun; and XIPE TOTEC, the god of spring and rebirth. They worshiped ancestors, and many local deities might have been (or were thought to be) ancestors; they held feasts or made pilgrimages to a mountaintop or other sacred place each year to bring gifts to it. They lived closely with nature and honored it, believing that drought came when nature was not respected. One story tells about this: Once, an evil demon lived in a cave and would not let it rain—his appearance outside the cave was enough to scare the clouds away. The 12 thunderbolts got together and wondered what to do. Finally, they hatched a plan. They assembled storm clouds, put them in jars, and placed them near the cave. Then they released them one by one to draw the demon out; and one by one, the thunderbolts struck the Earth. The first was killed by the demon's horns. The demon's horns also took part of the second, and it died, too. Then more thunderbolts hit the Earth, a little closer together. Eventually, six of them were killed but the demon was killed as well, and at last it began to rain.

The Spanish destroyed the Zapotec temples and used their stones to build Catholic churches. As the Zapotec adopted Catholicism, they substituted the Catholic saints for their own gods. Today, their religion is a mix of Catholicism and traditional beliefs.

ZEMI Wood, stone, or bone carvings of humans or animals worshiped by the ARAWAK of the Caribbean and other groups. *Zemi* were used during ceremonies to appeal to the gods to bring rain or sunshine, for example.

ZIPACNA A son of the giant VUKUB-CAKIX who appeared in the stories of the Quiché MAYA as told in the sacred book the *POPUL VUH*. After the HERO TWINS killed Zipacna's father and Zipacna killed the 400 young men who became the constellation PLEIADES, the Hero Twins decided that Zipacna should pay for the deaths of the young men. First, they constructed an object that looked like a crab in a small space under the overhanging ledge of a mountain. Then, they tracked Zipacna down and showed him the crab. At this point, Zipacna was very hungry and the crab looked tempting. When he tried to get the crab and bring it out, his struggling wedged the crab even tighter and he got stuck. All this activity loosened the mountain and it fell on top of Zipacna. He was turned to stone underneath it all. In other Mayan stories, Zipacna was the lord of dawn who killed 400 stars in the sky, which HUNAHPU, one of the Hero Twins, put back every night.

ZOTZ Another name for the Mayan bat god CAMAZOTZ; also known as Zotzilaha Chimalman.

SELECTED BIBLIOGRAPHY

Andrews, Tamra. *Legends of the Earth, Sea, and Sky: An Encyclopedia of Nature Myths*. Santa Barbara, California: ABC-CLO, Inc., 1998.

Ardagh, Philip. *World Book South American Myths & Legends*. Chicago: World Book, Inc., 1997.

Baird, Tony, et al. *Gods of Sun and Sacrifice: Aztec and Maya Myths*. London: Duncan Baird Publishers, 1997.

Bierhorst, John, ed. and trans. *Black Rainbow: Legends of the Incas and Myths of Ancient Peru*. New York: Farrar, Straus and Giroux, 1976.

Bierhorst, John, ed. *Latin American Folktales: Stories from Hispanic and Indian Traditions*. Pantheon Fairy Tale and Folklore Library. New York: Pantheon Books, 2001.

Bierhorst, John. *The Mythology of Mexico and Central America*. New York: William Morrow and Company, Inc., 1990.

Bierhorst, John. The *Mythology of South America*. New York: William Morrow and Company, Inc., 1988.

Bini, Renata. *A World Treasury of Myths, Legends and Folktales: Stories from Six Continents*. New York: Harry N. Abrams, Inc., 1999.

Casterton, Peter, Catherine Heallam, and Cynthia O'Neill, eds. *Goddesses, Heroes, and Shamans: A Young People's Guide to World Mythology*. New York: Kingfisher Books, 1994.

Guyana.ro. "The Legend of Kaieteur Falls," Guyana.ro. Available on-line. URL: http://www.Guyana.ro/facts/myths.htm. Downloaded on April 2, 2003.

———. "The Old Man's Fall," Guyana.ro. Available on-line. URL: http://www.Guyana.ro/facts/myths.htm. Downloaded on April 2, 2003.

Harris, Clyde. "Guyana Legends," A Guyana Scrapbook. Available on-line. URL: http://www.geocities.com/TheTropics/Shores/9253/index.html. Downloaded on July 21, 2003.

Instituto Socioambiental. "Indigenous Peoples in Brazil," Instituto Socioambiental. Available on-line. URL: http://www.socioambiental.org/website/pib/english/ others/ sitemap.htm. Downloaded on July 21, 2003.

Keenan, Sheila. *Gods, Goddesses, and Monsters: An Encyclopedia of World Mythology*. New York: Scholastic, 2000.

Lindemans, M. F. "Aztec Mythology," Encyclopedia Mythica. Available on-line. URL: http://www.pantheon.org/areas/mythology/americas/aztec/articles.html. Updated July 8, 2003.

————. "Inca Mythology," Encyclopedia Mythica. Available on-line. URL: http://www.pantheon.org/areas/mythology/americas/inca/articles.html. Updated July 8, 2003.

————. "Mayan Mythology," Encyclopedia Mythica. Available on-line. URL: http://www.pantheon.org/areas/mythology/americas/mayan/articles.html. Updated July 8, 2003.

Malinowski, Sharon, Anna Sheets, Jeffrey Lehman, and Melissa Walsh Doig, eds. *Gale Encyclopedia of Native American Tribes*. Vols. I and II. Detroit, Michigan: Gale, 1998.

Markowitz, Harvey, ed. *American Indians*. Vol. 1. Pasadena: Salem Press, Inc., 1995.

Monaghan, Patricia. *The New Book of Goddesses and Heroines*. St. Paul, Minnesota: Llewellyn Publications, 2000.

Owens, D. W. "Native American: Aztec Gods," Gods, Heroes, and Myth. Available on-line. URL: http://www.gods-heros-myth.com/namerican/aztec.html. Updated on July 18, 2003.

————. "Native American: Southern Gods," Gods, Heroes, and Myth. Available on-line. URL: http://www.gods-heros-myth.com/namerican/southern.html. Updated on July 18, 2003.

Read, Kay Almere, and Jason J. González. *Handbook of Mesoamerican Mythology*. Handbooks of World Mythology. Santa Barbara, California: ABC-CLIO, Inc., 2000.

Roberts, Timothy R. *Gods of the Maya, Aztecs, and Incas*. Myths of the World. New York: MetroBooks, 1996.

Smith, Nigel J. H. *The Enchanted Amazon Rain Forest: Stories from a Vanishing World*. Gainsville, Florida: The University Press of Florida, 1996.

Spence, Lewis. *The Myths of Mexico and Peru*. New York: Dover Publications, 1995.

Tedlock, Dennis, trans. *Popul Vuh: The Mayan Book of the Dawn of Life*. New York: Touchstone/Simon & Schuster, 1996.

Tenenbaum, Barbara A., and Georgette M. Dorn, eds. *Encyclopedia of Latin American History and Culture*. New York: Scribner's, 1996.

Turner, Patricia, and Charles Russell Coulter. *Dictionary of Ancient Deities*. New York: Oxford University Press, 2000.

Voorburg, René, and William Horden. "Introduction," Aztec Calendar. Available on-line. URL: http://www.azteccalendar.com. Downloaded April 4, 2003.

Willis, Roy, ed. *World Mythology*. New York: Henry Holt and Company, 1993.

INDEX

Boldface page numbers indicate main headings; *italic* page numbers indicate illustrations.

133